Your Custom Home

250+ Ready-to-Customize Home Plans

Your Custom Home

250+ Ready-to-Customize Home Plans

Published by Hanley Wood
One Thomas Circle, NW, Suite 600
Washington, DC 20005

Distribution Center
29333 Lorie Lane
Wixom, Michigan 48393

Group Vice President, General Manager, Andrew Schultz
Associate Publisher, Editorial Development, Jennifer Pearce
Managing Editor, Jason D. Vaughan
Senior Editor, Nate Ewell
Associate Editor, Simon Hyoun
Senior Plan Merchandiser, Morenci C. Clark
Plan Merchandiser, Nicole Phipps
Proofreader/Copywriter, Dyana Weis
Graphic Artist, Joong Min
Plan Data Team Leader, Ryan Emge
Production Manager, Brenda McClary

Vice President, Retail Sales, Scott Hill
National Sales Manager, Bruce Holmes
Director, Plan Products, Matt Higgins

Most Hanley Wood titles are available at quantity discounts
with bulk purchases for educational, business, or sales
promotional use. For information, please contact
Bruce Holmes at bholmes@hanleywood.com.

BIG DESIGNS, INC.
President, Creative Director, Anthony D'Elia
Vice President, Business Manager, Megan D'Elia
Vice President, Design Director, Chris Bonavita
Editorial Director, John Roach
Assistant Editor, Patricia Starkey
Senior Art Director, Stephen Reinfurt
Production Director, David Barbella
Photo Editor, Christine DiVuolo
Graphic Designer, Mary Ellen Mulshine
Graphic Designer, Billy Doremus
Graphic Designer, Jacque Young
Assistant Photo Editor, David Halpin
Assistant Production Manager, Rich Fuentes

PHOTO CREDITS
Front Cover (left to right):
Photo by Laurence Taylor. Find Design HPK1000168 on p. 193.
Photo by Donald A. Gardner Architects, Inc. Find Design HPK1000242
on p. 267.
Photo by Design Basics, Inc. Find Design HPK1000217 on p. 242.
Back Cover:
Photo by Judy Davis/Hoachlander Davis Photography

10 9 8 7 6 5 4 3 2 1

Printed in the United States of America

Library of Congress Control Number: 2004099005

ISBN: 1-931131-38-4

Contents

Introduction

Feature Houses

10   Eastern Shore Cottage
A four-bedroom hideaway inspires
ideas within reach

15   Form + Function
Great looks and a thoughtful layout
await final touches

22   Old World Revisited
A thoroughly modern plan strikes an
elegant pose

25   Luxury in Residence
Exuberant luxury fulfills big dreams

Case in Point

8   Made to Work
A mid-sized home finds great use in
dedicated utility rooms

19   Happy Family
Added bedrooms bring relief to a
growing family

32   Automatic for the People
How to make your home more efficient,
safe, and cool

Details

14   Walk-On Role
With today's flooring options, the sky's
the limit

31   Grand Opening
Beautify interior and exterior doors for
everyday elegance

Showcase of Plans

34   Bargain Bests
Budget-friendly designs for your
first home

73   Consumer Favorites
Our most requested designs

118   Perfect Starts
Homes up to 2,000 square feet

169   Just Right
Homes between 2,000 and
3,000 square feet

222   Bigger and Better
Homes over 3,000 square feet

278   Order Now!

A Home of One's Own

What is the essential difference between a bland, outdated, uninspired building listed for sale in the local paper and a newly built home that expresses our visions of fellowship and well-being? By what effort does a house become more than shelter, become something that responds to our personal hopes for security, prosperity, and legacy? What can a home teach us about our families and our communities? These are the questions we ask ourselves, if even for a brief moment, when trying to decide on a new home. We get the sense that these are fairly important questions—for one thing, we don't ask them when buying new shoes or assembling a new bookcase—but they're also quite difficult to keep in focus. They get lost in the fog of disappointments, half-measures, and disheartening compromises that characterize most home buying and home building experiences. Only six months after move-in, you're already thinking about how you'll get it right the next time.

Production-built homes and planned developments discourage the kind of natural variety that exists in older American neighborhoods. True community requires more than just proximity to your neighbors. It also requires an acceptance of differences that exist between families and homes.

©PHOTODISC BY GETTY IMAGES (2)

The Problem

A lot of the disappointment is caused by the reality of the housing market, which offers us few opportunities to fulfill the vision of the home we want at a reasonable expense.

For instance, most new homes on the market are production-built houses. Although builders are aware of current trends and tastes, their decisions are also affected by the priorities and habits of running a full-time business. In addition, the design options they can offer are limited by the plans *they* have chosen. Still, these houses account for most of the new home purchases made in the United States today, which speaks for their attractive prices.

On the other hand, a new home can also be custom designed from scratch by a residential architect. This is a reasonable choice for buyers who have a highly defined sense of aesthetic and want an artist's touch upon every square foot of their new home, or who are interested in progressive or experimental building methods. Of course, such devoted attention from an architect will carry a hefty price—typically 10-20 percent of the value of the home. As a result, only a small fraction of the new homes built in the United States today are custom-built residences.

What is the family's favorite room in your current house? And what rooms have never worked well? Hint: What room is your least favorite to clean?

A Better Option

This book proposes a third way to build a new home, one that allows you to tailor your home to suit your family's way of living without paying for the full services of a residential architect. Purchase a predrawn plan for a home that comes close to what you want, then have the plan modified by a designer or architect to incorporate desired changes—such as more overall square footage, another bedroom, a screen around the porch. Then find a builder to fulfill the plan, as for any new home construction. The architect has not drawn the plan from scratch, so your cost to him will be far less than the price of a custom designed home. At the same time, you've ensured that the design will satisfy what you've been looking for in your next home.

Improving on a predrawn plan is like choosing a car you nearly want, then upgrading or downgrading the features to perfection. Maybe you like the ride of a sports car but want more trunk space. Or maybe your family needs a minivan that can also tow a trailer. Car makers offer different editions—called "trims"—of their models to suit the buyer: a five-door trim or a one with a V8 engine. Modifying a predrawn plan is similar to choosing a trim, except the available features are much more numerous. Think of going to the car maker's manufacturing plant and being able to pick out from a lengthy list the moving parts, paints, features, size, materials, and interior that will be used in production of your vehicle. At the same time, you'd be saving time and money over the option of having your local auto mechanic conceptualize, design, test, and assemble a car from scratch.

Good Numbers

The typical savings over the cost of hiring a custom home architect are considerable and worth analyzing. Reflect on the following example. Hanley Wood offers a consultation with one of our designers for a nominal fee of $50 for prospective customers. The designer then works with you on a one-on-one basis to flesh out your ideas, then asks you to complete a checklist that reflects your final customization request. Based on the checklist, the designer makes the appropriate changes to the plan you have purchased (or intend to purchase, if it is a plan available through Hanley Wood) and gives you an estimate for the changes to be made. The average price for modifying a plan in this way is about $1,250, depending entirely on the complexity of the changes requested. The average cost of a reproducible set of blueprints from Hanley Wood is $1,200. Doing the math, the total bill for a reproducible set of your made-to-order home plans comes to about $2,750. By contrast, the market rate of a custom-designed home plan drawn from scratch by an architect is 10-20 percent of the total value of the home—that's $25,000-$50,000 for a $250,000 home. To be fair, this bill may also account for time spent by the architect working with the builder on-site or otherwise overseeing construction. But then again, predrawn plans have already been site-tested and don't normally require this kind of attention.

Using this Book

The first step to creating a home of dreams is to surrender the notion that there is one correct way to build a house and, therefore, you should keep your opinions to yourself. Everyone involved in the project—you, the designers, the builders, the contractors—should agree that the your home will be created only through collaboration between professionals and nonprofessionals.

The next two steps are what this book will prepare you for: choosing a stock house plan that most closely matches the home you want, then working with a designer to refine that plan to meet your particular concerns. The designer will then redraw the plans to accommodate your request. You can then take the customized home plan to your builder and, with his or her input, begin construction.

This book will not attempt to teach you the finer points of residential architecture and home construction with which you can draw your own home or act as your own general contractor. Sure, you can cut cost from the project by eliminating professional consultants and contractors. But a typical owner will outspend those savings with the cost of her own time and effort. Some work is better—and cheaper—left to the professionals.

The first part of this book features case studies and walk-throughs of real homes that underwent customizations led by the homeowners. The section also looks at homes before they've

Modification	Average Cost
Adding or removing living space (square footage)	Quote required
Adding or removing a garage	$400–$680
Garage: Front entry to side load or vice versa	Starting at $300
Adding a screened porch	$280–$600
Adding a bonus room in the attic	$450–$780
Changing a full basement to crawlspace or vice versa	Starting at $220
Changing a full basement to slab or vice versa	Starting at $260
Changing exterior building material	Starting at $200
Changing roof lines	$360–$630
Adjusting ceiling height	$280–$500
Adding, moving, or removing an exterior opening	$55 per opening
Adding or removing a fireplace	$90–$200
Modifying a nonbearing wall or room	$55 per room
Changing exterior walls from 2"x4" to 2"x6"	Starting at $200
Redesigning a bathroom or kitchen	$120–$280
Reverse plan right reading	Quote required
Adapting plans for local building code requirements	Quote required
Engineering stamping only	$450 / any state
Any other engineering services	Quote required
Adjust plan for handicapped accessibility	Quote required
Interactive illustrations (choices of exterior materials)	Quote required
Metric conversion of home plan	$400

The table at left lists frequently requested modifications and the average cost of incorporating them into a predrawn home plan. All estimates are based on modifications available currently through Hanley Wood.

©STONE +

The size of this home isn't as impressive as its distinguished looks and sense of history. See more of this plan on p. 217.

been customized and highlights areas that deserve attention. The book also suggests other options available to owners during construction, such as choice of flooring materials and door designs that over the life of the home can make a huge difference to the feel and function of living spaces.

The remainder of the book gives you an immediate opportunity to get started on the realization of your new home. Section One offers a selection of our most budget-friendly home plans—smaller, adaptable designs for you to build on. Section Two contains our best sellers—homes in a variety of architectural styles and sizes that have remained on the top of our clients' lists. Lastly, the remaining three sections have been arranged by total square footage. Look here first if you already know how much buildable space your lot presents and how big of a home your family wants.

Building a brand new home is one of the most complicated, expensive, and rewarding experiences of a person's life. We hope this book will help you overcome the potential pitfalls and ultimately arrive at the home of your dreams. ∎

ORIGINAL: 2,992 square feet, plus unfinished basement, 4 bedrooms, 3½ baths
MODIFIED: increased square footage of master suite, added office, added laundry room, added full bath, added screen to porch, exterior stone accents
COST OF PLAN: $1,080 (reproducible set, plus one mirror reverse set)
COST OF MODIFICATION: $1,138
TOTAL: $2,163*

Made to Work

Our first case study is of a house plan that has undergone a moderate degree of customization. Note also that the owners have chosen to use a mirror-reverse version of the original plan—an optional purchase from most home plans distributors. The decision may have been based on the advantages of the owners' lot, a superior vista they wanted to capture from certain parts of the home, for instance. Other typical reasons for using a mirror-reverse plan are to overcome obstacles present in the lot, such as large trees or a slope.

To begin, the owners chose an attractive two-story traditional design with a wealth of outdoor features: a wraparound porch, balcony, and a sun-loving array of windows. The kitchen and dining areas were adequate to the family's needs, as were the living spaces and three-car garage. What the owners really wanted were more working areas, such as a home office and a laundry room.

At the owners' request, three changes were made to the layout. On the first floor, a modest (86 sq. ft.) home office was added at the bottom of the plan, accessible from the foyer. Doing so has also given the exterior a more flushed appearance, so that the bottom left of the plan now comes to a single corner. A similar change was achieved at the top of the plan, where the owners desired more livable space in the master bedroom. The nearly 43 square feet of porch just outside the bedroom windows were reallocated to the bedroom itself, to match the depth of the master bath.

Upstairs, at the end of the brief hallway at the left of the plan, the designer converted the vanity area of a previously shared bath into a laundry room. A skylight origi-

SECOND FLOOR, BEFORE

FIRST FLOOR, BEFORE

*all prices based on 2005 pricing for plans and services available through Hanley Wood courtesy of Drummond Designs.

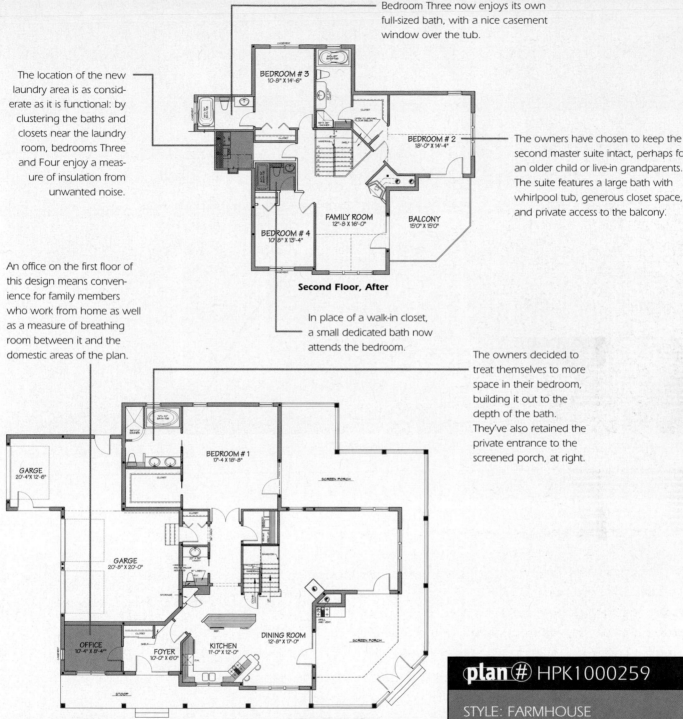

Bedroom Three now enjoys its own full-sized bath, with a nice casement window over the tub.

The location of the new laundry area is as considerate as it is functional: by clustering the baths and closets near the laundry room, bedrooms Three and Four enjoy a measure of insulation from unwanted noise.

The owners have chosen to keep the second master suite intact, perhaps for an older child or live-in grandparents. The suite features a large bath with whirlpool tub, generous closet space, and private access to the balcony.

BEDROOM # 3
10'-8" X 14'-6"

BEDROOM # 2
18'-0" X 14'-4"

BEDROOM # 4
10'-8" X 13'-4"

FAMILY ROOM
12'-8 X 16'-0"

BALCONY
15'0" X 15'0"

Second Floor, After

An office on the first floor of this design means convenience for family members who work from home as well as a measure of breathing room between it and the domestic areas of the plan.

In place of a walk-in closet, a small dedicated bath now attends the bedroom.

The owners decided to treat themselves to more space in their bedroom, building it out to the depth of the bath. They've also retained the private entrance to the screened porch, at right.

GARGE
20'-4"X 12'-6"

GARGE
20'-8" X 20'-0"

BEDROOM # 1
17'-4 X 18'-8"

SCREEN PORCH

OFFICE
10'-4" X 8'-4"

FOYER
10'-0" X 6'0"

KITCHEN
11'-0" X 12'-0"

DINING ROOM
12'-8" X 17'-0"

First Floor, After

nally meant for the vanity area has been retained to keep the room bright. But the addition of the family's new laundry room required another, separate modification. Since the vanity area served also as the way for Bedroom Three and Four to share the bath, Bedroom Four now required a bath of its own. The designer's solution was to convert the large walk-in closet into another full bath—the fourth in the home. The smaller closet now attending the bedroom was an acceptable trade-off.

Lastly, the owners specified for a screen to enclose the porch and stone accents on the exterior to bring more contrast to the shingles. ■

plan# HPK1000259

STYLE: FARMHOUSE
FIRST FLOOR: 1,654 SQ. FT.
SECOND FLOOR: 1,338 SQ. FT.
TOTAL: 2,992 SQ. FT.
BEDROOMS: 4
BATHROOMS: 3½
WIDTH: 72' - 0"
DEPTH: 52' - 0"
FOUNDATION: UNFINISHED BASEMENT

SEARCH ONLINE @ EPLANS.COM

PHOTOGRAPHY COURTESY OF WILLIAM E. POOLE DESIGNS, INC.;ISLANDS OF BEAUFORT—BEAUFORT, SC

Eastern Shore Cottage

A four-bedroom hideaway offers great looks and a sensible layout

The understated appeal of the home is reminiscent of a simpler life. The classic front porch and side-gabled roof achieve an old-style, neighborhood-friendly design.

The exterior of this home possesses an inviting, clean-cut appearance that doesn't try too hard to impress. A relaxing country porch and three charming dormers convey a classic American style that attains flair but remains accessible. Certainly this design will receive a warm welcome in any neighborhood. The side-loading garage at the bottom left of the plan preserves the integrity of the home's front exterior. But should your lot require the driveway to meet the front of the home, modifying the garage is possible. If you opt for a front-loading garage, we recommend separate doors for the cars. Avoid the look of an unadorned two-wide door by choosing two smaller carriage-style doors.

Left: High ceilings and dormer windows are complemented nicely by exposed beams. Matching furnishings and mantel complete the country look. On the other hand, bright windows and doors keep the space from seeming too rustic. Below: The picturesque breakfast nook and kitchen receive lots of sun during the day. Arched entryways frame attractive interior views, although families might prefer removing walls for a more open layout.

On the whole, lot orientation can greatly affect the personality and energy efficiency of your living spaces, and the advice of a professional landscape architect can be a worthwhile investment. For instance, a family of early risers will not mind east-facing bedrooms that allow in the morning sun. However, night owls may prefer their bedrooms to face north. Unless mediated by blinds or lighter colors, sun-loving rooms will also generate more heat in the home—good in the winter, but a burden on your air conditioning system in the summer. Similarly, keep in mind your landscaping and gardening plans. Facing the back of the house due south will allow the flowers and vegetables in your backyard to soak in the sun throughout the day. Based on the landscape architect's recommendations, a mirror-reverse layout of a plan might be more appropriate to your lot.

The 2,151-square-foot interior is perfectly suited for smaller families and presents customization opportunities for growing families. The master suite at the left of the plan is well appointed, featuring a whirlpool, compartmented toilet, dual-sink vanity, and walk-in closet. Owners in the suite will enjoy the privacy and quiet built into this part of the plan, but might also desire a larger bedroom or direct access to the backyard.

The design calls for three other bedrooms which can be retained as such. But families with work-at-home members should consider converting bedroom 2 into an office, which would remain far enough from the common areas of the home to ensure a quiet workspace. Bedroom Four on the second level can also fit the bill, and children of the home can be closely supervised as they play in the rec room nearby.

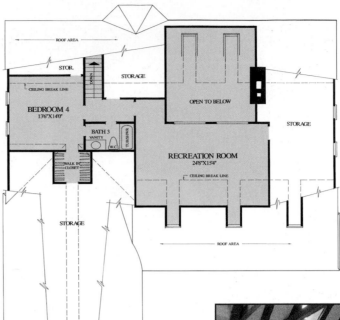

ROOF AREA

STOR.

STORAGE

CEILING BREAK LINE

DOWN

BEDROOM 4
13'6"X14'0"

OPEN TO BELOW

STORAGE

BATH 3
VANITY

W.C.

TUB/SHWR

RECREATION ROOM
24'8"X15'4"

WALK IN CLOSET

CEILING BREAK LINE

STORAGE

ROOF AREA

UP

BREAKFAST AREA
11'0"X10'4"

OPEN TO ABOVE

ENTERTAINMENT CENTER

BEDROOM 3
12'0"X12'0"

MASTER BEDROOM
13'6"X16'0"

OVEN

SHLVS

WALK IN CLOSET

BAR

SINK

VAULTED CEILING
GREAT ROOM
19'0"X22'0"

SEAT

SHOWER

VANITY

MASTER BATH

WHIRLPOOL TUB

STOR.

DRIP/DRY

PANTRY

KITCHEN
11'0"X11'0"

REFG.

TUB/SHWR

LINEN

LINEN

BATH 2
VANITY

W.C.

W.C.

HIS/HER WARDROBE

UTILITY

SINK

WASH

DRY

LINEN

DINING ROOM
14'0"X13'0"

FOYER
7'6"X13'0"

BEDROOM 2
12'0"X12'8"

COVERED PORCH

2 CAR GARAGE
23'0"X22'0"

© William E. Poole Designs

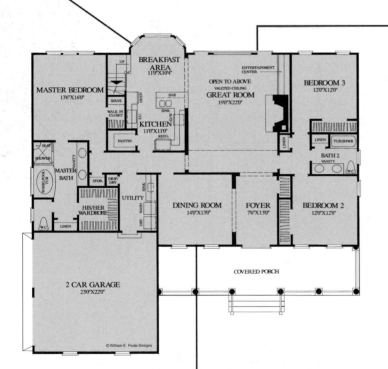

plan# HPK1000006

STYLE: COUNTRY COTTAGE
SQUARE FOOTAGE: 2,151
BONUS SPACE: 814 SQ. FT.
BEDROOMS: 3
BATHROOMS: 2
WIDTH: 61' - 0"
DEPTH: 55' - 8"
FOUNDATION: CRAWLSPACE, BASEMENT

SEARCH ONLINE @ EPLANS.COM

The great room calls for a large centerpiece fireplace, considered a must-have for some owners. Certainly, a family gathered around a crackling fire, sipping hot chocolate, and enjoying one another's company makes a fine picture. But if your family is more likely to gather around a large-screen television for movie nights, it makes sense to move the fireplace to a corner of the room. Direct-vent fireplaces are quite easy to relocate—to, say, the dining room. Of course, if you're not at all tempted by the sound and feel of a crackling fire, removing the fireplace is always an option.

The family-friendly kitchen and breakfast area are proportionate to the overall size of the home. The chef of the home will appreciate the straight-forward layout and abundance of natural light. The walk-in pantry is a welcome amenity, as is the serving bar.

The sprawling second floor specifies one more bedroom with bath and a large recreation area, leaving most of the level available for customization. Convenient storage spaces at the top, right, and bottom of the plan can be easily converted into additional bedrooms or utility spaces. This versatile layout is ideal for accomodating a recent grad who has returned home, a live-in relative, or frequent out-of-town guests. The storage area at the right, for instance, receives natural light from two large windows and a dormer that recommend the room be spared the fate of a typical dusty attic. ∎

Gentle arches and above-door fanlights bring a warm-hearted decorum to the dining room. This is a room where the work of an interior designer can really shine. Careful use of complementing and contrasting colors controls the perceived size and flow of the room.

A Step Ahead. Make a dramatic entrance with an exotic tiled staircase. Quarry tiles and other natural materials are great ways to bring the look of traditional Mediterranean design to your home. Terra-cotta-colored paving tiles beautifully complement the decorative tiling on the risers. Tiles offer an extensive color palette and can be applied within a contemporary or traditional space.

Tile Style. Duplicate the look of authentic sandstone with less expensive ceramic wall and floor tile. By working with mesh-backed tiles from the line, homeowners can also create borders and accents. Tiles also come in different sizes, so choose what looks right to you.

Sisal Surprise. Today, even your mother's vinyl floor has moved out of the kitchen. High-style designs like the one shown here, which resembles sisal carpeting, bring the look of natural materials to this low-maintenance favorite. It's the perfect choice for a sunroom, playroom, or entryway.

Vintage Favorite. There are now lines of laminate flooring that use a texturing technique to create the look and feel of real wood. This sun porch has all the style of a traditional space and takes advantage of laminate's durability and attractive cost. See also "Opulent Oak" (left) for more reasons to go laminate.

Flooring options run the gamut from tiles to laminate, vinyl, carpeting, and hardwood. What's popular often is associated with the part of the country you live in and the type of climate you experience. But no matter where you live, you'll find that flooring design is reaching new heights. What's particularly fun are the "true or faux" looks showing up in sheet vinyl. Who would have thought that simulated crocodile skin would become the latest flooring option, or that you could mop a woven "sisal" rug? On the more practical side, homeowners are considering the investment value of their flooring choices, and opting for long-term return options, like hardwood and natural stone.

Opulant Oak. Love the look of wood but worried about the upkeep? Modern laminate flooring offers the look of authentic wood but resists wear and tear better than the real thing. Laminate flooring such as the one shown here can feature a no-glue aluminum locking system that makes it a cinch to install, and a lifetime warranty covers joint integrity, fading, staining, wear, and water resistance.

Luxury Underfoot. Believe it or not, leather is one of the hottest trends in flooring. Ideal for low-traffic areas where you crave extra luxury (like the walk-in closet shown here) leather flooring feels soft and supple underfoot. And best of all, there's no maintenance—you can't clean it, and so it ages to a wonderful patina over time.

Tough Love. If you have a less-than-spotless track record with carpeting, choose stain-resistant brands for all high-traffic and utility areas in the home. Remember that height and density of the carpeting will also affect how well it holds up.

Grand Entrance. What an entrance a real hardwood floor like this makes. By using wood strips in varying natural colors, a diamond inlay was created in this foyer that achieves a dramatic visual impact. Your accountant would approve, too: Hardwood floors add to the value of your home (not to mention their durability, easy maintenance, and classic good looks).

Form + Function

Before modifying your new home plan, observe how your current home functions

Here is a one-story home that delivers the necessities without neglecting the ego. Gathering rooms are spacious enough for a family of four and refined by vaulted ceilings, full-height windows, and a centerpiece fireplace. The full-sized foyer takes advantage of a sunny entryway—thanks to side and transom lights—to create a warm homecoming for owners and guests.

The foyer also offers the home's formal gesture of welcome, which justifies the placement of the living room and dining room to the left and right. French doors open into the living room, lit well by bayed windows, and slender columns announce the formal dining room. Together, the three rooms reserve a sense of refinement in an otherwise family-oriented design.

A mix of materials and nested gables bring visual interest to the exterior. Large windows promote a bright interior, but coordinating their styles would achieve a more finished look.

The breakfast nook has become one of the hardest working rooms in the modern home and it receives well-deserved attention in this design. In most working families, the nook is where members gather first in the morning, if only for a moment, and again at dinner time before heading to the television room or to individual bedrooms. In other words, it functions in all the ways of a traditional dining room and often doubles as a family room—which frustrates some owners, who then feel as if the dining room and family room are being "wasted."

But instead of insisting that members conform their preferences to a home's layout, why not take cues from how spaces are serving the family currently? If the nook attracts members throughout the day, or if the breakfast table has been overrun with envelopes and magazines, leaving no room for place settings, perhaps nearby overflow space is what the home needs. The addition of a simple room near the kitchen and nook can bring a tremendous amount of utility to the heart of the home and relieve surrounding spaces of overuse. The added room pictured in this feature functions as a sitting room or den. Other uses include a nursery or playroom, media room, office, library, or pantry.

The left of the plan is occupied by an ample master suite. The tray ceiling and

Above: The bay window in the breakfast nook allows sunny casual meals. Right: The owners of this home added an attractive sitting room, just off the breakfast nook and kitchen. It becomes a comfy spot for reading and conversation.

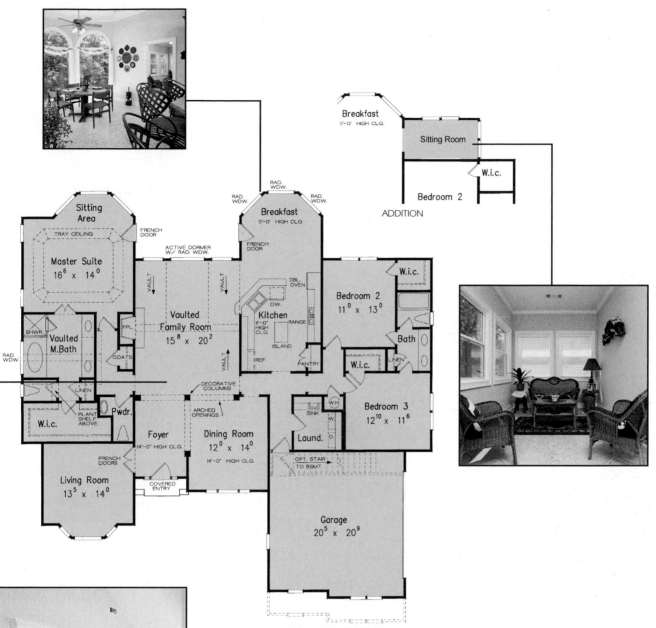

Breakfast
11'-0" HIGH CLG.

Sitting Room

W.i.c.

Bedroom 2

ADDITION

Sitting
Area

TRAY CEILING

Master Suite
16⁶ x 14⁰

FRENCH
DOOR

RAD.
WDW.

RAD.
WDW.

RAD.
WDW.

Breakfast
11'-0" HIGH CLG.

FRENCH
DOOR

ACTIVE DORMER
W/ RAD. WDW.

W.i.c.

Bedroom 2
11⁰ x 13⁰

SHWR.

Vaulted
M.Bath

FPL.

COATS

Vaulted
Family Room
15⁸ x 20²

DBL.
OVEN

DW.

Kitchen
11'-0"
HIGH
CLG.

RANGE

ISLAND

Bath

RAD.
WDW.

VAULT

VAULT

VAULT

I.REF.

PANTRY

W.i.c.

LINEN

LINEN

DECORATIVE
COLUMNS

Bedroom 3
12¹⁰ x 11⁶

W.i.c.

PLANT
SHELF
ABOVE

Pwdr.

ARCHED
OPENINGS

SINK

W.H.

W.

D.

Foyer
14'-0" HIGH CLG.

Dining Room
12⁰ x 14⁰
14'-0" HIGH CLG.

Laund.

RAD.
WDW.

FRENCH
DOORS

COVERED
ENTRY

OPT. STAIR
TO BSMT.

Living Room
13⁵ x 14⁰

Garage
20⁵ x 20⁹

GARAGE LOCATION WITH BASEMENT

plan# HPK100001

STYLE: COUNTRY COTTAGE
SQUARE FOOTAGE: 2,322
BEDROOMS: 3
BATHROOMS: 2½
WIDTH: 62'-0"
DEPTH: 61'-0"
FOUNDATION: SLAB,
CRAWLSPACE, UNFINISHED
WALKOUT BASEMENT

SEARCH ONLINE @ EPLANS.COM

Above: The vaulted family room is bright with arched windows and features a stone hearth.

bayed sitting area in the bedroom are luxury touches not usual for a home this size. The bath is equally ambitious: a large whirlpool beside the window, separate vanities, compartmented toilet, linen closet, and a gratifying walk-in closet. Notice the separate coat closet and powder room in the hallway just outside the suite, which help to reserve the suite for the owners.

At the other end of the plan, two bedrooms share one full bath. In such cases, converting one of the larger walk-in closets into a second bath is a popular customization request—an option we'll explore in more detail on page 8. The larger laundry area could also be turned into a bath, but only if room can be found elsewhere for a laundry and utility space. The two-car garage is adequate and loads from the side for a more pleasing exterior. A three-car option should preserve this feature.

A final consideration regards the home's foundation. When purchasing a predrawn home plan, be sure to ask what foundations are available for the design you have in mind. If your family does not require a basement, a slab or crawlspace foundation is an easy-to-build and cost-cutting option. The kind of lot you have purchased will also determine what foundations can be built, so be sure to consult with your builder, landscape architect, or plan sales representative. An unfinished (think: concrete walls and floors) walkout basement option is available for this plan, the entry to which would be from the garage. ■

ORIGINAL: 2,426 square feet, plus unfinished basement, 3 bedrooms, 2½ baths
MODIFIED: increased overall square footage, redesign of master suite, added bedroom, added extra room, converted basement into walk-out level, adjusted elevations
COST OF PLAN: $895 (reproducible set)
COST OF MODIFICATION: $1,375
TOTAL: $2,270*

Front Elevation, After

Happy Family

The owners of our next case home have really taken advantage of the modification option, bringing an extensive amount of custom changes to the original plan. Small changes—such as the removal of a fireplace and the reorientation of a stairway—as well as general changes—such as the addition of overall square footage and a walkout basement—have achieved the look and function the owners desired in their new home.

The second floor has seen far-reaching changes to the layout, such as the addition of two more rooms and a shared full bath at the bottom right of the plan. The previously diagonal walls of the existing rooms have been squared out to make way for the new spaces. Before modification, the second floor called for a small sitting area at the top of the stairs overlooking the downstairs living room—a good amount of vertical space at the heart of the home, but a design that did not meet the needs of a growing family. In its place, two sizeable rooms plus a bath were drawn to match the dimensions of the first-floor living room and dining area. Should the extra room become a bedroom in the future, the new bath would be shared between them. Whatever the case, the occupant in Bedroom Three will enjoy a cozy, cottage style feel in its sloped wall and dormer window.

At the top of the plan, a host of changes benefit the master suite. The owners have allotted the added square footage to an already spacious bath and walk-in closet. The result is an enviably luxurious spa, featuring an oversized shower, whirlpool, linen closet, and compartmented toilet. The walk-in has room enough for added shelving and a wraparound wardrobe. Lastly, owners have treated themselves to a private screened porch. ■

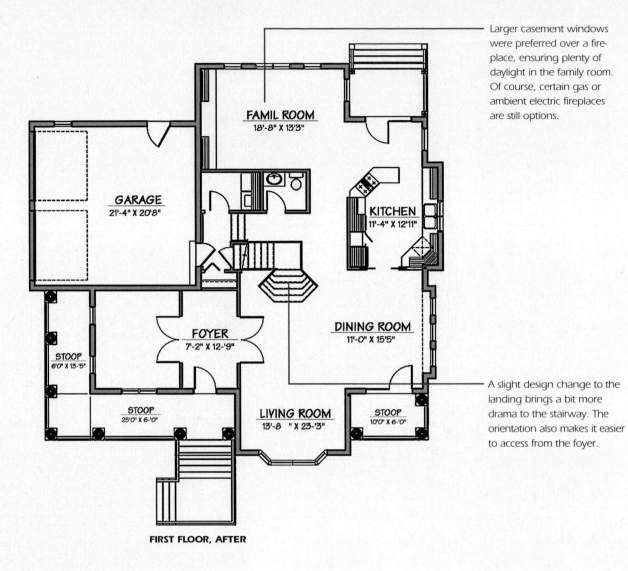

FAMIL ROOM
18'-8" X 13'3"

GARAGE
21'-4" X 20'8"

KITCHEN
11'-4" X 12'11"

FOYER
7'-2" X 12'-'9"

DINING ROOM
11'-0" X 15'5"

STOOP
6'0" X 13'-5"

STOOP
25'0" X 6'-0"

LIVING ROOM
13'-8 " X 23-'3"

STOOP
10'0" X 6'-0"

Larger casement windows were preferred over a fire-place, ensuring plenty of daylight in the family room. Of course, certain gas or ambient electric fireplaces are still options.

A slight design change to the landing brings a bit more drama to the stairway. The orientation also makes it easier to access from the foyer.

FIRST FLOOR, AFTER

Front Perspective, Before

FIRST FLOOR, BEFORE

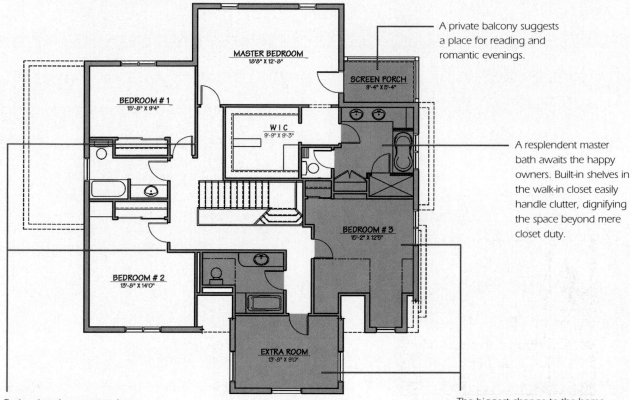

A private balcony suggests a place for reading and romantic evenings.

MASTER BEDROOM
18'8" X 12'-8"

SCREEN PORCH
9'-4" X 5'-4"

BEDROOM # 1
15'-8" X 9'4"

WIC
9'-9" X 9'-3"

A resplendent master bath awaits the happy owners. Built-in shelves in the walk-in closet easily handle clutter, dignifying the space beyond mere closet duty.

BEDROOM # 3
15'-2" X 12'5"

BEDROOM # 2
13'-8" X 14'0"

EXTRA ROOM
13'-8" X 9'0"

SECOND FLOOR, AFTER

Redrawing the rooms to be square with the exterior walls has reclaimed needed space for the additions on this level.

The biggest change to the home has been the addition of two rooms and a full bath on the second floor, taking the place of an overlook. Modifications here have brought new design to the front and side elevations.

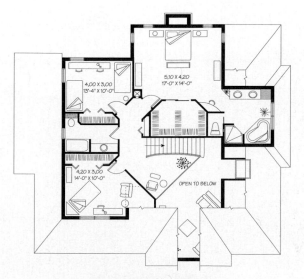

5,10 X 4,20
17'-0" X 14'-0"

4,00 X 3,00
13'-4" X 10'-0"

4,20 X 3,00
14'-0" X 10'-0"

OPEN TO BELOW

SECOND FLOOR, BEFORE

plan# HPK1000260

STYLE: TRADITIONAL
FIRST FLOOR: 1,319 SQ. FT.
SECOND FLOOR: 1,107 SQ. FT.
TOTAL: 2,426 SQ. FT.
BEDROOMS: 3
BATHROOMS: 2½
WIDTH: 52' - 0"
DEPTH: 46' - 8"
FOUNDATION: UNFINISHED BASEMENT

SEARCH ONLINE @ EPLANS.COM

Old World Revisited

A harmony of formal and casual spaces bring balance to the home

Miniature dormers, covered entry, and rustic materials complement the home's country manor style.

A home of this size has square footage enough to spare toward luxury spaces and specialized rooms, such as a game room or a library. Rooms we've already visited in the smaller featured homes are noticeably grander as well, such as the two-story foyer with vaulted ceiling. In addition, an eye-catching stairway makes a dramatic impression and announces the European look that guides the design of the home. Similar suggestions are found in the exterior materials, miniature dormers, and ornate windows with decorative shutters. Expressive rooflines and multiple front-facing gables establish an appealing curbside presence that will be a welcomed addition to any neighborhood.

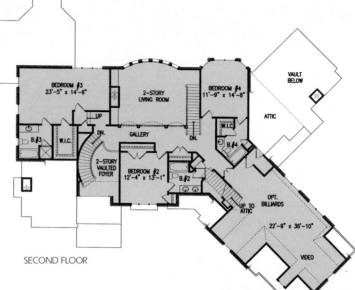

SECOND FLOOR

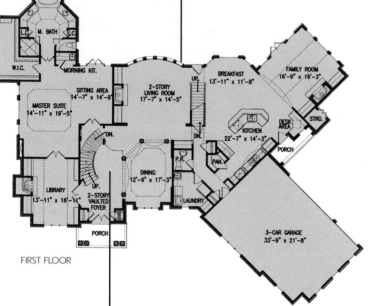

FIRST FLOOR

plan# HPK1006011

STYLE: FRENCH COUNTRY
FIRST FLOOR: 3,056 SQ. FT.
SECOND FLOOR: 1,307 SQ. FT.
TOTAL: 4,363 SQ. FT.
BONUS SPACE: 692 SQ. FT.
BEDROOMS: 4
BATHROOMS: 4½
WIDTH: 94'-4"
DEPTH: 79'-2"
FOUNDATION: CRAWLSPACE,
FINISHED BASEMENT,
UNFINISHED BASEMENT

SEARCH ONLINE @ EPLANS.COM

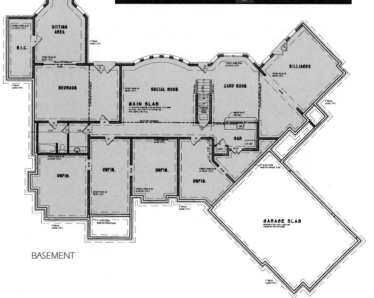

BASEMENT

Once again, the formal spaces dominate the bottom of the plan. The library to the left of the foyer is a luxurious spot for reading and office work. The fireplace here is a nice touch of nostalgia but can be replaced with more built-in shelving. The second entry into the library, from the master bedroom, is unusual but saves owners a trip through the foyer. On the other side of the foyer is the formal dining room, set off from the living room by decorative columns and a tray ceiling.

The remarkable two-story living room anchors the plan with a wall of windows and sheer size—about 240 square feet—which visually extend the room into the foyer and dining area. Built-in shelves and a fireplace mitigate the vast space by defining a cozy conversation area. In the home pictured here, high-contrast colors and molding also rein in space and bring visual interest to the walls.

The upstairs bedrooms are also suites and set apart for maximum privacy for occupants. Located at the corners and front of the plan, they also enjoy natural lighting and great views of the surrounding landscape. Of course, the addition of a bedroom is always possible, as is the conversion of the large billiards room above the garage. Such a large

Left: High-end materials and subtle detailing make the stairway a dramatic feature, not an overwhelming extravagance. Above: Perfectly chosen windows and decorative molding help control the vast space in the family room. Built-in cabinetry and just the right amount of furnishing keep the design coherent.

space could easily become a second-master suite or apartment space for an older child or live-in parent, complete with a separate entry.

It's hard to imagine homes of this size being modified for additional square footage, but it is still an option. For instance, owners may choose to build out the master bath to include an oversized shower and a second walk-in closet. More likely customizations will involve reassigning existing rooms to new tasks. Unfinished rooms in the basement can be recovered for living space, or for an impressive wine cellar.

If the floor plan of the home meets your needs, consider the materials being used in the interior of the home, which are as important to the use and enjoyment of a home as its layout. Consult with the builder about your preferences and get his or her advice on the balance between cost and benefit you want to maintain. There are materials available on the market that will deliver high quality at surprisingly low cost—and also are environmentally friendly. For example, wood floors are always a favorite among owners who want durability, low maintenance, and great looks. Mediate the high cost and environmental consequences of wood floors by choosing a builder-friendly and sustainable specie. See our guide to flooring on page 14 for more ideas. Similarly, windows and doors are parts of the home for which owners will find a wide variety of options—in fact, too many to cover fully in this book. See our review of popular doors and door products on page 31 and consult any popular home building and remodeling publication for more information. ■

Luxury in Residence

Thinking big? Find generous space
and sensitive details in this winning design.

A 5,500-square-foot plan isn't right for every neighborhood. But if you need your new home to stand a few feet taller above the ones next door, this plan takes luxury living to new heights. The revisited Southern plantation style is the perfect design theme to hold together the home's four bedrooms, soaring ceilings, robust stone columns, spiral stairway, and wealth of outdoor spaces. Exterior symmetry establishes a pleasing and dignified facade.

A low-pitch roof and crisp vertical lines bring a full-bodied look to the facade.

In the family room, veranda doors and windows echo the design of built-in cabinets. Crown molding and other decorative treatments control the room's height.

Right: The home's height advantage allows a dramatic stairway to sweep in at the center of the plan. Below: Observing the kitchen at night shows the designer's careful use of ambient and task lighting. Bottom: The handsome dining room can accommodate large families in comfort and style.

Hallways and overlooks control the real estate inside and help maintain healthy separations between shared and private spaces. For the effusive family room, however, the reins have been relaxed: 572 square feet of gathering and entertaining space with overflow options into the handsome veranda and breakfast nook. A large fireplace that would overwhelm lesser homes is gorgeous and correct here, as is the radial stairway at the center of the plan.

The library and dining room flank a prolonged foyer and announce an unaffected formal tone. Built-in shelves and art niches line the walls, between full-height windows. Casual versions of the two rooms are found at the rear of the home, near the kitchen—a design theme we've now seen in all our featured houses. The breakfast nook continues to be the daily gathering place for family members, and the nearby den complements its function. Note that the owners of this home have chosen to move the fireplace to the corner, perhaps to interrupt the geometry of a tile floor.

The island kitchen has been given an unorthodox shape but maintains proper distances between the main work stations: sink, stove, refrigerator, and prep areas. The angled layout also facilitates movement between stations. Aisles are wide enough to handle multiple chefs, but not wide enough

Right: In the master suite, columns establish a soft separation between the bed and sitting area. The private fireplace is an amenity that few owners can resist. Below: Moving the fireplace to the corner has made it less conspicuous, enabling a more restful sitting room.

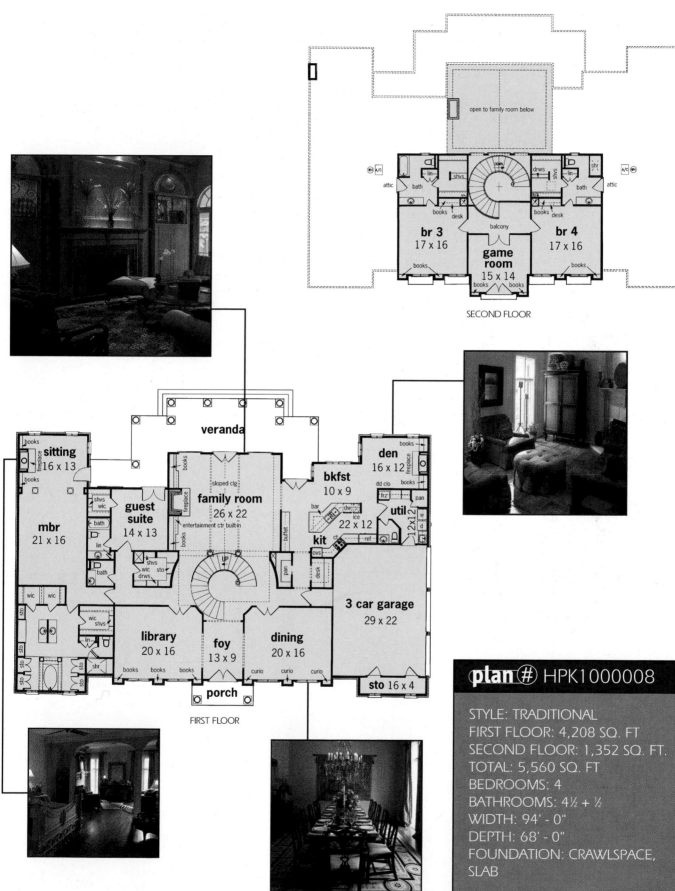

SECOND FLOOR

- br 3 17 x 16
- game room 15 x 14
- br 4 17 x 16
- open to family room below
- attic
- bath
- bath
- attic

FIRST FLOOR

- veranda
- sitting 16 x 13
- mbr 21 x 16
- guest suite 14 x 13
- family room 26 x 22
- sloped clg
- entertainment ctr built-in
- bkfst 10 x 9
- den 16 x 12
- util 12 x 12
- kit
- library 20 x 16
- foy 13 x 9
- dining 20 x 16
- 3 car garage 29 x 22
- sto 16 x 4
- porch

plan # HPK1000008

STYLE: TRADITIONAL
FIRST FLOOR: 4,208 SQ. FT
SECOND FLOOR: 1,352 SQ. FT.
TOTAL: 5,560 SQ. FT
BEDROOMS: 4
BATHROOMS: 4½ + ½
WIDTH: 94' - 0"
DEPTH: 68' - 0"
FOUNDATION: CRAWLSPACE, SLAB

SEARCH ONLINE @ EPLANS.COM

to feel awkward. Near-endless storage is provided by cabinets and pantry closets. Lighting—undeniably important in the kitchen but a detail often neglected by homeowners—consists of both ambient and task lighting. The first kind brightens the room and the second illuminates food preparation surfaces, usually as under-cabinet lighting. If not built during original construction, owners will need to install them after move in—often a more expensive option.

After baths, kitchens receive the most attention from homeowners. As a result, there is a vertiginous array of products and materials available to your builder and numerous ways to cater to your cooking style. Do you tend to cook with all your utensils and appliances out on the counter? Or do you clean as you cook, in smaller batches that don't require a lot of open space? The first kind of cook should invest in hardy, abuse-resistant surfaces and sinks. The second should ask for built-in conveniences and hide-away solutions. Think also about the kitchen floor: tile is a popular choice, but softer materials are less prone to cracking and easier on your feet.

Once again, the master suite is the star of the show. A 336-square-foot bedroom flows into a sizeable sitting area, complete with fireplace and private access to the veranda. Full-height windows bring in natural light and delicate columns softly separate the space from the rest of the suite. Dual vanities stand at the center of the master bath, surrounded by walk-ins and linen closets. At the bottom, a centerpiece whirlpool tub aspires to be a Roman bath. ■

Right: The kitchen shows good attention to lighting and a layout that can handle multiple chefs. Below: The master bath is a couple's paradise: separate vanities, but a whirlpool tub for two.

Grand Opening

The right doors add the perfect touch

Great Buy. With a beautiful six-paneled profile, the molded door above looks like a high-end wood door—yet it's surprisingly affordable. Be attentive to the design of interior doors and give your walls a truly finished look.

Glass Act. Including a walk-in pantry in your new kitchen? The right door can make it a strong design element, too. The pantry door above boasts an art-glass insert with a charming illustration of traditional pantry items.

Modern Love. For something more contemporary, consider the charming profile of this gorgeous entryway. The arched top is an understated but remarkable detail.

What a Treat. Owners can customize already purchased doors with handcrafted glass, such as this Craftsman-style geometric design. Patina or nickel finish caming (the metal between the pieces of glass) blends beautifully with surrounding details.

Rustic Rules. The perfect finishing touch for rustic-style interiors, the three-paneled interior door at right has an authentic, old-fashioned look. Be sure to choose matching door hardware.

Simple. For a look that's classic in its very simplicity, consider a Shaker-style door like the one at left. An understated door helps emphasize a room's existing design elements.

Elegant Entrance. This door enjoys all the weighty quality of a wood door, thanks to wood frame and a hearty core construction. A smooth finish makes it ideal for painting or staining.

Automatic for the People

HOME: 2,090 square-feet Country style, 3 bedrooms, 2½ baths
HOME PLAN: $950
DESIGN CONSULTATION: $250
EQUIPMENT: $29,223.70
INSTALLATION: $3,000*

Just as a well-planned layout can improve the everyday function of your home, a modern, intuitive wiring system can benefit your family's quality of life on a daily basis. Home automation—the integration of multiple electronics systems, such as lighting, climate control, telephone, home networking, and security—makes familiar and must-have household electronics work cooperatively and more intelligently than they can on their own. But unlike robot maids and other far-forward gadgets of an imagined future, home automation improves upon the functionality and convenience of devices you already depend on—televisions, smoke detectors, thermostats, speakers, security systems, and motion sensors.

For example, the door and window sensors of a typical home security system are triggered separately wherever monitored doors and windows open or close. Any motion sensors located in the property are also triggered wherever the hardware senses motion. In a typical system, the triggers are isolated, binary events and are not connected to provide a more meaningful report of the home environment. By contrast, an integrated home automation system achieves interpretive relationships between hardware components. The system can distinguish between "motion sensor triggered, window contact triggered" (homeowner walks across room, opens window) and "window contact triggered, motion sensor triggered" (someone opens window, enters home). The first event has bearing on the temperature system, which would compensate by lowering the thermostat in the affected area of the home. The second event concerns the security system, which would notify the monitoring center about a possible break-in.

Home automation providers can work with predrawn plans to provide a whole-house wiring map and components list in the same way modification designers provide customized blueprints. The components list also serves as a cost estimate and payment schedule that the subcontractor or "system integrator" will use to order the hardware specified in the design. The integrator will, of course, also charge for labor and any additional design that becomes necessary on site. Typically, the cost of installing a whole-house automation system comes to about 10 percent of the value of the home. See the info box at the top of the page for an estimated cost of the automation system featured at right. For more information on how to order a home automation estimate for your plan, turn to page 281. ■

Smoke detected in one room triggers a house-wide alarm. Consult the nearest control panel to confirm a possible emergency.

Built-in home and network hookups in every bedroom mean no unsightly wires running along floors or risky wireless networking.

The temperature sensors monitor and react in a measured way to changing situations by considering the comfort level of the entire home. For instance, opening a window in one room will be interpreted by the system as a voluntary act and will not cause the furnace to overreact to the drop in temperature.

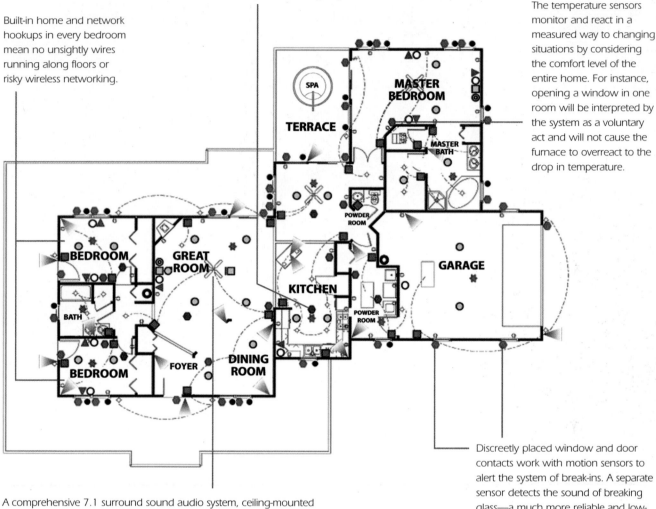

Discreetly placed window and door contacts work with motion sensors to alert the system of break-ins. A separate sensor detects the sound of breaking glass—a much more reliable and low-maintenance solution than traditional on-the-glass break sensors.

A comprehensive 7.1 surround sound audio system, ceiling-mounted projection unit, and drop-down screen enable theater-quality movie watching. Access controls for lights and curtains from the same wall-mounted control panel. Program the same controls to switch on/open at different times of the day to adjust automatically to changing temperature and light conditions.

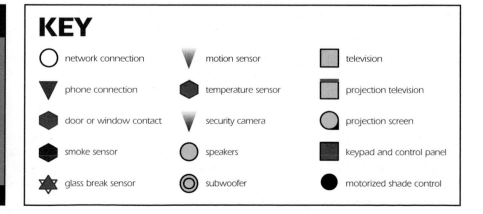

plan ⊕ HPK1000261

STYLE: FARMHOUSE
SQUARE FOOTAGE: 2,090
BEDROOMS: 3
BATHROOMS: 2½
WIDTH: 84' - 6"
DEPTH: 64' - 0"
FOUNDATION: CRAWLSPACE

SEARCH ONLINE @ EPLANS.COM

KEY

○ network connection
▼ phone connection
⬡ door or window contact
⬢ smoke sensor
✶ glass break sensor

▼ motion sensor
⬢ temperature sensor
▽ security camera
○ speakers
◎ subwoofer

◻ television
◻ projection television
○ projection screen
◼ keypad and control panel
● motorized shade control

Siding and stone and traditional dormers add country style to this lovely design. A covered front porch welcomes you inside to a foyer flanked by an octagonal study and a formal dining room. The family room is warmed by a fireplace and overlooks the back deck. The island kitchen easily serves the breakfast room. The master suite is secluded for privacy and includes a pampering bath and walk-in closet. Two additional family bedrooms are located on the opposite side of the plan and share a Jack-and-Jill bath. The two-car garage provides extra storage space. Upstairs, the bonus room easily converts to a home office or fourth bedroom and accesses the second-floor attic space.

plan# HPK1000009

STYLE: COUNTRY COTTAGE
SQUARE FOOTAGE: 1,991
BONUS SPACE: 462 SQ. FT.
BEDROOMS: 3
BATHROOMS: 2½
WIDTH: 60' - 0"
DEPTH: 57' - 6"
FOUNDATION: CRAWLSPACE, SLAB, UNFINISHED BASEMENT

SEARCH ONLINE @ EPLANS.COM

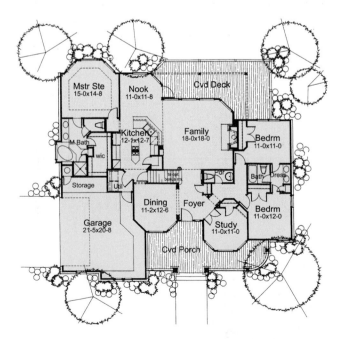

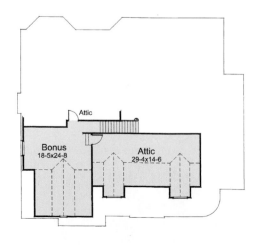

plan # HPK1000010

STYLE: TRADITIONAL
SQUARE FOOTAGE: 1,834
BEDROOMS: 3
BATHROOMS: 2
WIDTH: 55' - 0"
DEPTH: 60' - 4"
FOUNDATION: SLAB

SEARCH ONLINE @ EPLANS.COM

Corner quoins, French shutters, and rounded windows provide an Old World feel to this modern cottage design. A stunning brick facade hints at the exquisite beauty of the interior spaces. The great room is warmed by a fireplace and accesses the rear porch. The casual kitchen/dinette area provides pantry space. The master suite offers a private bath and enormous walk-in closet. Two family bedrooms on the opposite side of the home share a full hall bath and linen storage. A double garage and laundry room are located nearby.

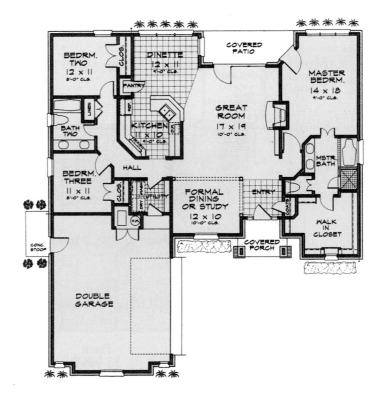

Run up a flight of stairs to an attractive four-bedroom home! The living room features a fireplace and easy access to the L-shaped kitchen. Here, a work island makes meal preparation a breeze. Two family bedrooms share a full bath and access to the laundry facilities. Upstairs, a third bedroom offers a private bath and two walk-in closets. The master suite is complete with a pampering bath, two walk-in closets, and a large private balcony.

plan# HPK1000013

STYLE: SEASIDE
FIRST FLOOR: 1,056 SQ. FT.
SECOND FLOOR: 807 SQ. FT.
TOTAL: 1,863 SQ. FT.
BEDROOMS: 4
BATHROOMS: 3
WIDTH: 33' - 0"
DEPTH: 54' - 0"
FOUNDATION: CRAWLSPACE, PIER

SEARCH ONLINE @ EPLANS.COM

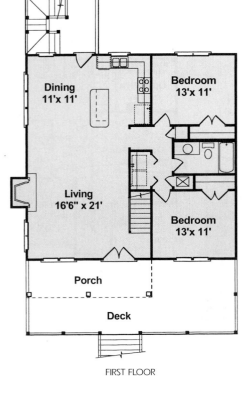

FIRST FLOOR

SECOND FLOOR

plan# HPK1000014

STYLE: TRADITIONAL
SQUARE FOOTAGE: 2,001
BEDROOMS: 3
BATHROOMS: 2
WIDTH: 60' - 0"
DEPTH: 50' - 0"
FOUNDATION: CRAWLSPACE

SEARCH ONLINE @ EPLANS.COM

Reminiscent of the security and comfort found in traditional American homes, this lovely design combines fresh country style with old-fashioned values. From the arched entry, the foyer leads inside to a sprawling great room, aptly named, with vaulted ceilings, a fireplace, and an optional media center. The open, unique kitchen easily serves the dining area, complete with a hutch area (or choose built-ins). Looking out over the rear property, the master suite enjoys a vaulted ceiling, pampering spa bath, and abundant closet space. Two bedrooms at the front of the home share an angled bath; a nearby den may also be used as a fourth bedroom. A two- or three-car garage accommodates a shop area for the do-it-yourselfer.

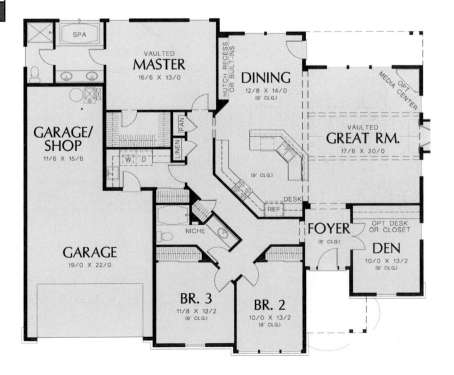

Varying rooflines and strong brick columns leading to the entrance provide bold first impressions to visitors of this home. Come inside to find a practical and inviting floor plan filled with thoughtful touches. Secluded to the far left of the plan are two bedrooms which share a full bath; the master suite is tucked away in the back right corner of the plan with an enormous walk-in closet and master bath. Living spaces are open to each other, with the kitchen easily serving the nook and living room—adorned with a lovely plant ledge—and a dining room nearby. Venture upstairs to the optional game room and finish it at your leisure.

plan # HPK1000015

STYLE: EUROPEAN COTTAGE
SQUARE FOOTAGE: 1,595
BONUS SPACE: 312 SQ. FT.
BEDROOMS: 3
BATHROOMS: 2
WIDTH: 49' - 0"
DEPTH: 60' - 0"

SEARCH ONLINE @ EPLANS.COM

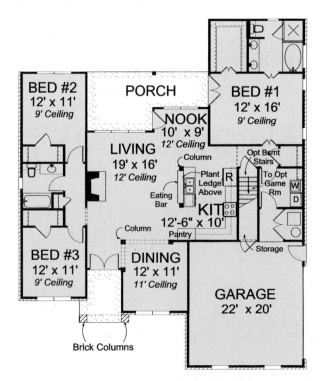

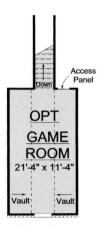

plan # HPK1000016

STYLE: CRAFTSMAN
FIRST FLOOR: 1,711 SQ. FT.
SECOND FLOOR: 773 SQ. FT.
TOTAL: 2,484 SQ. FT.
BONUS SPACE: 323 SQ. FT.
BEDROOMS: 4
BATHROOMS: 3½
WIDTH: 50' - 8"
DEPTH: 62' - 0"
FOUNDATION: CRAWLSPACE,
SLAB, UNFINISHED BASEMENT

SEARCH ONLINE @ EPLANS.COM

A rustic blend of Craftsman and farmhouse styles envelops a surprisingly comfortable floor plan with an open layout and abundant natural light. A wrapping front porch opens to the foyer, which leads to a parlor (or make it a formal dining room). Ahead, the great room is lit by a beautiful arched window and enjoys the warmth of a fireplace. The kitchen and family dining room are assisted by a serving-bar island. A home office is nearby. The master suite is located for privacy and delights in French doors, dual vanities, linen closets, walk-in closets with built-in seats, and a spectacular whirlpool tub and separate shower. Three upstairs bedrooms (one with a full bath and two sharing a bath) access optional bonus space, perfect as a playroom.

A rustic exterior of shingles, siding, and stone provides a sweet country look. Inside, the foyer is flanked by a dining room and family bedrooms. Bedrooms 2 and 3 share a full hall bath. The master suite, located on the opposite side of the home for privacy, boasts a tray ceiling and a pampering bath with an oversized tub. The kitchen opens to a breakfast room that accesses the rear sun deck. The enormous living room is warmed by a central fireplace. The laundry room and double-car garage complete this plan.

plan # HPK1000017

STYLE: TRADITIONAL
SQUARE FOOTAGE: 1,869
BONUS SPACE: 336 SQ. FT.
BEDROOMS: 3
BATHROOMS: 2
WIDTH: 54' - 0"
DEPTH: 60' - 6"
FOUNDATION: UNFINISHED
WALKOUT BASEMENT,
CRAWLSPACE, SLAB

SEARCH ONLINE @ EPLANS.COM

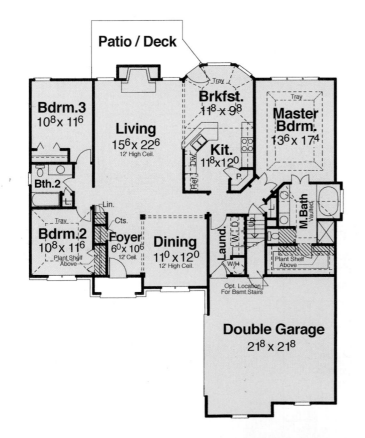

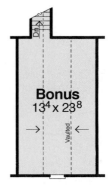

plan # HPK1000018

STYLE: MOUNTAIN
MAIN LEVEL: 790 SQ. FT.
UPPER LEVEL: 299 SQ. FT.
LOWER LEVEL: 787 SQ. FT.
TOTAL: 1,876 SQ. FT.
BEDROOMS: 3
BATHROOMS: 2
WIDTH: 32' - 4"
DEPTH: 24' - 4"
FOUNDATION: UNFINISHED
WALKOUT BASEMENT

SEARCH ONLINE @ EPLANS.COM

Here's a mountain cabin with plenty of space for entertaining. Three levels include a loft with space for computers, books, and games. The main level features an open living area set off with views from tall windows. The kitchen embraces a casual eating space and provides sliding glass doors that lead to the wraparound deck. Double doors open from the living room to a master bedroom. The lower level creates a thoughtful arrangement of secondary sleeping quarters and a sitting room with a fireplace.

UPPER LEVEL

MAIN LEVEL

LOWER LEVEL

This comfortable vacation design provides two levels of relaxing family space. The main level offers a spacious wrapping front porch and an abundance of windows, filling interior spaces with the summer sunshine. A two-sided fireplace warms the living room/dining room combination and a master bedroom that features a roomy walk-in closet. Nearby, the hall bath offers a relaxing whirlpool tub. The kitchen is open and features an island snack bar and pantry storage. A cozy sunroom accesses the wrapping deck. Upstairs, two additional bedrooms feature ample closet space and share a second-floor bath.

plan # HPK1000019

STYLE: LAKEFRONT
FIRST FLOOR: 1,212 SQ. FT.
SECOND FLOOR: 620 SQ. FT.
TOTAL: 1,832 SQ. FT.
BEDROOMS: 3
BATHROOMS: 2
WIDTH: 38' - 0"
DEPTH: 40' - 0"
FOUNDATION: UNFINISHED
WALKOUT BASEMENT

SEARCH ONLINE @ EPLANS.COM

4,50 X 4,40
15'-0" X 14'-8"

4,10 X 3,40
13'-8" X 11'-4"

3,60 X 4,80
12'-0" X 16'-0"

4,10 X 4,40
13'-8" X 14'-8"

3,30 X 4,80
11'-0" X 16'-0"

FIRST FLOOR

3,60 X 3,90
12'-0" X 13'-0"

4,90 X 3,60
16'-4" X 12'-0"

SECOND FLOOR

plan # HPK1000020

STYLE: COUNTRY COTTAGE
SQUARE FOOTAGE: 1,884
BEDROOMS: 3
BATHROOMS: 2½
WIDTH: 50' - 0"
DEPTH: 55' - 4"
FOUNDATION: SLAB,
CRAWLSPACE, UNFINISHED
WALKOUT BASEMENT

SEARCH ONLINE @ EPLANS.COM

Arched openings, decorative columns, and elegant ceiling details throughout highlight this livable floor plan. The country kitchen includes a spacious work area, preparation island, serving bar to the great room, and a breakfast nook with a tray ceiling. Set to the rear for gracious entertaining, the dining room opens to the great room. Note the warming fireplace and French-door access to the backyard in the great room. The master suite is beautifully appointed with a tray ceiling, bay window, compartmented bath, and walk-in closet. Two family bedrooms, a laundry room, and a powder room complete this gracious design.

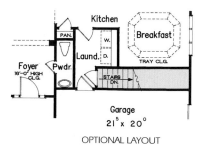

OPTIONAL LAYOUT

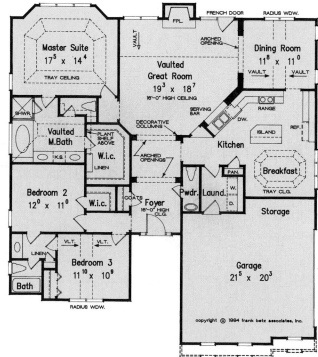

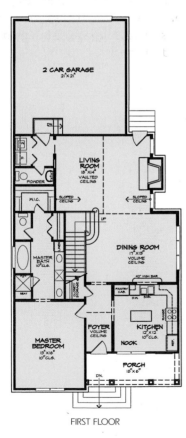

FIRST FLOOR

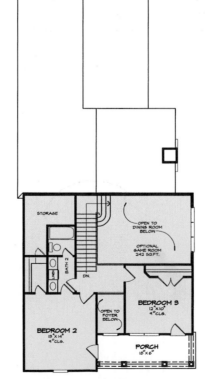

SECOND FLOOR

plan ⊕ HPK1000021

STYLE: TRADITIONAL
FIRST FLOOR: 1,347 SQ. FT.
SECOND FLOOR: 537 SQ. FT.
TOTAL: 1,884 SQ. FT.
BEDROOMS: 3
BATHROOMS: 2½
WIDTH: 32' - 10"
DEPTH: 70' - 10"
FOUNDATION: CRAWLSPACE

SEARCH ONLINE @ EPLANS.COM

This old-fashioned townhouse design features an attractive two-story floor plan. Two front covered porches enhance the traditional facade. Inside, the foyer introduces an island kitchen that overlooks the dining room. A formal two-story living room, located at the rear of the plan, is warmed by a fireplace. The first-floor master suite enjoys a private bath and huge walk-in closet. A powder room, laundry room, and two-car garage complete the first floor. Upstairs, two secondary bedrooms—one with a walk-in closet—share a full hall bath. Bedroom 3 features a private balcony overlooking the front property. Optional storage is available on the second floor.

plan # HPK1000022

STYLE: SW CONTEMPORARY
SQUARE FOOTAGE: 1,899
BEDROOMS: 3
BATHROOMS: 2
WIDTH: 43' - 4"
DEPTH: 79' - 6"
FOUNDATION: SLAB

SEARCH ONLINE @ EPLANS.COM

Long and slender, this pueblo-style home is perfect for a narrow lot. A facade graced with stepped rooflines and vigas brings the Southwest to your neighborhood. The well-lit entry begins with a columned living room—enclose the space for a generous bedroom. Ahead, the wet bar and dining room are ready to serve guests in style. Continue through arches to the hearth-warmed great room and breakfast nook, both with veranda access. The secluded master suite is located to the far left, splendid with an indulgent bath and private patio.

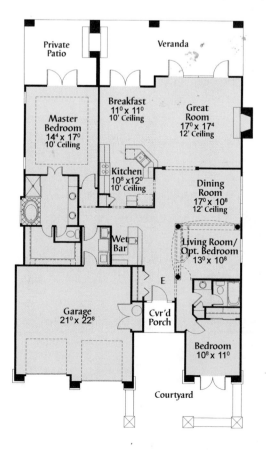

In the Craftsman tradition, this one-story home is enhanced by rubblework masonry and multipaned windows. The covered porch leads into the entry, flanked by the living room and formal dining room. The hearth-warmed family room enjoys views to the rear screened porch. The island kitchen provides plenty of counter space and close proximity to the breakfast nook. All bedrooms reside on the left side of the plan. The master bedroom boasts a private covered patio and lavish full bath, and two family bedrooms share a full bath. A unique shop area attached to the two-car garage completes the plan.

plan # HPK1000023

STYLE: BUNGALOW
SQUARE FOOTAGE: 1,922
BEDROOMS: 3
BATHROOMS: 2½
WIDTH: 79' - 3"
DEPTH: 40' - 0"
FOUNDATION: SLAB

SEARCH ONLINE @ EPLANS.COM

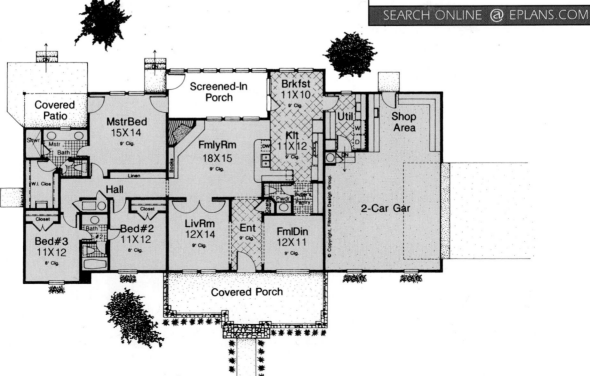

plan # HPK1000024

STYLE: SANTA FE
SQUARE FOOTAGE: 1,934
BEDROOMS: 3
BATHROOMS: 2½
WIDTH: 61' - 6"
DEPTH: 67' - 4"
FOUNDATION: SLAB

SEARCH ONLINE @ EPLANS.COM

Graceful curves welcome you into the courtyard of this Santa Fe home. Inside, a gallery directs traffic to the work zone on the left or the sleeping zone on the right. The wide covered rear porch is accessible from the dining room, the gathering room with fireplace, and the secluded master bedroom. The master bath features a whirlpool tub, separate shower, double vanity, and a spacious walk-in closet. Two additional bedrooms share a full bath with separate vanities. Extra storage space is provided in the two-car garage.

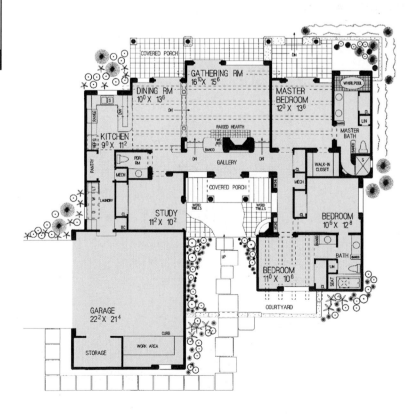

Craftsman-style windows decorate the facade of this beautiful bungalow design. Inside, the formal dining room, to the left of the foyer, can double as a study; the family room offers a sloping ceiling and a fireplace option. In the breakfast nook, a window seat and sliding glass doors that open to the covered patio provide places to enjoy the outdoors. The master bedroom dominates the right side of the plan, boasting a walk-in closet and private bath. Upstairs, two secondary bedrooms—both with walk-in closets, and one with a private bath—sit to either side of a game room.

plan # HPK1000025

STYLE: FARMHOUSE
FIRST FLOOR: 1,305 SQ. FT.
SECOND FLOOR: 636 SQ. FT.
TOTAL: 1,941 SQ. FT.
BEDROOMS: 4
BATHROOMS: 2½
WIDTH: 42' - 4"
DEPTH: 46' - 10"
FOUNDATION: CRAWLSPACE, SLAB, UNFINISHED BASEMENT

SEARCH ONLINE @ EPLANS.COM

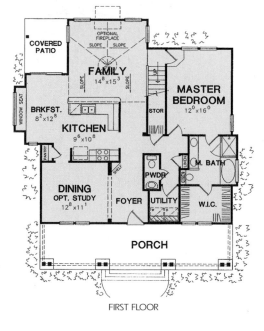

FIRST FLOOR

SECOND FLOOR

plan # HPK1000026

STYLE: SW CONTEMPORARY
SQUARE FOOTAGE: 1,949
BEDROOMS: 3
BATHROOMS: 2
WIDTH: 56' - 0"
DEPTH: 69' - 4"
FOUNDATION: SLAB

SEARCH ONLINE @ EPLANS.COM

Wide wall bases provide a sturdy appearance to this modern Southwestern home. Inside, the dining room is located off the entry, defined by a rounded tray ceiling. Just ahead, a large, modified-galley kitchen serves the breakfast nook with ease; a serving counter overlooks the great room's striking fireplace. A wet bar is an added benefit, great for entertaining. The nearby master suite enjoys French-door veranda access and a vaulted bath. Two additional bedrooms share a hall bath to the left of the plan.

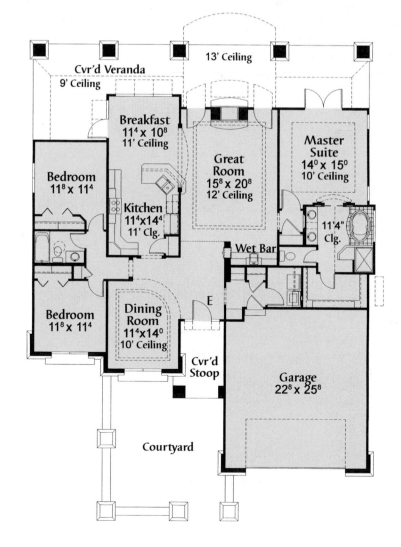

A double window highlighted by country shutters is the focal point of this home's facade, which also includes plenty of distinctive stone accents. Inside, the family room features a wall of windows that overlooks the rear covered porch. Lots of counter space, a pantry, and an island cooktop enhance the kitchen; the nearby breakfast nook opens to the porch. Two walk-in closets, a corner tub, and separate shower accent the master bath; the spacious master bedroom, like the great room, is brightened by a wall of windows. Two family bedrooms, one with a walk-in closet, reside upstairs.

plan# HPK1000027

STYLE: COUNTRY
FIRST FLOOR: 1,510 SQ. FT.
SECOND FLOOR: 442 SQ. FT.
TOTAL: 1,952 SQ. FT.
BEDROOMS: 3
BATHROOMS: 2½
WIDTH: 54' - 7"
DEPTH: 60' - 3"
FOUNDATION: SLAB,
UNFINISHED BASEMENT,
CRAWLSPACE

SEARCH ONLINE @ EPLANS.COM

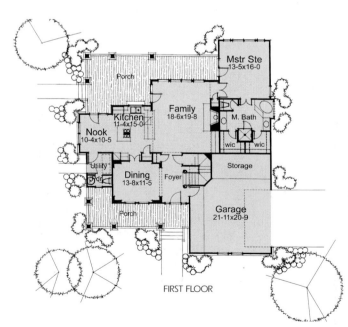

FIRST FLOOR

SECOND FLOOR

plan # HPK1000028

STYLE: CRAFTSMAN
FIRST FLOOR: 970 SQ. FT.
SECOND FLOOR: 988 SQ. FT.
TOTAL: 1,958 SQ. FT.
BEDROOMS: 3
BATHROOMS: 2½
WIDTH: 40' - 0"
DEPTH: 43' - 0"
FOUNDATION: CRAWLSPACE

SEARCH ONLINE @ EPLANS.COM

A sensible floor plan, with living spaces on the first floor and bedrooms on the second floor, is the highlight of this Craftsman home. Elegance reigns in the formal living room, with a vaulted ceiling and columned entry; this room is open to the dining room, which is brightened by natural light from two tall windows. Ideal for informal gatherings, the family room boasts a fireplace flanked by built-in shelves. The efficient kitchen includes a central island and double sink, and the nearby nook features easy access to the outdoors through sliding glass doors. The master suite includes a lavish bath with a corner spa tub and compartmented toilet; two additional bedrooms, one with a walk-in closet, share a full bath.

SECOND FLOOR

FIRST FLOOR

This mid-size ranch offers plentiful amenities all wrapped into a new compact design. The elegant brick exterior is accented by a Palladian window, multilevel trim, and an inviting front porch. The exquisite master suite, the three-car garage, and a large screened porch make this home irresistible. The exceptional master retreat provides direct access to the deck, a sitting area, a full-featured bath, and a spacious walk-in closet. A bay window brightens the breakfast room and kitchen. Vaulted or trayed ceilings adorn the living, family, and dining rooms, along with the master suite. Other rooms offer nine-foot ceilings. The secondary bedrooms provide walk-in closets and share a His and Hers bath.

plan # HPK1000029

STYLE: TRADITIONAL
SQUARE FOOTAGE: 1,992
BEDROOMS: 3
BATHROOMS: 2½
WIDTH: 63' - 0"
DEPTH: 57' - 2"
FOUNDATION: SLAB,
UNFINISHED BASEMENT,
CRAWLSPACE

SEARCH ONLINE @ EPLANS.COM

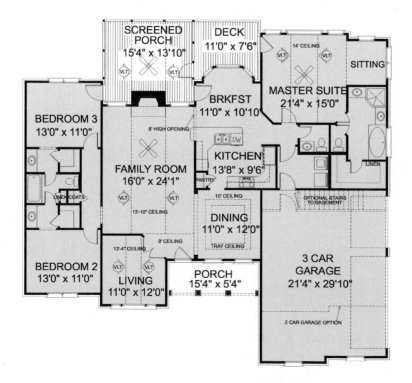

plan# HPK1000030

STYLE: TRADITIONAL
SQUARE FOOTAGE: 1,787
BONUS SPACE: 263 SQ. FT.
BEDROOMS: 3
BATHROOMS: 2
WIDTH: 55' - 8"
DEPTH: 56' - 6"
FOUNDATION: UNFINISHED
WALKOUT BASEMENT, SLAB,
CRAWLSPACE

SEARCH ONLINE @ EPLANS.COM

This striking and distinctive ranch home includes all the frills. From the inviting front porch to the screened porch and deck, this home provides dramatic spaces, luxurious appointments, and spacious living areas. It's carefully designed to provide the feel and features of a much larger home. The bonus room and basement provide plenty of space for expansion, so this home is one that won't soon be outgrown. Soaring ceilings enhance the entryway. To the left is the dining room—open to the entry and family room. The kitchen is open and provides both a breakfast and serving bar. The dramatic master suite is loaded with amenities such as a double step tray ceiling, direct access to the screened porch, a sitting room, deluxe bath, and His and Hers walk-in closets. The secondary bedrooms share a second bath.

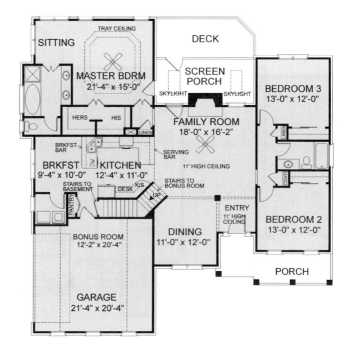

The wide front steps, columned porch, and symmetrical layout give this charming home a Georgian appeal. The large kitchen, with its walk-in pantry, island/snack bar, and breakfast nook, will gratify any cook. The central great room offers radiant French doors on both sides of the fireplace. Outside those doors is a comfortable covered porch with two skylights. To the left of the great room reside four bedrooms—three secondary bedrooms and a master bedroom. The master bedroom enjoys a walk-in closet, twin-vanity sinks, a separate shower and tub, and private access to the rear porch.

plan# HPK1000033

STYLE: COLONIAL
SQUARE FOOTAGE: 1,997
BEDROOMS: 4
BATHROOMS: 2½
WIDTH: 56' - 4"
DEPTH: 67' - 4"
FOUNDATION: CRAWLSPACE, SLAB, UNFINISHED BASEMENT

SEARCH ONLINE @ EPLANS.COM

Storage
17-4x5-8

Garage
20-4x21-4

Master Bedroom
12-0x17-1

Bath

Porch
17-4x10-0

1/2 Bath

Laundry
7-4x6-3

Bedroom
11-4x10-0

Bath

Greatroom
17-4x17-4

Pantry

Bedroom
11-4x11-4

Bedroom
11-3x10-1

Foyer

Dining
11-3x13-4

Kitchen/Breakfast
11-4x20-5

©Larry James Designs

Porch
31-0x8-0

1/2 Bath

Greatroom

Kitchen

Basement Stair Location

OPTIONAL LAYOUT

plan # HPK1000034

STYLE: COUNTRY COTTAGE
SQUARE FOOTAGE: 1,549
BONUS SPACE: 247 SQ. FT.
BEDROOMS: 3
BATHROOMS: 2
WIDTH: 52' - 4"
DEPTH: 49' - 0"
FOUNDATION: CRAWLSPACE,
UNFINISHED WALKOUT
BASEMENT

SEARCH ONLINE @ EPLANS.COM

The cozy comfort of the covered porch invites visitors through a short foyer and into the vaulted-ceilinged family room, complete with a central fireplace. The open floor plans allows the fireplace to warm the adjoining dining room, kitchen, and breakfast nook. A serving bar conveniently serves the area. Access to the rear covered porch is available from the breakfast nook. A short hallway leads to the master suite, two additional family bedrooms, and a full bath. French doors lead from the master bedroom into the master bath. Options include a bonus room/office and an additional full bath. The two-car garage offers convenient extra storage space.

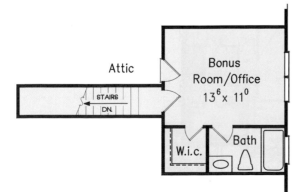

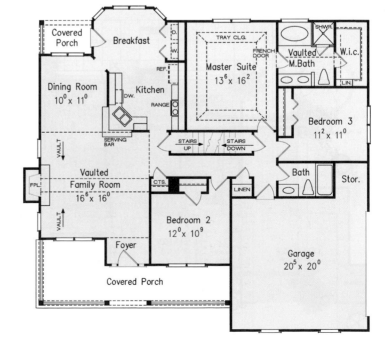

A portico entry, graceful arches, and brick detailing provide appeal and a low-maintenance exterior for this design. A half-circle transom over the entry lights the two-story foyer, and a plant shelf lines the hallway to the sunken family room. This living space holds a vaulted ceiling, masonry fireplace, and French-door access to the railed patio. The nearby kitchen has a center prep island, built-in desk overlooking the family room, and extensive pantries in the breakfast area. The formal dining room has a tray ceiling and access to the foyer and the central hall. The master suite is on the first level for privacy and convenience. It features a walk-in closet and lavish bath with twin vanities, a whirlpool tub, and separate shower. Three family bedrooms, two of which feature built-in desks, are on the second floor.

plan # HPK1000037

STYLE: TRADITIONAL
FIRST FLOOR: 1,445 SQ. FT.
SECOND FLOOR: 652 SQ. FT.
TOTAL: 2,097 SQ. FT.
BEDROOMS: 4
BATHROOMS: 2½
WIDTH: 56' - 8"
DEPTH: 48' - 4"
FOUNDATION: CRAWLSPACE,
UNFINISHED BASEMENT

SEARCH ONLINE @ EPLANS.COM

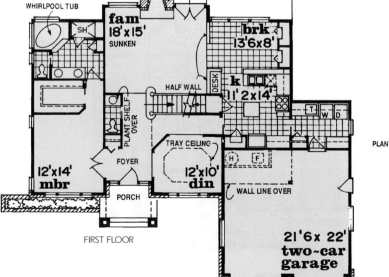

FIRST FLOOR

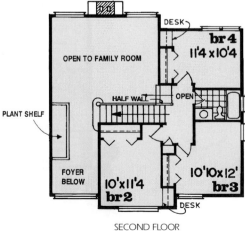

SECOND FLOOR

plan# HPK1000038

STYLE: CRAFTSMAN
FIRST FLOOR: 1,252 SQ. FT.
SECOND FLOOR: 985 SQ. FT.
TOTAL: 2,237 SQ. FT.
BONUS SPACE: 183 SQ. FT.
BEDROOMS: 4
BATHROOMS: 3
WIDTH: 40' - 0"
DEPTH: 51' - 0"
FOUNDATION: CRAWLSPACE, UNFINISHED BASEMENT

SEARCH ONLINE @ EPLANS.COM

This cozy Craftsman plan conveniently separates living and sleeping quarters, with family living areas on the first floor and bedrooms on the second. The plan begins with a vaulted living/dining room, and moves on to a great room that provides a fireplace flanked by built-ins. The adjacent kitchen includes a built-in desk and adjoins a breakfast nook that opens to the rear property. To the rear of the plan, the den can be converted to a fourth bedroom. Upstairs, a master suite—with a spa tub and walk-in closet with built-in shelves—joins two bedrooms and a vaulted bonus room.

SECOND FLOOR

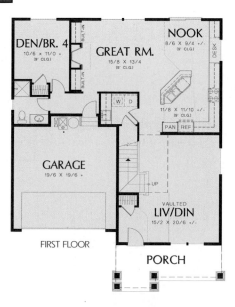

FIRST FLOOR

This home's facade employs an elegant balance of country comfort and traditional grace. Inside, the foyer opens to the formal dining room that features a coffered ceiling. Straight ahead, the great room offers a warm fireplace and open flow to the breakfast and kitchen areas. Two secondary bedrooms and a full bath can be found just off the kitchen. A bonus room, near the master suite, can be used as a nursery or den. The private master bath enjoys dual vanities, two walk-in closets, and a compartmentment toilet. Upstairs, unfinished space is ready for expansion.

plan # HPK1000039

STYLE: TRADITIONAL
SQUARE FOOTAGE 2,127
BEDROOMS: 3
BATHROOMS: 2½
WIDTH: 69' - 0"
DEPTH: 67' - 4"
FOUNDATION: UNFINISHED
BASEMENT, SLAB, CRAWLSPACE

SEARCH ONLINE @ EPLANS.COM

plan # HPK1000040

STYLE: TRADITIONAL
FIRST FLOOR: 1,112 SQ. FT.
SECOND FLOOR: 1,070 SQ. FT.
TOTAL: 2,182 SQ. FT.
BEDROOMS: 3
BATHROOMS: 3½
WIDTH: 57' - 0"
DEPTH: 48' - 8"
FOUNDATION: UNFINISHED
BASEMENT

SEARCH ONLINE @ EPLANS.COM

Symmetrically grand, this home features large windows which flood the interior with natural light. The massive sunken great room with a vaulted ceiling includes an exciting balcony overlook of the towering atrium window wall. The open breakfast nook and hearth room adjoin the kitchen. Four fireplaces throughout the house create an overall sense of warmth. A colonnade, a private entrance to the rear deck, and a sunken tub with a fireplace complement the master suite. Two family bedrooms share a dual-vanity bath between them.

This delightful country home is sure to please with the welcoming touch of the broad wraparound porch. Once inside, the open floor plan adjoins the living room, dining room, and kitchen areas, rather than designating formal quarters. A raised snack bar in the kitchen offers convenient service to the dining room. The master suite, a second bedroom, and a full bath complete the first floor. Upstairs, there is a loft with a view of the living room below, and an optional full bathroom for a possible future bedroom.

plan # HPK1000041

STYLE: COUNTRY COTTAGE
SQUARE FOOTAGE: 1,250
BONUS SPACE: 341 SQ. FT.
BEDROOMS: 2
BATHROOMS: 2
WIDTH: 52' - 6"
DEPTH: 45' - 8"
FOUNDATION: CRAWLSPACE, SLAB

SEARCH ONLINE @ EPLANS.COM

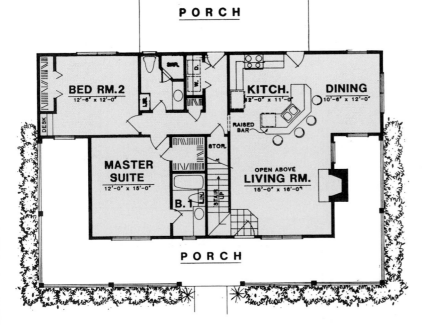

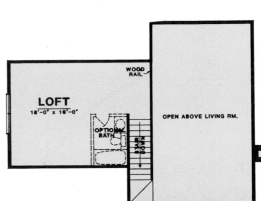

plan # HPK1000042

STYLE: TRADITIONAL
SQUARE FOOTAGE: 1,342
BONUS SPACE: 350 SQ. FT.
BEDROOMS: 3
BATHROOMS: 2
WIDTH: 52' - 6"
DEPTH: 39' - 10"
FOUNDATION: CRAWLSPACE,
UNFINISHED WALKOUT
BASEMENT, SLAB

SEARCH ONLINE @ EPLANS.COM

This striking brick home will immediately impress you with its ceilings. A 14-foot-high vaulted ceiling rises above the great room, which, with its warming fireplace, will be the center of all entertaining; the master suite enjoys a majestic tray ceiling. A handy serving bar separates the kitchen from the formal dining area, which opens to the great room. In addition to the lavish master suite, two other bedrooms share a bath. Additional space is available above the garage to build a fourth bedroom.

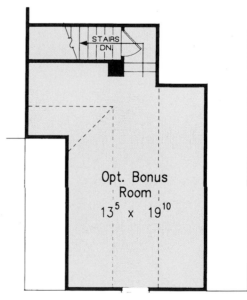

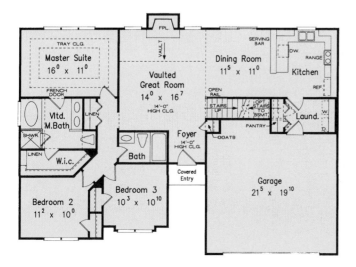

Enjoy an exciting floor plan that flows exceptionally well for lots of entertainment possibilities. High-volume ceilings throughout accentuate this open plan. A large gathering room off the full kitchen includes a magnificent Palladian window. An octagonal tray ceiling reflects the bay-window shape in the dining room. The master suite, located away from the other bedrooms for enhanced privacy, features its own private sitting area and morning bar, along with huge dual walk-in closets. The master retreat and gathering room are connected by a covered lanai complete with a skylight. A private deck is located off Suite 2.

plan# HPK1000043

STYLE: TRANSITIONAL
SQUARE FOOTAGE: 2,398
BEDROOMS: 3
BATHROOMS: 2½
WIDTH: 58' - 0"
DEPTH: 76' - 0"
FOUNDATION: CRAWLSPACE, UNFINISHED BASEMENT

SEARCH ONLINE @ EPLANS.COM

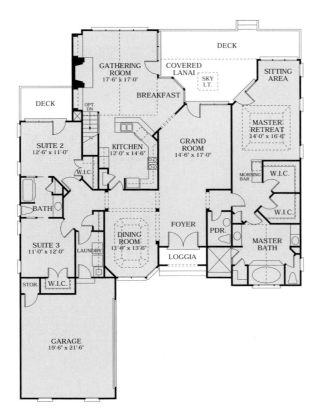

plan # HPK1000044

STYLE: COUNTRY COTTAGE
FIRST FLOOR: 812 SQ. FT.
SECOND FLOOR: 786 SQ. FT.
TOTAL: 1,598 SQ. FT.
BEDROOMS: 3
BATHROOMS: 2½
WIDTH: 52' - 0"
DEPTH: 28' - 0"
FOUNDATION: SLAB,
CRAWLSPACE

SEARCH ONLINE @ EPLANS.COM

This lovely Victorian home has a perfect balance of ornamental features making it irresistible, yet affordable. The beveled-glass front door invites you into a roomy foyer. The open kitchen and breakfast room and abundant counter space make cooking a pleasure. A large family room with a warming fireplace is convenient for either informal family gatherings or formal entertaining. The upper level includes a master suite with a multifaceted vaulted ceiling, a separate shower, and a six-foot garden tub. Two additional bedrooms share a conveniently located bath. A special feature is the large, closed-in storage space at the back of the two-car garage.

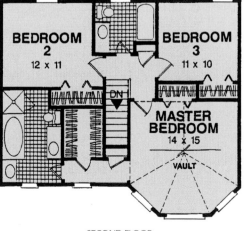

SECOND FLOOR

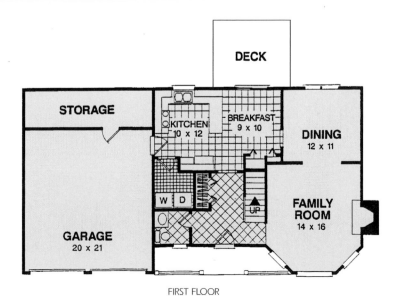

FIRST FLOOR

This charming design is accented with an array of country complements. The front porch welcomes you inside to a foyer flanked on either side by a dining room and study. The family room features a fireplace and views of the rear deck. Two family bedrooms sharing a Jack-and-Jill bath are located to the right of the plan. The island kitchen easily serves the breakfast nook. The master bedroom enjoys a private bath and walk-in closet. The garage features extra storage space. The second-floor option provides plans for two more bedrooms, a hall bath, and a game room.

plan# HPK1000045

STYLE: COUNTRY COTTAGE
SQUARE FOOTAGE: 1,991
BONUS SPACE: 938 SQ. FT.
BEDROOMS: 3
BATHROOMS: 2½
WIDTH: 60' - 0"
DEPTH: 57' - 6"
FOUNDATION: CRAWLSPACE, SLAB, UNFINISHED BASEMENT

SEARCH ONLINE @ EPLANS.COM

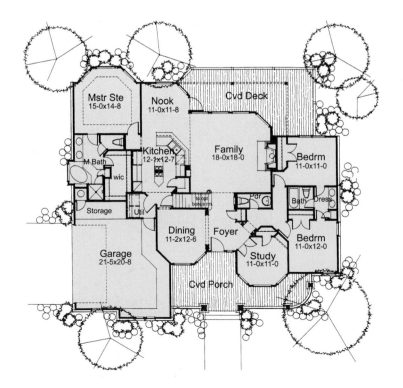

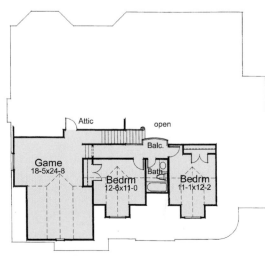

plan# HPK1000046

STYLE: COUNTRY COTTAGE
SQUARE FOOTAGE: 2,414
BEDROOMS: 3
BATHROOMS: 2½
WIDTH: 65' - 0"
DEPTH: 62' - 0"
FOUNDATION: SLAB

SEARCH ONLINE @ EPLANS.COM

Amenities abound in the efficient design of this country cottage. The fireplace in the great room provides warmth to the adjacent kitchen, breakfast nook, and dining room. If the warmth from the fireplace isn't enough, a sunroom is located off of the kitchen. A rear screened porch can be accessed from the breakfast nook and the master suite. The left side of the plan is dominated by the master suite. Features include a tray ceiling, a walk-in closet, dual vanities, a garden tub, a separate shower, and a compartmented toilet. Two additional family bedrooms share a full bath. A two-car garage equipped with extra storage space completes this plan.

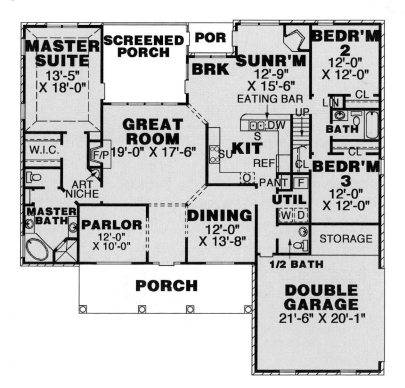

True country living is the feeling you get when you see this wrapped front porch and dormered front. An open flow leads you through the living room to the dining room where access through the bay opens to a sundeck. A friendly kitchen, which looks out to the front of the house, connects to a bayed breakfast area. The first floor master bedroom features a front porch view and a comfortable master bath suite with all the amenities. The garage entry can lead you to the kitchen, the back deck, a very spacious laundry room, or stairs that take you to a room above the garage. This space can be anything from a home office to a teen suite. The second floor provides two spacious bedrooms with a shared study or computer room.

plan# HPK1000047

STYLE: COUNTRY COTTAGE
FIRST FLOOR: 1,362 SQ. FT.
SECOND FLOOR: 729 SQ. FT.
TOTAL: 2,091 SQ. FT.
BONUS SPACE: 384 SQ. FT.
BEDROOMS: 3
BATHROOMS: 2½
WIDTH: 72' - 0"
DEPTH: 38' - 0"
FOUNDATION: UNFINISHED BASEMENT, SLAB, CRAWLSPACE

SEARCH ONLINE @ EPLANS.COM

Sundeck
16-8 x 14-0

Stor.
7-0 x 9-4

Dining
13-0 x 13-6

Brkfst.
10-0 x 9-4

Laund.

M.Bath

Lav.

Kit.
12-0 x 8-0

Master Bdrm.
13-6 x 17-0

Living Area
20-0 x 13-6

Double Garage
21-4 x 21-8

Foyer

Porch

FIRST FLOOR

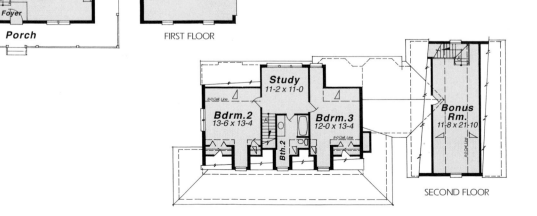

Study
11-2 x 11-0

Bdrm.2
13-6 x 13-4

Bdrm.3
12-0 x 13-4

Bth.2

Bonus Rm.
11-8 x 21-10

SECOND FLOOR

plan# HPK1000048

STYLE: TRADITIONAL
FIRST FLOOR: 906 SQ. FT.
SECOND FLOOR: 798 SQ. FT.
TOTAL: 1,704 SQ. FT.
BEDROOMS: 3
BATHROOMS: 2½
WIDTH: 29' - 8"
DEPTH: 33' - 10"
FOUNDATION: UNFINISHED
BASEMENT

SEARCH ONLINE @ EPLANS.COM

Elements of farmhouse style grace the facade of this rustic design. Inside, the floor plan is all modern. A huge great room in the rear is complemented by both a formal dining room and a casual breakfast room with a snack bar through to the kitchen. A corner fireplace in the great room warms a cozy gathering area. The two-car garage is easily accessed through a service entrance near the laundry. Bedrooms on the second floor consist of a master suite and two family bedrooms. The master suite enjoys a private bath; family bedrooms share a full bath.

SECOND FLOOR

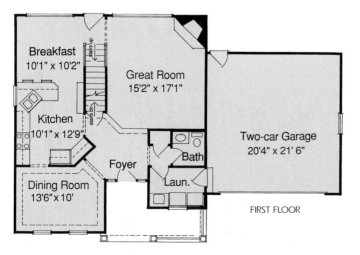

FIRST FLOOR

This fascinating Northwest Contemporary home enjoys two balcony-style decks and a master suite all to its own floor. The great room, dining area, and kitchen are joined together in a flexible and aesthetically pleasing open layout. French doors lead to both decks from the great room, warmed by a cozy fireplace. Two family bedrooms both have direct access to the same bath. Upstairs, the resplendent master suite reigns. A three-car garage, a workshop, and loads of unfinished storage space are located on the basement level.

plan# HPK1000049

STYLE: NW CONTEMPORARY
FIRST FLOOR: 1,538 SQ. FT.
SECOND FLOOR: 628 SQ. FT.
TOTAL: 2,166 SQ. FT.
BEDROOMS: 3
BATHROOMS: 2½
WIDTH: 53' - 0"
DEPTH: 35' - 0"
FOUNDATION: CRAWLSPACE,
UNFINISHED BASEMENT

SEARCH ONLINE @ EPLANS.COM

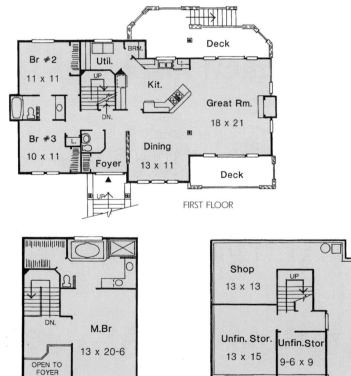

FIRST FLOOR

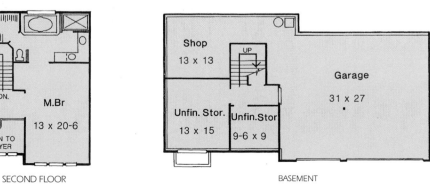

SECOND FLOOR

BASEMENT

plan # HPK1000050

STYLE: EUROPEAN COTTAGE
SQUARE FOOTAGE: 2,168
BONUS SPACE: 308 SQ. FT.
BEDROOMS: 3
BATHROOMS: 2
WIDTH: 44' - 10"
DEPTH: 79' - 10"
FOUNDATION: SLAB

SEARCH ONLINE @ EPLANS.COM

A touch of Tudor and a touch of the English cottage—this home is designed for comfort. A tiled entry, gallery, kitchen, and breakfast nook give a sense of casual space. The formal dining area is set to the right and enjoys a bumped-out bay window. Two bedrooms share a hall bath on the right of the plan. The master suite looks out to the rear covered patio and is pampered by a full bath and walk-in closet. The great room is the hub of this plan, featuring a warm fireplace and patio access. A bonus room is perfect for a guest bedroom or recreation room.

This beautiful three-bedroom home boasts many attractive features. Two covered porches will entice you outside; inside, a special sunroom on the first floor brings the outdoors in. The foyer opens on the right to a comfortable family room that may be used as a home office. On the left, the living area is warmed by the sunroom and a cozy corner fireplace. A formal dining area lies adjacent to an efficient kitchen with a central island and breakfast nook overlooking the back porch. The second level offers two family bedrooms served by a full bath. A spacious master suite with a walk-in closet and luxurious bath completes the second floor.

plan# HPK1000051

STYLE: VICTORIAN
FIRST FLOOR: 1,232 SQ. FT.
SECOND FLOOR: 951 SQ. FT.
TOTAL: 2,183 SQ. FT.
BONUS SPACE: 365 SQ. FT.
BEDROOMS: 3
BATHROOMS: 2½
WIDTH: 56' - 0"
DEPTH: 38' - 0"
FOUNDATION: UNFINISHED BASEMENT

SEARCH ONLINE @ EPLANS.COM

FIRST FLOOR

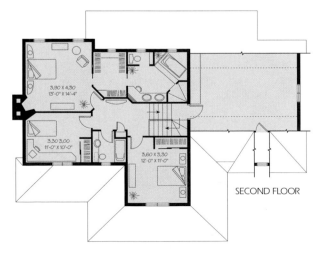

SECOND FLOOR

© William E. Poole Designs, Inc.

plan# HPK1000052

STYLE: GEORGIAN
FIRST FLOOR: 1,209 SQ. FT.
SECOND FLOOR: 1,005 SQ. FT.
TOTAL: 2,214 SQ. FT.
BONUS SPACE: 366 SQ. FT.
BEDROOMS: 3
BATHROOMS: 2½
WIDTH: 65' - 4"
DEPTH: 40' - 4"
FOUNDATION: CRAWLSPACE

SEARCH ONLINE @ EPLANS.COM

The rebirth of a style—this design salutes the look of Early America. From the porch, step into the two-story foyer, and either venture to the left towards the living room and dining room, or to the right where the family room sits. A central fireplace in the family room warms the island kitchen. The open design allows unrestricted interaction. Upstairs, the master suite boasts a roomy bath with a dual-sink vanity, a whirlpool tub, a private toilet, a separate shower, and His and Hers walk-in closets. Two additional family bedrooms share a full bath. Future expansion space completes this level.

SECOND FLOOR

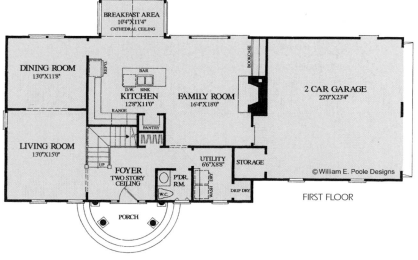

© William E. Poole Designs

FIRST FLOOR

Steeply pitched gables on this home's facade bring to mind quaint country churches, but this home takes quaint and pushes it to comfortable luxury. The formal dining room sits across the tiled gallery from the spacious great room. Plenty of natural light filters in from the wall of windows in the great room. To the right, two family bedrooms share a Jack-and-Jill bath and feature walk-in closets. A large kitchen, breakfast area and utility room serve both casual and formal areas. The master suite enjoys a roomy bath and walk-in closet. An extra bedroom or study is just down the hall, close to a full bath.

plan # HPK1000053

STYLE: EUROPEAN COTTAGE
SQUARE FOOTAGE: 2,288
BEDROOMS: 4
BATHROOMS: 3
WIDTH: 57' - 5"
DEPTH: 57' - 10"
FOUNDATION: SLAB

SEARCH ONLINE @ EPLANS.COM

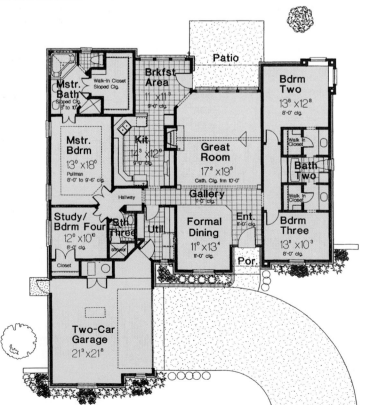

plan # HPK1000054

STYLE: TRADITIONAL
SQUARE FOOTAGE: 2,311
BEDROOMS: 3
BATHROOMS: 2½
WIDTH: 64' - 0"
DEPTH: 57' - 2"

SEARCH ONLINE @ EPLANS.COM

Interesting details on the front porch add to the appeal of this ranch home. The great room is highlighted by a pass-through wet bar/buffet and sits just across the hall from the formal dining room. The bedrooms are found in a cluster to the right of the home: a master suite, and two family bedrooms sharing a full bath. The private master suite contains a shower with glass-block detailing, a whirlpool tub, and dual vanities.

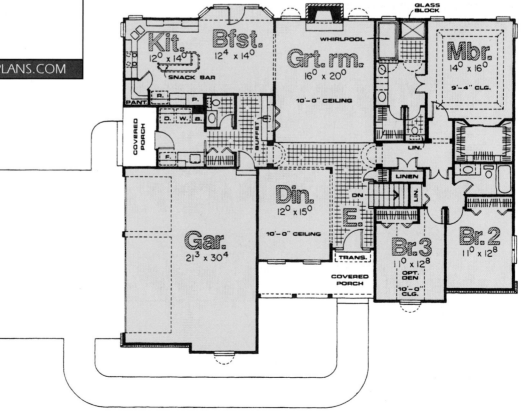

A hipped roof, siding, and stone accents bring a Neoclassical element to this traditional family home. Inside, the two-story great room is inviting, with a fireplace and lots of natural light. The living room/study is entered through French doors and is set in a box-bay window. A country kitchen serves the dining room and breakfast area with ease; covered-porch access beckons outdoor meals. The second-floor master suite enjoys a sitting area and a vaulted bath with a garden tub. Two bedrooms, one with a sitting area and a walk-in closet, share a full bath.

plan# HPK1000055

STYLE: TRADITIONAL
FIRST FLOOR: 1,208 SQ. FT.
SECOND FLOOR: 1,137 SQ. FT.
TOTAL: 2,345 SQ. FT.
BEDROOMS: 3
BATHROOMS: 3
WIDTH: 38' - 6"
DEPTH: 51' - 4"
FOUNDATION: CRAWLSPACE,
UNFINISHED WALKOUT
BASEMENT

SEARCH ONLINE @ EPLANS.COM

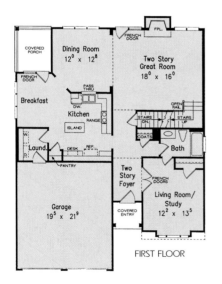

FIRST FLOOR

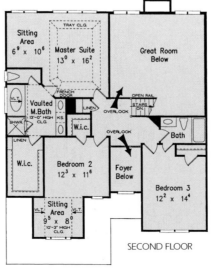

SECOND FLOOR

plan # HPK1000057

STYLE: EUROPEAN COTTAGE
SQUARE FOOTAGE: 2,388
BEDROOMS: 3
BATHROOMS: 2 1/2
WIDTH: 63' - 0"
DEPTH: 60' - 0"
FOUNDATION: CRAWLSPACE,
UNFINISHED WALKOUT
BASEMENT, SLAB

SEARCH ONLINE @ EPLANS.COM

This three-bedroom home brings the past to life with Tuscan columns, dormers, and fanlight windows. The entrance is flanked by the dining room and study. The great room boasts cathedral ceilings and a fireplace, with an open design that connects to the kitchen area. The spacious kitchen adjoins a breakfast nook and accesses the rear covered veranda. The master bedroom enjoys a sitting area, access to the covered veranda, and a spacious bathroom. This home is complete with two family bedrooms.

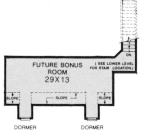

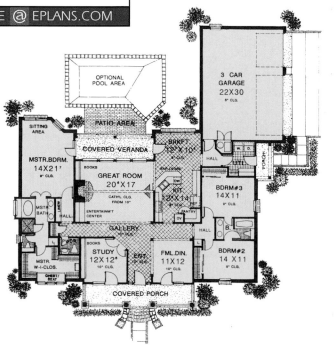

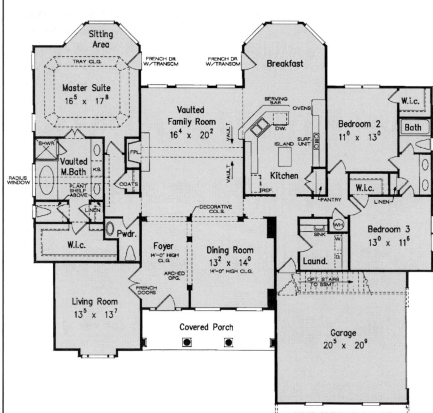

Master Suite
16⁵ x 17⁸

Sitting Area

TRAY CLG.

FRENCH DR. W/TRANSOM

FRENCH DR. W/TRANSOM

Breakfast

SERVING BAR

OVENS

W.i.c.

Bath

Bedroom 2
11⁰ x 13⁰

Vaulted Family Room
16⁴ x 20²

VAULT

VAULT

DW.

ISLAND

SURF. UNIT

SHWR.

KS.

Vaulted M.Bath

FPL.

COATS

Kitchen

REF.

RADIUS WINDOW

PLANT SHELF ABOVE

LINEN

DECORATIVE COLS.

PANTRY

W.i.c.

LINEN

Pwdr.

W.i.c.

Foyer
14'-0" HIGH CLG.

Dining Room
13² x 14⁰
14'-0" HIGH CLG.

SINK

Laund.

WH

Bedroom 3
13⁰ x 11⁵

ARCHED OPG.

OPT. STAIRS TO BSMT.

Living Room
13⁵ x 13⁷

FRENCH DOORS

Covered Porch

Garage
20⁵ x 20⁹

GARAGE LOCATION WITH BASEMENT

plan# HPK1000057

STYLE: EUROPEAN COTTAGE
SQUARE FOOTAGE: 2,388
BEDROOMS: 3
BATHROOMS: 2½
WIDTH: 63' - 0"
DEPTH: 60' - 0"
FOUNDATION: CRAWLSPACE, UNFINISHED WALKOUT BASEMENT, SLAB

SEARCH ONLINE @ EPLANS.COM

Quoins, arched lintels, and twin pedimented dormers lend this house a sweet country feel. Columns and a vaulted ceiling make the interior elegant. French doors lead to a living room found at the left of the entrance, and decorative columns adorn the elegant dining room. The spacious family room is enhanced by the vaulted ceiling and cozy fireplace. Two lovely bay windows embellish the rear of the house. The island kitchen features a roomy pantry, a serving bar, and a breakfast area with a French door that opens to the outside through a transom. The master suite boasts a tray ceiling, sitting area, a deluxe bath with built-in plant shelves, a radius window, dual vanities, and a large walk-in closet.

plan# HPK1000058

STYLE: VICTORIAN
FIRST FLOOR: 1,600 SQ. FT.
SECOND FLOOR: 790 SQ. FT.
TOTAL: 2,390 SQ. FT.
BEDROOMS: 4
BATHROOMS: 3½
WIDTH: 45' - 0"
DEPTH: 54' - 0"
FOUNDATION: CRAWLSPACE

SEARCH ONLINE @ EPLANS.COM

Queen Anne houses, with their projecting bays, towers, and wraparound porches, are the apex of the Victorian era. This up-to-date rendition of the beloved style captures a floor plan that is as dramatic on the inside as it is on the outside. The front-facing pediment ornamented with typical gable detailing highlights the front doorway and provides additional welcome to this enchanted abode. The angles and bays that occur in every first-floor room add visual excitement to formal and informal living and dining areas. A well-lit breakfast bay with its soaring ceiling is a spectacular addition to this classic plan. The first-floor master suite features two walk-in closets. Three upstairs bedrooms also have spacious walk-in closets.

FIRST FLOOR

SECOND FLOOR

plan # HPK1000059

STYLE: FRENCH
FIRST FLOOR: 1,566 SQ. FT.
SECOND FLOOR: 837 SQ. FT.
TOTAL: 2,403 SQ. FT.
BEDROOMS: 5
BATHROOMS: 4½
WIDTH: 116' - 3"
DEPTH: 55' - 1"
FOUNDATION: UNFINISHED BASEMENT

SEARCH ONLINE @ EPLANS.COM

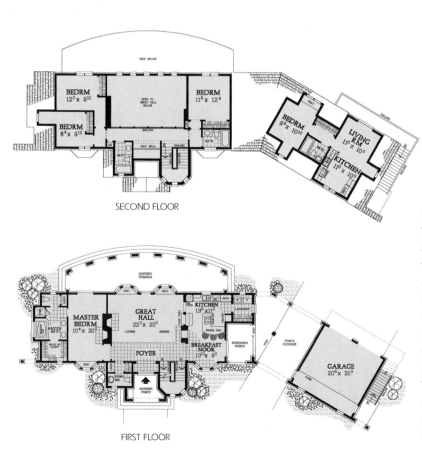

SECOND FLOOR

FIRST FLOOR

Be the owner of your own country estate—this two-story home gives the look and feel of grand-style living without the expense of large square footage. The entry leads to a massive foyer and great hall. There's space enough here for living and dining areas. Two window seats in the great hall overlook the rear veranda. One fireplace warms the living area, another looks through the dining room to the kitchen and breakfast nook. A screened porch offers casual dining space for warm weather. The master suite has another fireplace and a window seat and adjoins a luxurious master bath with a separate tub and shower. The second floor contains three family bedrooms and two full baths. A separate apartment over the garage includes its own living room, kitchen, and bedroom.

plan # HPK1000060

STYLE: TRADITIONAL
SQUARE FOOTAGE: 2,517
BEDROOMS: 3
BATHROOMS: 2½
WIDTH: 77' - 0"
DEPTH: 59' - 0"

SEARCH ONLINE @ EPLANS.COM

This European stucco home is a well-designed one-story villa. Turrets top identical bayed rooms that are enclosed behind double doors just off the entry. The formal dining room and study are situated in the window-filled turrets. The family room is a spacious entertaining area with a fireplace and built-ins. An efficient kitchen is uniquely designed with its island and angular shape. The split-bedroom floor plan places the master suite away from the two family bedrooms.

With a solid exterior of rough cedar and stone, this new French Country design will stand the test of time. A wood-paneled study in the front features a large bay window. The heart of the house is found in a large open great room with a built-in entertainment center. The spacious master bedroom features a corner reading area and access to an adjacent covered patio. A three-car garage and three additional bedrooms complete this generous family home.

plan# HPK1000061

STYLE: FRENCH
SQUARE FOOTAGE: 2,590
BEDROOMS: 4
BATHROOMS: 3½
WIDTH: 73' - 6"
DEPTH: 64' - 10"
FOUNDATION: SLAB

SEARCH ONLINE @ EPLANS.COM

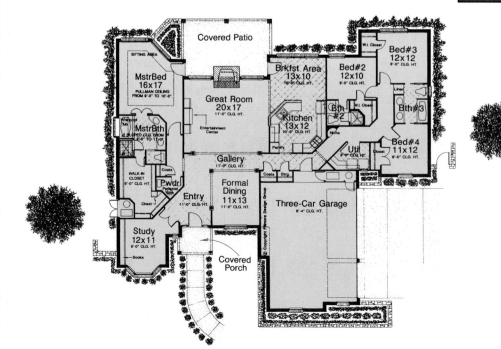

plan# HPK1000062

STYLE: MEDITERRANEAN
SQUARE FOOTAGE: 2,831
BEDROOMS: 4
BATHROOMS: 3
WIDTH: 84' - 0"
DEPTH: 77' - 0"
FOUNDATION: SLAB

SEARCH ONLINE @ EPLANS.COM

Besides great curb appeal, this home has a wonderful floor plan. The foyer features a fountain that greets visitors and leads to a formal dining room on the right and a living room on the left. A large family room at the rear has a built-in entertainment center and a fireplace. The U-shaped kitchen is perfectly located for servicing all living and dining areas. To the right of the plan, away from the central entertaining spaces, are three family bedrooms sharing a full bath. On the left side, with solitude and comfort for the master suite, are a large sitting area, an office, and an amenity-filled bath. A deck with a spa sits outside the master suite.

Loft

Open to Below

Opt. Bath

Bonus Room
29'-6" x 20'-0"

CL

CL CL

Dn

CL

CL

Bath 1

Bedroom 1
12'-10" x 10'-10"

art niche

Bedroom 2
12'-10" x 13'-2"

Whirlpool

SECOND FLOOR

plan# HPK1000063

STYLE: FARMHOUSE
FIRST FLOOR: 2,151 SQ. FT.
SECOND FLOOR: 738 SQ. FT.
TOTAL: 2,889 SQ. FT.
BONUS SPACE: 534 SQ. FT.
BEDROOMS: 3
BATHROOMS: 2½
WIDTH: 99' - 0"
DEPTH: 56' - 0"
FOUNDATION: CRAWLSPACE

SEARCH ONLINE @ EPLANS.COM

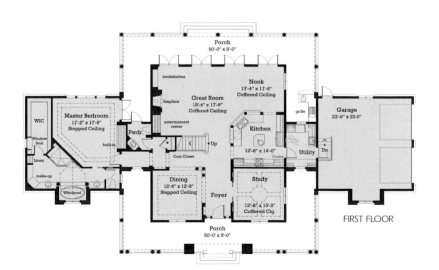

Porch
50'-0" x 8'-0"

bookshelves

Nook
13'-4" x 11'-6"
Coffered Ceiling

Great Room
18'-4" x 17'-6"
Coffered Ceiling

fireplace

WIC

Master Bedroom
17'-2" x 17'-6"
Stepped Ceiling

Window Seat

Linen

make-up

Whirlpool

entertainment center

built-in

Pwdr.

Coat Closet

Up

Kitchen

12'-8" x 14'-0"

Pantry

Utility

grille

Garage
23'-6" x 23'-0"

Dn

Dining
12'-6" x 12'-8"
Stepped Ceiling

Foyer

Study

12'-8" x 13'-2"
Coffered Clg.

Porch
50'-0" x 8'-0"

FIRST FLOOR

A wide, welcoming porch and plenty of stone accents highlight the facade of this charming symmetrical design. Inside, coffered ceilings enhance the study, great room, and breakfast nook; the dining room and master suite both boast stepped ceilings. From the great room, four sets of French doors open to a wraparound rear porch with a grilling area. The master bedroom, also with porch access, includes built-in shelves, a walk-in closet with a window seat, and a luxurious bath with a whirlpool tub. On the second floor, two family bedrooms share a full bath with a whirlpool tub; a loft area and a bonus room offer extra space.

© William E. Poole Designs, Inc.

plan # HPK1000064

STYLE: FARMHOUSE
FIRST FLOOR: 1,913 SQ. FT.
SECOND FLOOR: 997 SQ. FT.
TOTAL: 2,910 SQ. FT.
BONUS SPACE: 377 SQ. FT.
BEDROOMS: 4
BATHROOMS: 3½
WIDTH: 63' - 0"
DEPTH: 59' - 4"
FOUNDATION: CRAWLSPACE,
UNFINISHED BASEMENT

SEARCH ONLINE @ EPLANS.COM

This enchanting farmhouse brings the past to life with plenty of modern amenities. An open-flow kitchen/breakfast area and family room combination is the heart of the home, opening up to the screened porch and enjoying the warmth of a fireplace. For more formal occasions, the foyer is flanked by a living room on the left and a dining room on the right. An elegant master bedroom, complete with a super-size walk-in closet, is tucked away quietly behind the garage. Three more bedrooms reside upstairs, along with two full baths and a future recreation room.

SECOND FLOOR

FIRST FLOOR

Distinctive windows, round columns, and well-planned projections lend a touch of grandeur to the charming front porch of this alluring home. Horizontal siding and a stone chimney provide captivating complements to the exterior. The living room opens to the great room and includes two sets of doors to the front porch. The great room features built-in bookshelves and a fireplace. A large kitchen, adjacent to a compact office, easily serves the breakfast room and the dining room. Upstairs, a spacious master suite features a tray ceiling and a walk-in closet. Three additional bedrooms and a bonus room with access to a rear staircase complete the upper floor.

plan# HPK1000065

STYLE: FARMHOUSE
FIRST FLOOR: 1,652 SQ. FT.
SECOND FLOOR: 1,460 SQ. FT.
TOTAL: 3,112 SQ. FT.
BONUS SPACE: 256 SQ. FT.
BEDROOMS: 4
BATHROOMS: 3½
WIDTH: 48' - 0"
DEPTH: 78' - 4"
FOUNDATION: UNFINISHED
WALKOUT BASEMENT

SEARCH ONLINE @ EPLANS.COM

Two Car Garage 22³ x 21³

Porch

Kitchen 14⁶ x 13⁰

Breakfast 14⁹ x 12⁰

Great Room 16⁰ x 19³

Office

Foyer

Dining Room 12³ x 15⁹

Living Room 13⁶ x 13⁶

Covered Porch

FIRST FLOOR

Future Bonus Room 12⁶ x 22⁶

WIC

Master Suite 14⁹ x 21⁶

Master Bath

Bedroom #4 13⁶ x 12⁹

Bedroom #2 13⁶ x 12⁹

Bedroom #3 13⁶ x 11⁶

SECOND FLOOR

plan # HPK1000066

STYLE: FRENCH COUNTRY
FIRST FLOOR: 2,390 SQ. FT.
SECOND FLOOR: 765 SQ. FT.
TOTAL: 3,155 SQ. FT.
BONUS SPACE: 433 SQ. FT.
BEDROOMS: 4
BATHROOMS: 3½
WIDTH: 87' - 11"
DEPTH: 75' - 2"
FOUNDATION: CRAWLSPACE

SEARCH ONLINE @ EPLANS.COM

The grand exterior of this Normandy country design features a steeply pitched gable roofline. Arched dormers repeat the window accents. Inside, the promise of space is fulfilled with a large gathering room that fills the center of the house and opens to a long trellised veranda. The den or guest suite with a fireplace, the adjacent powder room, and the master suite with a vaulted ceiling and access to the veranda reside in the right wing. Two additional bedrooms with two baths and a loft overlooking the gathering room are upstairs. A large bonus room is found over the garage and can be developed later as office or hobby space.

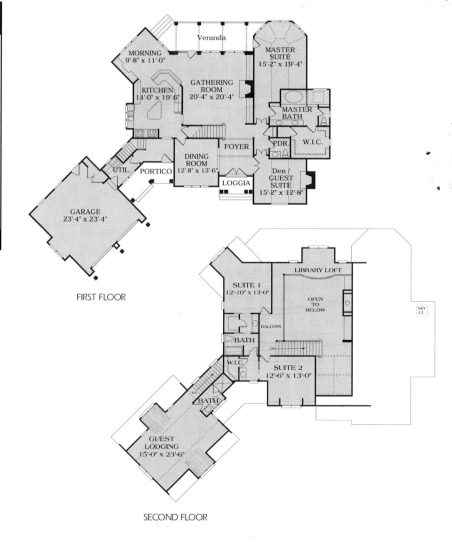

FIRST FLOOR

SECOND FLOOR

Perfect for a sloping lot, this Craftsman design boasts two levels of living space. Plenty of special amenities—vaulted ceilings in the living, dining, and family rooms, as well as in the master bedroom; built-ins in the family room and den; a large island cooktop in the kitchen; and an expansive rear deck—make this plan stand out. All three of the bedrooms—a main-level master suite and two lower-level bedrooms—include walk-in closets. Also on the lower level, find a recreation room with built-ins and a fireplace.

plan# HPK1000067

STYLE: CRAFTSMAN
MAIN LEVEL: 2,170 SQ. FT.
LOWER LEVEL: 1,076 SQ. FT.
TOTAL: 3,246 SQ. FT.
BEDROOMS: 3
BATHROOMS: 2½
WIDTH: 74' - 0"
DEPTH: 54' - 0"
FOUNDATION: SLAB, FINISHED WALKOUT BASEMENT

SEARCH ONLINE @ EPLANS.COM

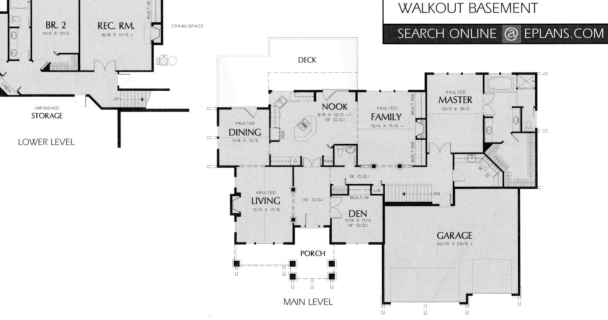

plan# HPK1000068

STYLE: TRADITIONAL
FIRST FLOOR: 2,292 SQ. FT.
SECOND FLOOR: 1,028 SQ. FT.
TOTAL: 3,320 SQ. FT.
BEDROOMS: 5
BATHROOMS: 3½ + ½
WIDTH: 68' - 0"
DEPTH: 56' - 6"
FOUNDATION: UNFINISHED
BASEMENT

SEARCH ONLINE @ EPLANS.COM

This majestic brick home fits new traditional neighborhoods perfectly, with an inviting front porch and a side-loading garage. Formal and flex rooms accommodate modern lifestyles and allow space for surfing online or even a home office. The foyer opens to the dining room and a study—or make it a guest bedroom. The gourmet kitchen boasts an island counter and opens to an old-fashioned keeping room, which features a fireplace. The breakfast room offers a bay window to let the sunlight in and opens to an expansive deck. The master suite sports a tray ceiling and a bath that provides more than just a touch of luxury. Upstairs, two family bedrooms share a full bath; a guest bedroom features a private bath.

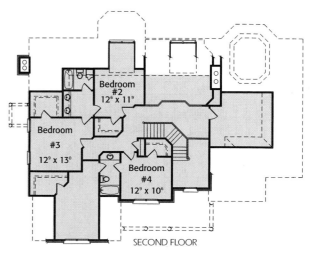

SECOND FLOOR

Bedroom #2
12⁶ x 11⁹

Bedroom #3
12⁹ x 13⁰

Bedroom #4
12⁹ x 10⁶

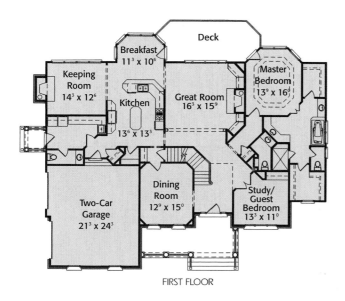

Deck

Breakfast
11³ x 10⁶

Keeping Room
14³ x 12⁶

Kitchen
13⁶ x 13³

Great Room
16³ x 15⁹

Master Bedroom
13⁹ x 16⁰

Two-Car Garage
21³ x 24³

Dining Room
12⁹ x 15⁰

Study/Guest Bedroom
13³ x 11⁰

FIRST FLOOR

This uniquely designed home is dazzled in Mediterranean influences and eye-catching luxury. A grand arching entrance welcomes you inside to a spacious foyer that introduces a curved staircase and flanking living and dining rooms on either side. Casual areas of the home are clustered to the rear left of the plan and include a kitchen, nook, and family room warmed by a fireplace. The professional study is a quiet retreat. The three-car garage offers spacious storage. Upstairs, the master bedroom enjoys a private bath and roomy walk-in closet. Three additional bedrooms share a hall bath and open playroom.

plan # HPK1000069

STYLE: TRADITIONAL
FIRST FLOOR: 1,923 SQ. FT.
SECOND FLOOR: 1,710 SQ. FT.
TOTAL: 3,633 SQ. FT.
BEDROOMS: 4
BATHROOMS: 2½
WIDTH: 66' - 0"
DEPTH: 60' - 0"
FOUNDATION: CRAWLSPACE

SEARCH ONLINE @ EPLANS.COM

FIRST FLOOR

SECOND FLOOR

plan# HPK1000070

STYLE: EUROPEAN COTTAGE
FIRST FLOOR: 2,612 SQ. FT.
SECOND FLOOR: 1,300 SQ. FT.
TOTAL: 3,912 SQ. FT.
BONUS SPACE: 330 SQ. FT.
BEDROOMS: 4
BATHROOMS: 3½
WIDTH: 95' - 6"
DEPTH: 64' - 0"
FOUNDATION: UNFINISHED BASEMENT

SEARCH ONLINE @ EPLANS.COM

Lovely stucco columns and a copper standing-seam roof highlight this stone-and-brick facade. An elegant New World interior starts with a sensational winding staircase, a carved handrail, and honey-hued hardwood floor. An open, two-story formal dining room enjoys front-property views and leads to the gourmet kitchen through the butler's pantry, announced by an archway. Beyond the foyer, tall windows brighten the two-story family room and bring in a sense of the outdoors; a fireplace makes the space cozy and warm. The center food-prep island counter overlooks a breakfast niche that offers wide views through walls of windows and access to the rear porch.

SECOND FLOOR

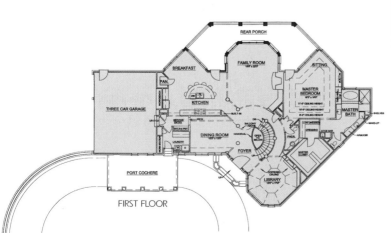

FIRST FLOOR

© William E. Poole Designs, Inc.

Memories of Christmases at home with the large tree greeting you upon entering the gracious foyer, garland hanging along the curved staircase, carols being sung around the piano in the library, turkey and pumpkin pie baking in the kitchen—these are what the Evergreen is all about. With the curved and columned front porch, authentic detail, and gracious flow, family and neighbors gather with joy in this 'home for all seasons' throughout the year and especially for holidays.

plan # HPK1000071

STYLE: GEORGIAN
FIRST FLOOR: 2,767 SQ. FT.
SECOND FLOOR: 1,179 SQ. FT.
TOTAL: 3,946 SQ. FT.
BONUS SPACE: 591 SQ. FT.
BEDROOMS: 4
BATHROOMS: 3½ + ½
WIDTH: 79' - 11"
DEPTH: 80' - 6"
FOUNDATION: CRAWLSPACE

SEARCH ONLINE @ EPLANS.COM

FIRST FLOOR

SECOND FLOOR

plan# HPK1000072

STYLE: FRENCH
FIRST FLOOR: 1,685 SQ. FT.
SECOND FLOOR: 1,596 SQ. FT.
TOTAL: 3,281 SQ. FT.
BEDROOMS: 5
BATHROOMS: 4½
WIDTH: 51' - 0"
DEPTH: 66' - 10"
FOUNDATION: CRAWLSPACE,
UNFINISHED WALKOUT
BASEMENT

SEARCH ONLINE @ EPLANS.COM

Strong lines lead the eye upwards toward this home's varied roofline. The formal dining room enjoys views from the two-story turret. The breakfast room opens to a glorious sun room with access to the rear property. The two-story family room enjoys a curved wall of windows and a double-sided fireplace. At the right of the plan, a study and powder room share space with a comfortable guest suite. Upstairs, three family bedrooms with ample closet space share two baths. The sumptuous master suite boasts a sitting room, vaulted bath, and His and Hers walk-in closets.

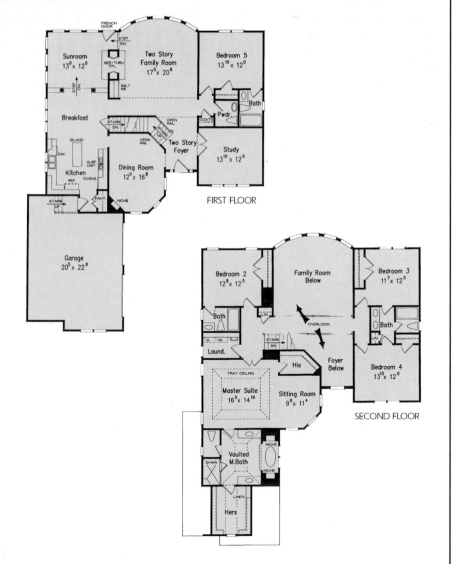

FIRST FLOOR

SECOND FLOOR

A brick and stone exterior with a tower and recessed entry creates a strong, solid look to this enchanting home. The large foyer introduces the great room with beamed ceiling and tall windows for a rear view. The dining room is defined by columns and topped with a coffered ceiling. Complementing the kitchen is a convenient walk-in pantry and center island with seating. An extra-large hearth room with gas fireplace and access to the rear deck provides a comfortable family gathering place. The master bedroom with sloped ceiling and a spacious dressing area offers a relaxing retreat. Split stairs located for family convenience introduce the spectacular lower level with a wine room, exercise room, wet bar, and two additional bedrooms.

plan# HPK1000073

STYLE: TRANSITIONAL
MAIN LEVEL: 2,562 SQ. FT.
LOWER LEVEL: 1,955 SQ. FT.
TOTAL: 4,517 SQ. FT.
BEDROOMS: 3
BATHROOMS: 2½ + ½
WIDTH: 75' - 8"
DEPTH: 70' - 6"
FOUNDATION: FINISHED
WALKOUT BASEMENT

SEARCH ONLINE @ EPLANS.COM

MAIN LEVEL

LOWER LEVEL

plan# HPK1000074

STYLE: MEDITERRANEAN
SQUARE FOOTAGE: 3,398
BEDROOMS: 3
BATHROOMS: 3½
WIDTH: 121' - 5"
DEPTH: 96' - 2"
FOUNDATION: SLAB, SLAB

SEARCH ONLINE @ EPLANS.COM

Bringing the outdoors in through a multitude of bay windows is what this design is all about. The grand foyer opens to the living room with a magnificent view to the covered lanai. The study and dining room flank the foyer. The master suite is found on the left with an opulent private bath and views of the private garden. To the right, the kitchen adjoins the nook that boasts a mitered-glass bay window overlooking the lanai. Beyond the leisure room are two guest rooms, each with private baths.

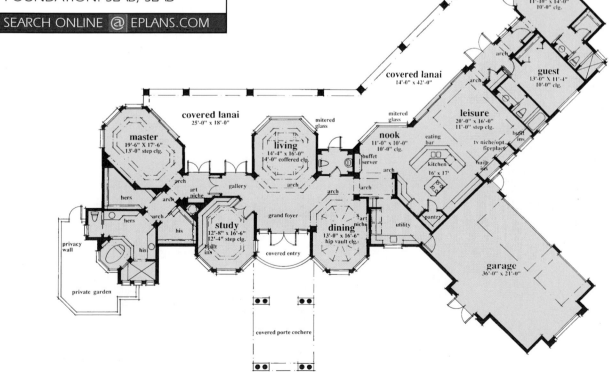

This captivating luxury home puts a contemporary spin on Old World style. Stucco provides a wonderful complement to multiple arched windows on the exterior; inside, natural light streams into the two-story entry. Just ahead, the living room is graced with a rear window bay and a warming fireplace. The professional-grade kitchen is ready to serve the elegant dining room and bright breakfast nook, both set in bays. A built-in entertainment center in the family room gives the space a definite focus. The right wing is devoted to the master suite: a bayed window lets in the light, as the dazzling bath soothes with a whirlpool tub and room-size walk-in closet. Follow the U-shaped staircase to a mid-level study; three grand bedrooms, a lofty game room, and a sun deck complete the plan.

plan # HPK1000075

STYLE: CONTEMPORARY
FIRST FLOOR: 2,489 SQ. FT.
SECOND FLOOR: 1,650 SQ. FT.
TOTAL: 4,139 SQ. FT.
BONUS SPACE: 366 SQ. FT.
BEDROOMS: 4
BATHROOMS: 3½
WIDTH: 72' - 8"
DEPTH: 77' - 0"

SEARCH ONLINE @ EPLANS.COM

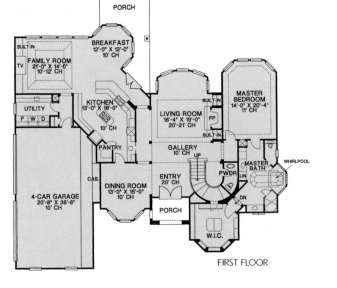

FIRST FLOOR

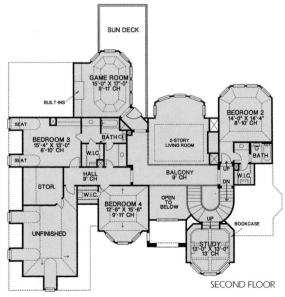

SECOND FLOOR

plan# HPK1000076

STYLE: COUNTRY COTTAGE
FIRST FLOOR: 1,050 SQ. FT.
SECOND FLOOR: 458 SQ. FT.
TOTAL: 1,508 SQ. FT.
BEDROOMS: 3
BATHROOMS: 2½
WIDTH: 35' - 6"
DEPTH: 39' - 9"
FOUNDATION: PIER

SEARCH ONLINE @ EPLANS.COM

This adorable abode could serve as a vacation cottage, guest house, starter home, or in-law quarters. The side-gabled design allows for a front porch with a "down-South" feel. Despite the small size, this home is packed with all the necessities. The first-floor master suite has a large bathroom and a walk-in closet. An open, functional floor plan includes a powder room, a kitchen/breakfast nook area, and a family room with a corner fireplace. Upstairs, two additional bedrooms share a bath. One could be used as a home office.

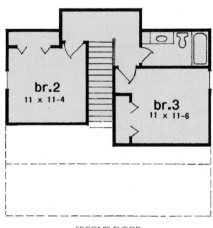

SECOND FLOOR

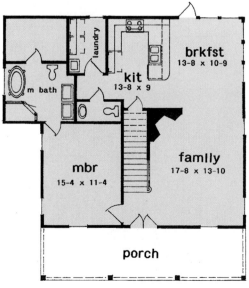

FIRST FLOOR

This sweeping European facade, featuring a majestic turret-style bay, will easily be a stand-out in the neighborhood and a family favorite. The foyer opens to a spacious formal receiving area. Double doors from the living room open to the rear porch for outdoor activities. The master wing features a sitting area, a luxurious master bath, and two walk-in closets. The spacious island kitchen works with the bayed breakfast room for more intimate meals. The family room offers a warm and relaxing fireplace. A private raised study, three-car garage, and utility room complete the first floor. Upstairs, three additional family bedrooms share the second floor with a music loft, hobby room, and game room.

plan# HPK1000077

STYLE: FRENCH
FIRST FLOOR: 3,058 SQ. FT.
SECOND FLOOR: 2,076 SQ. FT.
TOTAL: 5,134 SQ. FT.
BEDROOMS: 4
BATHROOMS: 4½
WIDTH: 79' - 6"
DEPTH: 73' - 10"
FOUNDATION: SLAB,
UNFINISHED BASEMENT,
CRAWLSPACE

SEARCH ONLINE @ EPLANS.COM

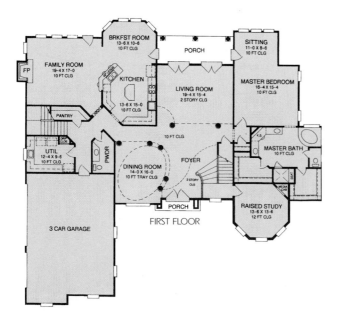

FIRST FLOOR

SECOND FLOOR

plan# HPK1000078

STYLE: FARMHOUSE
FIRST FLOOR: 1,320 SQ. FT.
SECOND FLOOR: 433 SQ. FT.
TOTAL: 1,753 SQ. FT.
BONUS SPACE: 209 SQ. FT.
BEDROOMS: 3
BATHROOMS: 2½
WIDTH: 51' - 11"
DEPTH: 50' - 0"
FOUNDATION: CRAWLSPACE,
SLAB, UNFINISHED BASEMENT

SEARCH ONLINE @ EPLANS.COM

Truly a sight to behold, this home borrows elements from the Colonial styling of the South. Flagstone enhances the facade, while a two-story porch brings out the uniqueness of the design. Enter through the foyer to find a dining room, hearth-warmed great room, and kitchen/nook area; the nook opens to a rear porch. The right side of the plan is home to the master suite with a full bath. Upstairs, two additional bedrooms, a full bath, a covered porch, and a balcony open to the great room below can be found.

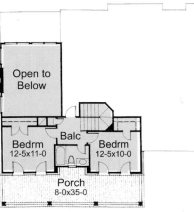

SECOND FLOOR

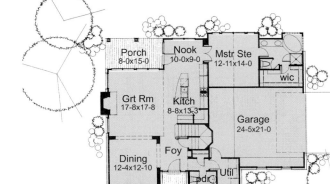

FIRST FLOOR

With its brick facade and gables, this home brings great curb appeal to any neighborhood. This one-story home features a great room with a cozy fireplace, a laundry room tucked away from the spacious kitchen, and a breakfast area accessing the screened porch. Completing this design are two family bedrooms and an elegant master bedroom suite featuring an ample walk-in closet. A dressing area in the master bathroom is shared by a dual vanity and a step-up tub.

plan# HPK1000079

STYLE: CRAFTSMAN
SQUARE FOOTAGE: 1,759
BEDROOMS: 3
BATHROOMS: 2
WIDTH: 82' - 10"
DEPTH: 47' - 5"
FOUNDATION: UNFINISHED BASEMENT

SEARCH ONLINE @ EPLANS.COM

Patio

Screened Porch
15'9" x 18 Irr.
← 15' →
← 7' →

Breakfast
12'8" x 9'11"

Great Room
16' x 16'6"

Dressing

Master Bedroom
15' x 13'

Kitchen
17' x 11'5"

12' ceiling height

stairs down

Niche

Two Car Garage
20' x 23'

Laun.

Dining Room
11' x 12'10"

Foyer
10' center ceiling ht.

Bedroom
13'3" x 11'10"

Bath

Bedroom
10'8" x 14'1"

sloped ceiling

soffit

Porch

sloped ceiling

plan# HPK1000080

STYLE: SOUTHERN COLONIAL
SQUARE FOOTAGE: 1,688
BEDROOMS: 3
BATHROOMS: 2
WIDTH: 70' - 1"
DEPTH: 48' - 0"
FOUNDATION: CRAWLSPACE,
SLAB, UNFINISHED BASEMENT

SEARCH ONLINE @ EPLANS.COM

Dormers and columns decorate the exterior of this three-bedroom country home. Inside, the foyer has immediate access to one family bedroom and the formal dining area. Ahead is the great room with a warming fireplace and ribbon of windows for natural lighting. The master suite is set to the back of the plan and has a lavish bath with a garden tub, separate shower, and two vanities.

Laun.
8-6x5-6
Storage

Basement Stair
Option

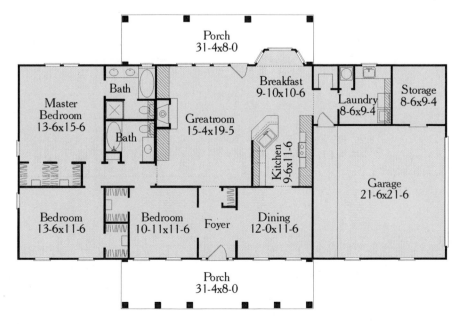

Porch
31-4x8-0

Master
Bedroom
13-6x15-6

Bath

Bath

Greatroom
15-4x19-5

Breakfast
9-10x10-6

Laundry
8-6x9-4

Storage
8-6x9-4

Kitchen
9-6x11-6

Garage
21-6x21-6

Bedroom
13-6x11-6

Bedroom
10-11x11-6

Foyer

Dining
12-0x11-6

Porch
31-4x8-0

The amazing turret/gazebo porch on this classy home has an authentic Victorian flavor. Exceptional details accent this classic view. The bedroom on the first level offers a protruding balcony, which adds appeal both inside and outside. The entrance leads to the living room, located just left of the dining area and L-shaped kitchen. The master suite features a walk-in closet and a private bath with dual sinks. Two more family bedrooms are located on the second level.

plan# HPK1000081

STYLE: VICTORIAN
FIRST FLOOR: 840 SQ. FT.
SECOND FLOOR: 757 SQ. FT.
TOTAL: 1,597 SQ. FT.
BEDROOMS: 3
BATHROOMS: 3
WIDTH: 26' - 0"
DEPTH: 32' - 0"
FOUNDATION: UNFINISHED BASEMENT

SEARCH ONLINE @ EPLANS.COM

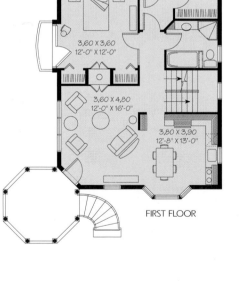

FIRST FLOOR

SECOND FLOOR

plan# HPK1000082

STYLE: COUNTRY COTTAGE
FIRST FLOOR: 1,570 SQ. FT.
SECOND FLOOR: 1,650 SQ. FT.
TOTAL: 3,220 SQ. FT.
BEDROOMS: 5
BATHROOMS: 4
WIDTH: 55' - 6"
DEPTH: 60' - 0"
FOUNDATION: CRAWLSPACE,
UNFINISHED WALKOUT
BASEMENT

SEARCH ONLINE @ EPLANS.COM

A side-loading garage and stunning country details make this home perfect for a corner lot. Formal rooms at the front of the plan border the two-story foyer. The two-story family room is an inviting gathering place. A C-shaped serving-bar kitchen is well-planned and ready to serve the breakfast nook and dining room. A quiet den with a semi-private bath completes this level. On the second floor, two bedrooms (one with a lovely box-bay window) share a full bath. An additional bedroom has a private bath. The master suite will amaze, with a splendid bath and vast walk-in closet. Extra storage space is an added asset

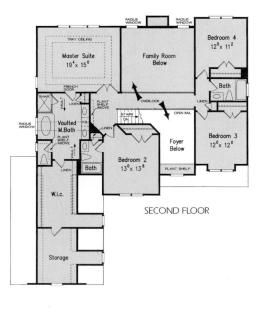

SECOND FLOOR

FIRST FLOOR

© The Sater Design Collection, Inc.

© The Sater Design Collection, Inc.

SECOND FLOOR

Bedroom 2
13'-0" x 12'-0"
9'-0" Clg.

Open to Below
21'-0" to 21'-8"
Coffered Clg.

Bonus Room
13'-8" x 14'-0"
Vault to 10'-2" Clg.

Computer Loft
9'-0" Clg.

Bath 1
9'-0" Clg.

Walk-In Shower

WIC

WIC

Walk-In Shower

Bonus Bath
10'-2" Clg.

Bath 2
9'-0" Clg.

Walk-In Shower

WIC

Bedroom 1
13'-0" x 12'-6"
12'-4" Clg.

Desk

Niche

Dn

Guest Suite
13'-0" x 11'-8"
9'-0" Clg.

Deck

FIRST FLOOR

Veranda
37'-2" x 12'-8"
12'-0" Clg.

Outdoor Grille

Breakfast
13'-0" x 9'-0"
9'-4" to 10'-0"
Beamed Clg.

Built-Ins

Great Room
21'-0" x 17'-2"
Open to Above

Fireplace

Kitchen
14'-6" x 10'-6"
9'-4" to 10'-0"
Beamed Clg.

Master Suite
14'-8" x 17'-0"
12'-0" to 13'-0"
Tray Clg.

WIC

Entertainment Center

Storage

Garage
23'-0" x 24'-0"
10'-2" Clg.

Art Niche

Foyer
9'-4" x 10'-0"
Stepped Clg.

Dining
13'-0" x 12'-10"
9'-0" to 10'-0"
Stepped Clg.

Pantry
8'-8" Clg.

Utility
9'-0" x 6'-4"
8'-0" Clg.

Up

Dn

Master Bath
11'-0" Clg.

Whirlpool

Walk-In Shower

Powder Bath
9'-4" Clg.

Study/Office
13'-0" x 13'-8"
9'-4" to 10'-0"
Beamed Clg.

Portico
10'-0" Clg.

plan# HPK1000083

STYLE: EUROPEAN COTTAGE
FIRST FLOOR: 2,219 SQ. FT.
SECOND FLOOR: 1,085 SQ. FT.
TOTAL: 3,304 SQ. FT.
BONUS SPACE: 404 SQ. FT.
BEDROOMS: 4
BATHROOMS: 3½
WIDTH: 91' - 0"
DEPTH: 52' - 8"
FOUNDATION: SLAB

SEARCH ONLINE @ EPLANS.COM

This home features two levels of pampering luxury filled with the most up-to-date amenities. Touches of Mediterranean detail add to the striking facade. A wrapping front porch welcomes you inside to a formal dining room and two-story great room warmed by a fireplace. Double doors from the master suite, great room, and breakfast nook access the rear veranda. The first-floor master suite enjoys a luxury bath, roomy walk-in closet, and close access to the front-facing office/study. Three additional bedrooms reside upstairs. The bonus room above the garage is great for an apartment or storage space.

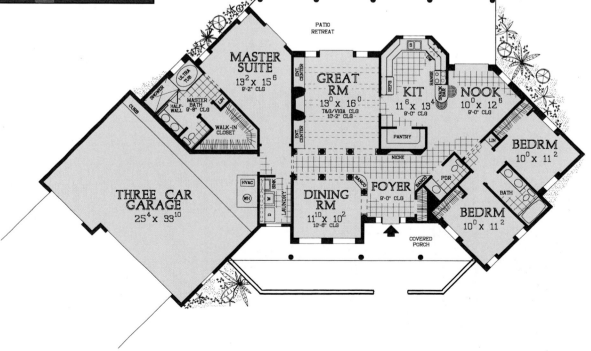

plan # HPK1000084

STYLE: SW CONTEMPORARY
SQUARE FOOTAGE: 2,015
BEDROOMS: 3
BATHROOMS: 2½
WIDTH: 96' - 5"
DEPTH: 54' - 9"
FOUNDATION: SLAB

SEARCH ONLINE @ EPLANS.COM

This Santa Fe-style home is as warm as a desert breeze and just as comfortable. Outside details are reminiscent of old-style adobe homes, and the interior caters to convenient living. The front covered porch leads to an open foyer. Columns define the formal dining room and the giant great room. The kitchen has an enormous pantry and a snack bar and is connected to a breakfast nook with rear-patio access. Two family bedrooms on the right side of the plan share a full bathroom that includes twin vanities. The master suite on the left side of the plan has a monstrous walk-in closet and a bath with a spa-style tub and a separate shower.

This charming one-story plan features a facade that is accented by a stone pediment and a shed-dormer window. Inside, elegant touches grace the efficient floor plan. Vaulted ceilings adorn the great room and master bedroom, and a 10-foot tray ceiling highlights the foyer. One of the front bedrooms makes a perfect den; another accesses a full hall bath with a linen closet. The great room, which opens to the porch, includes a fireplace and a media niche. The dining room offers outdoor access and built-ins for ultimate convenience.

plan# HPK1000085

STYLE: COUNTRY COTTAGE
SQUARE FOOTAGE: 1,580
BEDROOMS: 3
BATHROOMS: 2½
WIDTH: 50' - 0"
DEPTH: 48' - 0"
FOUNDATION: CRAWLSPACE

SEARCH ONLINE @ EPLANS.COM

PORCH

DINING
11/2 X 12/8
(9' CLG.)

SHELVES

VAULTED
MASTER
12/8 X 15/2

BUILT-INS

VAULTED
GREAT RM.
16/8 X 17/0

MEDIA

11/4 X 12/10

REF.

LIN. LIN.

P.

W D

FOYER
(10' CLG.)

BR. 3/
DEN
10/6 X 11/4
(9' CLG.)

GARAGE
20/6 X 21/0

BR. 2
11/0 X 10/0
(9' CLG.)

PORCH

plan # HPK1000086

STYLE: TRADITIONAL
SQUARE FOOTAGE: 1,643
BEDROOMS: 3
BATHROOMS: 2
WIDTH: 62' - 2"
DEPTH: 51' - 4"
FOUNDATION: CRAWLSPACE,
SLAB, UNFINISHED BASEMENT

SEARCH ONLINE @ EPLANS.COM

Two covered porches lend a relaxing charm to this three-bedroom ranch home. Inside, the focal point is a warming fireplace with windows framing each side. The vaulted ceiling in the great room adds spaciousness to the adjoining kitchen and dining areas. A tray ceiling decorates the master suite, which also sports two walk-in closets. Two family bedrooms are located on the opposite side of the house.

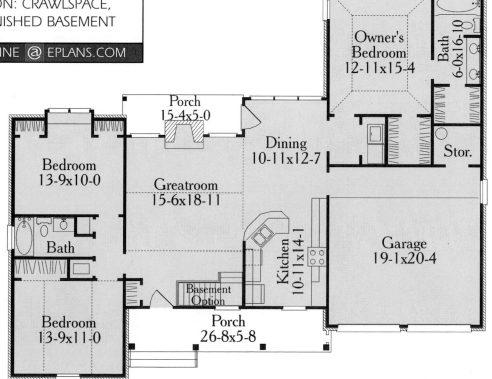

A brick/stone facade creates the solid exterior of this French Country design. Inside, a library in the front is warmed by a fireplace, but the heart of the house is found in a large, open great room with a second fireplace. The spacious gourmet kitchen enjoys warmth from the grand room to the left and a third fireplace in the adjoining family room on the right. Access to a rear covered porch and deck/patio can be gained from the family room. There are three bedrooms upstairs and a bonus room/optional fifth bedroom. Each bedroom boasts a walk-in closet and convenient access to a full bath.

plan# HPK1000087

STYLE: NORMAN
FIRST FLOOR: 3,121 SQ. FT.
SECOND FLOOR: 1,278 SQ. FT.
TOTAL: 4,399 SQ. FT.
BEDROOMS: 4
BATHROOMS: 3½ + ½
WIDTH: 86' - 7"
DEPTH: 81' - 4"
FOUNDATION: FINISHED BASEMENT, UNFINISHED BASEMENT

SEARCH ONLINE @ EPLANS.COM

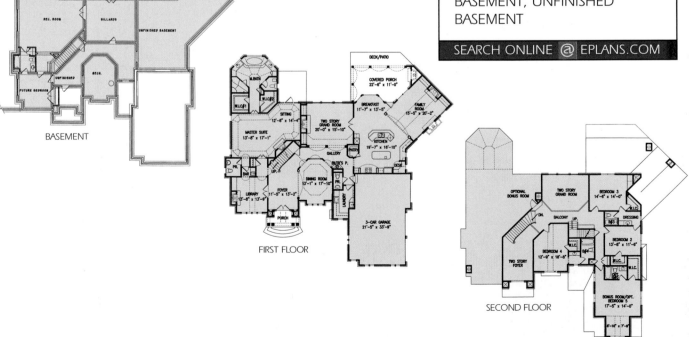

BASEMENT

FIRST FLOOR

SECOND FLOOR

plan ⊕ # HPK1000088

STYLE: COUNTRY COTTAGE
SQUARE FOOTAGE: 1,583
BONUS SPACE: 544 SQ. FT.
BEDROOMS: 3
BATHROOMS: 2
WIDTH: 54' - 0"
DEPTH: 47' - 0"
FOUNDATION: CRAWLSPACE,
UNFINISHED WALKOUT
BASEMENT, SLAB

SEARCH ONLINE @ EPLANS.COM

This comfortable cottage is well suited to an alpine environment, yet, with its flexible interior and superior architecture, can be built anywhere. Open living and dining space is anchored by a decorative column and a fireplace surrounded by views. A well-planned kitchen features a food-preparation island and a serving bar. A triple window in the breakfast area brightens the kitchen; a French door allows access to the rear property. To the right of the plan, the master suite boasts a vaulted bath, a plant shelf, and a walk-in closet. Two secondary bedrooms share a full bath.

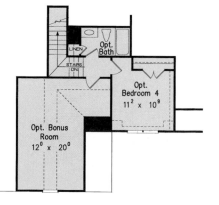

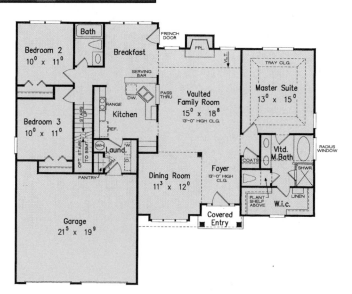

A hint of Moroccan architecture, with columns, arches, and walls of glass, makes an arresting appearance in this home. It allows a diverse arrangement of space inside, for a dynamic floor plan. The foyer spills openly into the immense living area and sunken dining room. A stair encircles the sunken library/great space for a home theater. Beyond is the family room with a two-story high media wall and built-ins, plus the circular breakfast room and island kitchen. A maid's room, or guest room, has a full circular wall of glass and leads to the garage through a covered entry and drive-through area. The master suite is true luxury: circular sitting area, His and Hers facilities, and a private garden. Upstairs is a game room, plus two family bedrooms with private, amenity-filled baths.

plan # HPK1000089

STYLE: MEDITERRANEAN
FIRST FLOOR: 4,284 SQ. FT.
SECOND FLOOR: 1,319 SQ. FT.
TOTAL: 5,603 SQ. FT.
BEDROOMS: 4
BATHROOMS: 4½ + ½
WIDTH: 109' - 4"
DEPTH: 73' - 2"
FOUNDATION: SLAB

SEARCH ONLINE @ EPLANS.COM

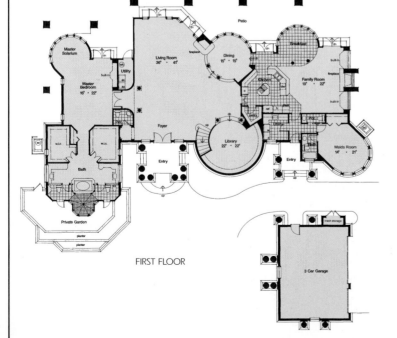

FIRST FLOOR

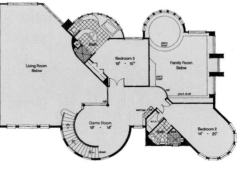

SECOND FLOOR

plan # HPK1000090

STYLE: EUROPEAN COTTAGE
SQUARE FOOTAGE: 2,007
BEDROOMS: 3
BATHROOMS: 2½
WIDTH: 40' - 0"
DEPTH: 94' - 10"
FOUNDATION: SLAB

SEARCH ONLINE @ EPLANS.COM

An ornate stucco facade with brick highlights refines this charming French cottage. The double-door entrance sits to the side—perfect for a courtyard welcome. A dining and family room utilize an open layout for easy traffic flow. The circular kitchen space features an island and complementary breakfast bay. Bedrooms 2 and 3 share a hall bath. The master suite, apart from the main living areas, enjoys privacy and a full bath with a spacious walk-in closet. The rear porch encourages outdoor relaxation.

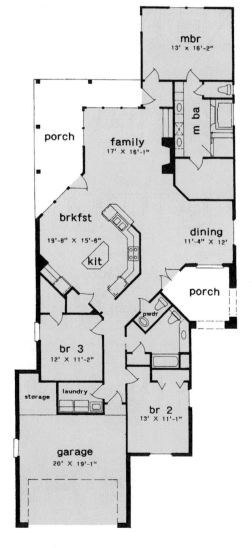

Six columns and a steeply pitched roof lend elegance to this four-bedroom home. To the right of the foyer, the dining area sits conveniently near the efficient island kitchen that enjoys plenty of work space. Natural light will flood the breakfast nook through a ribbon of windows facing the rear yard. Escape to the relaxing master bedroom, with its luxurious bath set between His and Hers walk-in closets. The great room is complete with a warming fireplace and built-ins. Three family bedrooms enjoy private walk-in closets and share a fully appointed bath.

plan# HPK1000091

STYLE: COUNTRY COTTAGE
SQUARE FOOTAGE: 2,267
BEDROOMS: 4
BATHROOMS: 2½
WIDTH: 71' - 2"
DEPTH: 62' - 0"
FOUNDATION: UNFINISHED
BASEMENT, CRAWLSPACE, SLAB

SEARCH ONLINE @ EPLANS.COM

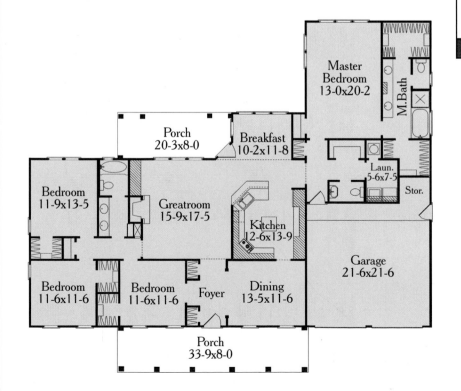

Basement Stair
Location

OPTIONAL LAYOUT

plan# HPK1000092

STYLE: COUNTRY COTTAGE
FIRST FLOOR: 1,290 SQ. FT.
SECOND FLOOR: 985 SQ. FT.
TOTAL: 2,275 SQ. FT.
BONUS SPACE: 186 SQ. FT.
BEDROOMS: 4
BATHROOMS: 3
WIDTH: 45' - 0"
DEPTH: 43' - 4"
FOUNDATION: CRAWLSPACE,
UNFINISHED WALKOUT
BASEMENT, SLAB,

SEARCH ONLINE @ EPLANS.COM

This casually elegant European Country-style home offers more than just a slice of everything you've always wanted: it is designed with room to grow. Formal living and dining rooms are defined by decorative columns and open from a two-story foyer, which leads to open family space. A two-story family room offers a fireplace and shares a French door to the rear property with the breakfast room. A gallery hall with a balcony overlook connects two sleeping wings upstairs. The master suite boasts a vaulted bath, and the family hall leads to bonus space.

SECOND FLOOR

FIRST FLOOR

With brick, wood, and siding, this home will captivate interest right away. An efficient layout reveals two family bedrooms—or use one as a study—at the front of the home; the master suite is tucked at the rear for privacy. The master bath will soothe and revitalize, and the large walk-in closet is sure to please. The family room opens to the dining room, with easy access to the open kitchen. The convenient laundry room is hidden in one wall of the kitchen.

plan # HPK1000093

STYLE: TRANSITIONAL
SQUARE FOOTAGE: 1,151
BEDROOMS: 3
BATHROOMS: 2
WIDTH: 39' - 3"
DEPTH: 42' - 1"
FOUNDATION: SLAB

SEARCH ONLINE @ EPLANS.COM

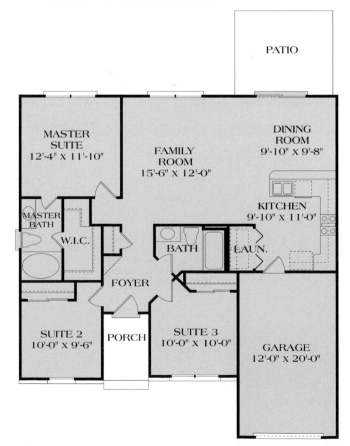

PATIO

MASTER SUITE
12'-4" x 11'-10"

FAMILY ROOM
15'-6" x 12'-0"

DINING ROOM
9'-10" x 9'-8"

MASTER BATH

W.I.C.

KITCHEN
9'-10" x 11'-0"

BATH

LAUN.

FOYER

SUITE 2
10'-0" x 9'-6"

PORCH

SUITE 3
10'-0" x 10'-0"

GARAGE
12'-0" x 20'-0"

plan# HPK1000094

STYLE: TRADITIONAL
FIRST FLOOR: 120 SQ. FT.
SECOND FLOOR: 512 SQ. FT.
TOTAL: 632 SQ. FT.
BEDROOMS: 1
BATHROOMS: 1
WIDTH: 28' - 0"
DEPTH: 26' - 0"
FOUNDATION: SLAB

SEARCH ONLINE @ EPLANS.COM

This two-car garage offers a farmhouse exterior with a bonus! A one-bedroom apartment with a spacious vaulted living room, full kitchen, separate bath and a rear deck takes up the 512-square-foot second floor. The downstairs entry offers a coat closet and garage and laundry access.

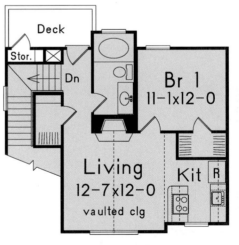

SECOND FLOOR

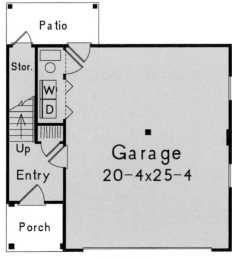

FIRST FLOOR

Traditional and Craftsman elements shape the exterior of this lovely family home. The two-story foyer leads down the hall to a great room with a warming fireplace. The U-shaped kitchen includes a window sink and is open to the breakfast nook. A powder room is located near the garage. Upstairs, the master suite provides a private bath and walk-in closet. The two family bedrooms share a full hall bath across from the second-floor laundry room. Linen closets are available in the hall and inside the full hall bath.

plan# HPK1000095

STYLE: CRAFTSMAN
FIRST FLOOR: 636 SQ. FT.
SECOND FLOOR: 830 SQ. FT.
TOTAL: 1,466 SQ. FT.
BEDROOMS: 3
BATHROOMS: 2½
WIDTH: 28' - 0"
DEPTH: 43' - 6"
FOUNDATION: CRAWLSPACE

SEARCH ONLINE @ EPLANS.COM

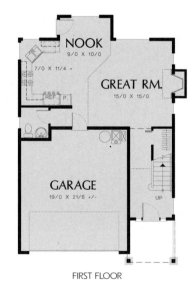

NOOK
9/0 X 10/0
7/0 X 11/4

GREAT RM.
15/0 X 15/0

REF. P.

GARAGE
19/0 X 21/6 +/-

UP

FIRST FLOOR

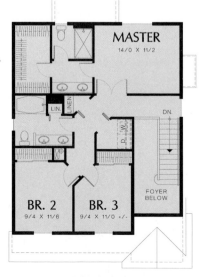

MASTER
14/0 X 11/2

LIN.
LINEN

D. W

DN.

BR. 2
9/4 X 11/6

BR. 3
9/4 X 11/0 +/-

FOYER
BELOW

SECOND FLOOR

plan ⊕ HPK1000096

STYLE: EUROPEAN COTTAGE
SQUARE FOOTAGE: 1,964
BEDROOMS: 3
BATHROOMS: 2
WIDTH: 38' - 10"
DEPTH: 90' - 1"
FOUNDATION: SLAB

SEARCH ONLINE @ EPLANS.COM

This narrow-lot plan has all the appeal and romance of a European cottage. The front porch welcomes you to a charming set of double doors. Two family bedrooms, a hall bath, a laundry room, and the two-car garage with storage are located at the front of the plan. The island kitchen easily serves the dining room, which accesses a private garden and the casual breakfast room. The spacious family room offers a warming fireplace, built-ins, and back-porch access. The plan is completed by the master suite, which features a private bath and walk-in closet.

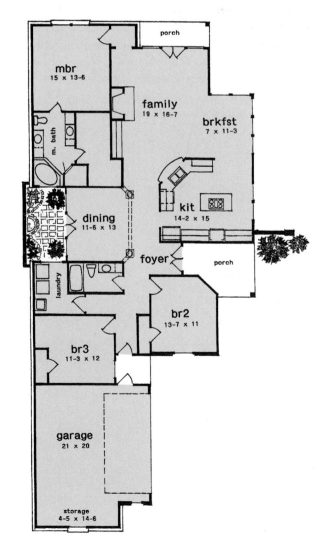

Traditional in every sense of the word, you can't go wrong with this charming country cottage. The foyer opens on the right to a columned dining room, and ahead to the family room. Here, a raised ceiling and bright radius windows expand the space, and a warming fireplace lends a cozy touch. A sunny bayed breakfast nook flows into the angled kitchen for easy casual meals. Down the hall, two bedrooms share a full bath, tucked behind the two-car garage to protect the bedrooms from street noise. The master suite is indulgent, pampering homeowners with a bayed sitting area, tray ceiling, vaulted spa bath, and an oversized walk-in closet. A fourth bedroom and bonus space are available to grow as your family does.

plan# HPK1000097

STYLE: COUNTRY COTTAGE
SQUARE FOOTAGE: 1,933
BONUS SPACE: 519 SQ. FT.
BEDROOMS: 3
BATHROOMS: 2½
WIDTH: 62' - 0"
DEPTH: 50' - 0"
FOUNDATION: CRAWLSPACE, UNFINISHED WALKOUT BASEMENT

SEARCH ONLINE @ EPLANS.COM

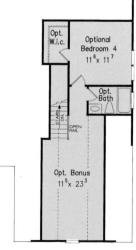

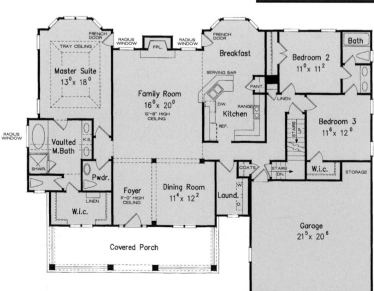

plan # HPK1000098

STYLE: TRADITIONAL
SQUARE FOOTAGE: 1,746
BEDROOMS: 3
BATHROOMS: 2
WIDTH: 58' - 0"
DEPTH: 59' - 4"
FOUNDATION: SLAB

SEARCH ONLINE @ EPLANS.COM

Wooden window accents bring a rustic flavor to this warm Santa Fe design. Double doors open to the foyer: to the right, a vaulted dining room is enhanced by bright multipane windows. The study opens to the left through stylish French doors. Ahead, the vaulted great room ushers in natural light. An efficient kitchen easily serves the bayed breakfast nook for simple casual meals. Two family bedrooms share a full bath, creating a quiet zone for the master suite. A corner whirlpool tub, oversized walk-in closet, and sliding-glass-door access to the lanai make this retreat a true haven.

This stellar single-story symmetrical home offers plenty of living space for any family. The front porch and rear deck make outdoor entertaining delightful. The living and dining rooms are open and spacious for family gatherings. A well-organized kitchen with an abundance of cabinetry and a built-in pantry completes the functional plan. The three bedrooms reside to the left of the plan.

plan # HPK1000099

STYLE: TRADITIONAL
SQUARE FOOTAGE: 1,140
BEDROOMS: 3
BATHROOMS: 2
WIDTH: 44' - 0"
DEPTH: 27' - 0"
FOUNDATION: UNFINISHED BASEMENT

SEARCH ONLINE @ EPLANS.COM

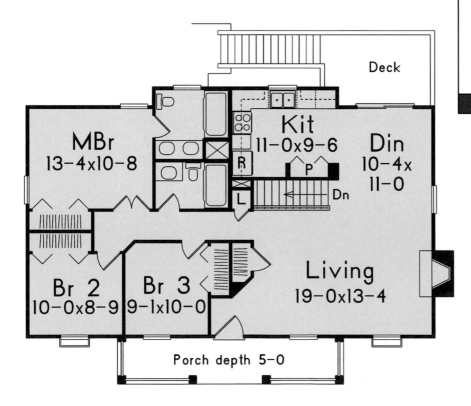

plan# HPK1000100

STYLE: COUNTRY COTTAGE
SQUARE FOOTAGE: 1,477
BONUS SPACE: 283 SQ. FT.
BEDROOMS: 3
BATHROOMS: 2
WIDTH: 51' - 0"
DEPTH: 51' - 4"
FOUNDATION: CRAWLSPACE,
UNFINISHED WALKOUT
BASEMENT

SEARCH ONLINE @ EPLANS.COM

This adorable three-bedroom home will provide a pleasant atmosphere for your family. The communal living areas reside on the left side of the plan. The L-shaped kitchen includes a serving bar that opens to the dining area. The vaulted family room features a fireplace and leads to the sleeping quarters. A master suite and vaulted master bath will pamper homeowners. Two family bedrooms reside across the hall and share a full hall bath. Upstairs, an optional fourth bedroom and full bath are perfect for guests.

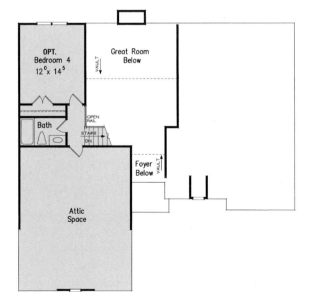

LIN.

MASTER BATH

DN

SUITE 2
12'-2" x 13'-4"

W.I.C.

LAUN

BATH

ATTIC STOR.

MASTER SUITE
14'-0" x 15'-8"

W.I.C.

ATTIC STOR.

SECOND FLOOR

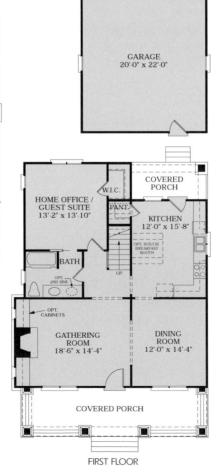

GARAGE
20'-0" x 22'-0"

COVERED PORCH

HOME OFFICE / GUEST SUITE
13'-2" x 13'-10"

W.I.C.

PANT.

KITCHEN
12'-0" x 15'-8"

OPT. BUILTIN BREAKFAST BOOTH

BATH

UP

OPT. 2ND SINK

OPT. CABINETS

GATHERING ROOM
18'-6" x 14'-4"

DINING ROOM
12'-0" x 14'-4"

COVERED PORCH

FIRST FLOOR

plan# HPK1000101

STYLE: CRAFTSMAN
FIRST FLOOR: 1,060 SQ. FT.
SECOND FLOOR: 914 SQ. FT.
TOTAL: 1,974 SQ. FT.
BEDROOMS: 3
BATHROOMS: 3
WIDTH: 32' - 0"
DEPTH: 35' - 0"
FOUNDATION: CRAWLSPACE

SEARCH ONLINE @ EPLANS.COM

This charming Craftsman design offers a second-story master bedroom with four windows under the gabled dormer. The covered front porch displays column and pier supports. The hearth-warmed gathering room opens to the dining room on the right, where the adjoining kitchen offers enough space for an optional breakfast booth. A home office/guest suite is found in the rear. The second floor holds the lavish master suite and a second bedroom suite with its own private bath.

plan# HPK1000102

STYLE: COUNTRY COTTAGE
FIRST FLOOR: 947 SQ. FT.
SECOND FLOOR: 981 SQ. FT.
TOTAL: 1,928 SQ. FT.
BEDROOMS: 4
BATHROOMS: 2½
WIDTH: 41' - 0"
DEPTH: 39' - 4"
FOUNDATION: CRAWLSPACE,
UNFINISHED WALKOUT
BASEMENT

SEARCH ONLINE @ EPLANS.COM

A brick one-story garage with a flowerbox window lends this two-story home a cottage feel. Inside, efficient use of space and flexibility adds to the appeal. A formal dining room opens from the two-story foyer, and leads to a cleverly designed kitchen. A serving bar connects the kitchen and breakfast nook. The hearth-warmed family room is just steps away. Four bedrooms—three family bedrooms and a roomy master suite—fill the second level. Note the option of turning Bedroom 4 into a sitting area for the master suite.

SECOND FLOOR

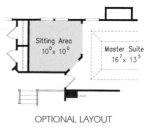

OPTIONAL LAYOUT

FIRST FLOOR

Simplicity is often the best approach to design. Twin chimneys serve as anchors to the home, while a deep front porch welcomes visitors. Inside, the cathedral ceiling and natural light from the dormers above enliven the great room. The well-appointed master suite also enjoys a private fireplace. Two additional bedrooms are located on the second floor along with the bonus room, which will add 115 square feet if finished.

plan# HPK1000103

STYLE: COUNTRY COTTAGE
FIRST FLOOR: 1,152 SQ. FT.
SECOND FLOOR: 567 SQ. FT.
TOTAL: 1,719 SQ. FT.
BONUS SPACE: 115 SQ. FT.
BEDROOMS: 3
BATHROOMS: 2½
WIDTH: 36' - 0"
DEPTH: 64' - 0"
FOUNDATION: CRAWLSPACE,
UNFINISHED BASEMENT

SEARCH ONLINE @ EPLANS.COM

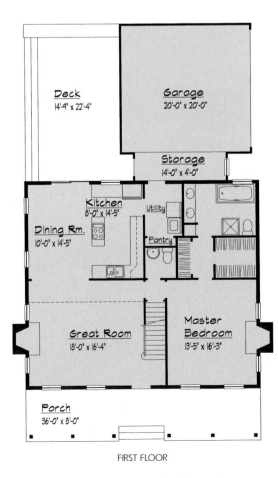

FIRST FLOOR

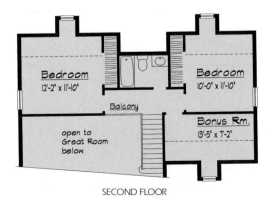

SECOND FLOOR

plan # HPK1000104

STYLE: TRADITIONAL
SQUARE FOOTAGE: 1,721
BEDROOMS: 3
BATHROOMS: 2
WIDTH: 83' - 0"
DEPTH: 42' - 0"
FOUNDATION: UNFINISHED
WALKOUT BASEMENT

SEARCH ONLINE @ EPLANS.COM

This home offers a beautifully textured facade. Keystones and lintels highlight the beauty of the windows. The vaulted great room and dining room are immersed in light from the atrium window wall. The breakfast bay opens to the covered porch in the backyard. A curved counter connects the kitchen to the great room. Three bedrooms, including a deluxe master suite, share the right side of the plan. All enjoy large windows of their own. The garage is designed for two cars, plus space for a motorcycle or yard tractor.

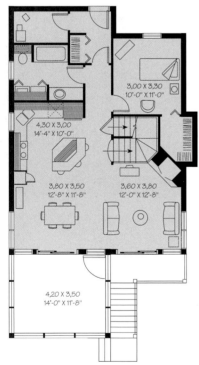

FIRST FLOOR

3,00 X 3,30
10'-0" X 11'-0"

4,30 X 3,00
14'-4" X 10'-0"

3,80 X 3,50
12'-8" X 11'-8"

3,60 X 3,80
12'-0" X 12'-8"

4,20 X 3,50
14'-0" X 11'-8"

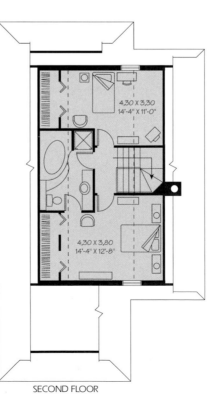

SECOND FLOOR

4,30 X 3,30
14'-4" X 11'-0"

4,30 X 3,80
14'-4" X 12'-8"

plan# HPK1000105

STYLE: RESORT LIFESTYLES
FIRST FLOOR: 908 SQ. FT.
SECOND FLOOR: 576 SQ. FT.
TOTAL: 1,484 SQ. FT.
BEDROOMS: 3
BATHROOMS: 2
WIDTH: 26' - 0"
DEPTH: 36' - 0"
FOUNDATION: UNFINISHED
WALKOUT BASEMENT

SEARCH ONLINE @ EPLANS.COM

This vacation home enjoys a screened porch and sits on stilts to avoid any water damage. Truly a free-flowing plan, the dining room, living room, and kitchen share a common space, with no walls separating them. An island snack counter in the kitchen provides plenty of space for food preparation. A family bedroom and full bath complete the first level. Upstairs, two additional bedrooms—with ample closet space—share a lavish bath, which includes a whirlpool tub and separate shower.

plan # HPK1000106

STYLE: COUNTRY COTTAGE
FIRST FLOOR: 576 SQ. FT.
SECOND FLOOR: 489 SQ. FT.
TOTAL: 1,065 SQ. FT.
BEDROOMS: 1
BATHROOMS: 1½
WIDTH: 24' - 0"
DEPTH: 31' - 0"
FOUNDATION: CRAWLSPACE

SEARCH ONLINE @ EPLANS.COM

The steep rooflines on this home offer a sophisticated look that draws attention. Three dormers flood the home with light. The covered porch adds detailing to the posts. The entry leads to the two-story living room complete with a fireplace. The dining room is quite spacious and contains convenient access to the kitchen where a pantry room and plenty of counter space make cooking a treat in this home. The stairs to the second floor wrap around the fireplace and take the homeowners to the master bedroom and loft area.

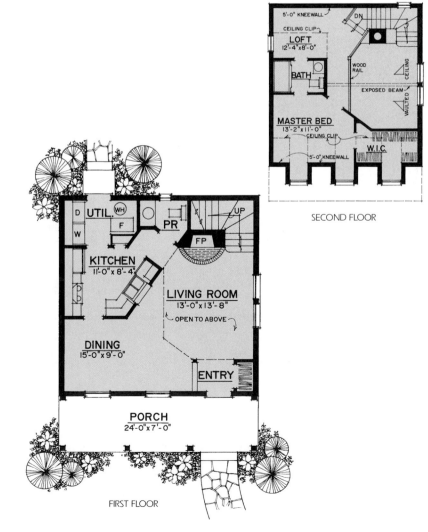

SECOND FLOOR

FIRST FLOOR

Welcome home to a petite cottage that is economical to build and has plenty to offer. Enter from the covered porch to a family room with great views and a warming fireplace. The sunny dining area is adjacent and can be as formal or casual as you wish. The kitchen is planned for efficiency and hosts a serving bar and rear-porch access, perfect for outdoor dining. Three family bedrooms include a master suite with a private bath and two additional bedrooms that share a full bath.

plan# HPK1000107

STYLE: CRAFTSMAN
SQUARE FOOTAGE: 1,195
BEDROOMS: 3
BATHROOMS: 2
WIDTH: 40' - 0"
DEPTH: 48' - 8"

SEARCH ONLINE @ EPLANS.COM

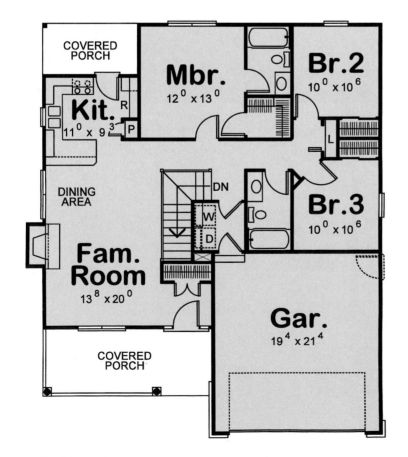

plan # HPK1000108

STYLE: SOUTHERN COLONIAL
FIRST FLOOR: 1,071 SQ. FT.
SECOND FLOOR: 924 SQ. FT.
TOTAL: 1,995 SQ. FT.
BONUS SPACE: 280 SQ. FT.
BEDROOMS: 3
BATHROOMS: 2½
WIDTH: 55' - 10"
DEPTH: 38' - 6"
FOUNDATION: CRAWLSPACE,
UNFINISHED WALKOUT
BASEMENT, SLAB

SEARCH ONLINE @ EPLANS.COM

Move-up buyers can enjoy all the luxuries of this two-story home highlighted by an angled staircase separating the dining room from casual living areas. A private powder room is tucked away behind the dining room—convenient for formal dinner parties. A bay window and built-in desk in the breakfast area are just a few of the plan's amenities. The sleeping zone occupies the second floor—away from everyday activities—and includes a master suite and two secondary bedrooms.

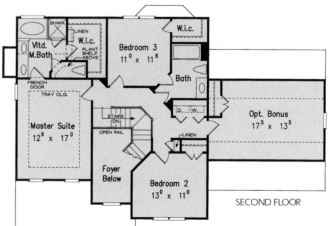

SECOND FLOOR

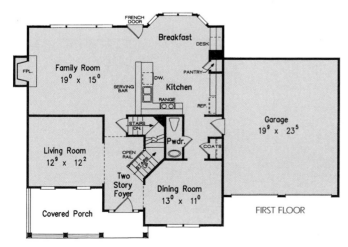

FIRST FLOOR

This charming country home speaks well of an American vernacular style, with classic clapboard siding, shutters, and sash windows—all dressed up for 21st-Century living. A flex room on the first floor can be a study, playroom, or fourth bedroom. The casual living space enjoys a fireplace, wide views of the rear property, and a French door to the outside. Upstairs, the master suite features a vaulted bath with separate shower, dual vanity, and walk-in closet with linen storage.

plan # HPK1000109

STYLE: SOUTHERN COLONIAL
FIRST FLOOR: 1,103 SQ. FT.
SECOND FLOOR: 759 SQ. FT.
TOTAL: 1,862 SQ. FT.
BONUS SPACE: 342 SQ. FT.
BEDROOMS: 4
BATHROOMS: 3
WIDTH: 50' - 4"
DEPTH: 35' - 0"
FOUNDATION: CRAWLSPACE,
UNFINISHED WALKOUT
BASEMENT, SLAB

SEARCH ONLINE @ EPLANS.COM

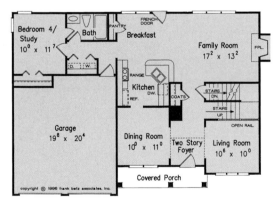

FIRST FLOOR

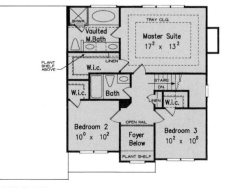

SECOND FLOOR

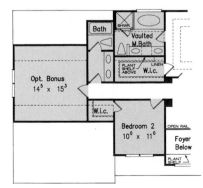

OPTIONAL LAYOUT

plan# HPK1000110

STYLE: FARMHOUSE
FIRST FLOOR: 716 SQ. FT.
SECOND FLOOR: 754 SQ. FT.
TOTAL: 1,470 SQ. FT.
BEDROOMS: 3
BATHROOMS: 2½
WIDTH: 45' - 4"
DEPTH: 38' - 0"

SEARCH ONLINE @ EPLANS.COM

This compact traditional home offers an attractive exterior and a comfortable floor plan. The front door opens directly to the family room, which includes a fireplace and a built-in entertainment center. Just beyond, the kitchen features a walk-in pantry and adjoins a sunlit dining bay with access to the backyard. A two-car garage completes the first floor. Upstairs, three bedrooms are conveniently close to the laundry area. The master suite and Bedroom 2 provide walk-in closets.

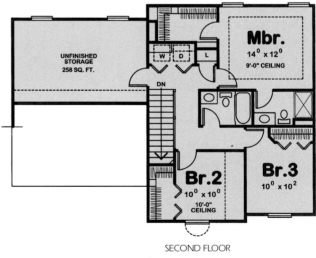

SECOND FLOOR

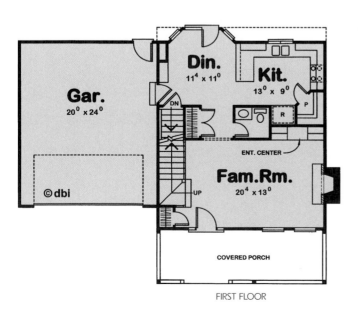

FIRST FLOOR

This ranch-style home offers a comfortable atmosphere. The center highlight of this plan may just as well be the kitchen/dining area with a work island and plenty of preparation and eating space. A large walk-in closet and private bath make the master bedroom that much more enjoyable. The laundry room is adjacent to the kitchen for easy access. The garage includes a convenient workshop.

plan# HPK1000111

STYLE: TRADITIONAL
SQUARE FOOTAGE: 1,360
BEDROOMS: 3
BATHROOMS: 2
WIDTH: 68' - 0"
DEPTH: 30' - 0"
FOUNDATION: CRAWLSPACE, SLAB, UNFINISHED BASEMENT

SEARCH ONLINE @ EPLANS.COM

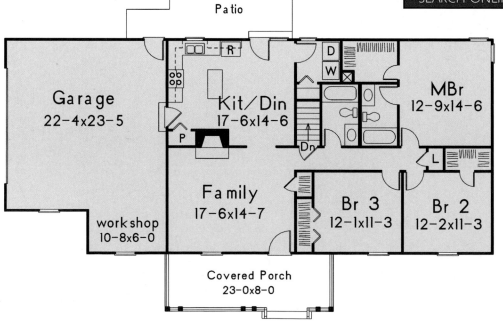

68'-0"
Patio

Garage
22-4x23-5

Kit/Din
17-6x14-6

MBr
12-9x14-6

D
W

Dn

Family
17-6x14-7

Br 3
12-1x11-3

Br 2
12-2x11-3

P

workshop
10-8x6-0

Covered Porch
23-0x8-0

plan # HPK1000112

STYLE: COUNTRY COTTAGE
SQUARE FOOTAGE: 1,832
BONUS SPACE: 68 SQ. FT.
BEDROOMS: 3
BATHROOMS: 2½
WIDTH: 59' - 6"
DEPTH: 52' - 6"
FOUNDATION: CRAWLSPACE, SLAB, UNFINISHED WALKOUT BASEMENT

SEARCH ONLINE @ EPLANS.COM

This compact one-story has plenty of living in it. The master suite features an optional sun-washed sitting area with views to the rear of the home. A vaulted great room with fireplace conveniently accesses the kitchen via a serving bar. Meals can also be taken in the cozy breakfast area. For formal occasions the dining room creates opulence with its decorative columns. Two family bedrooms flank the right of the home with a shared bath, linen storage, and easy access to laundry facilities.

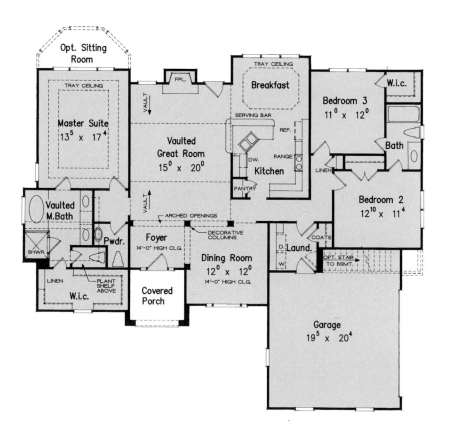

This two-story, European-style home has plenty of livability within a minimum of square footage. Open planning gives a feeling of spaciousness—the entry opens to the living area, which flows into the rear-facing dining room. Conveniently located nearby is the kitchen with its breakfast island and pantry. An enormous master suite occupies one-half of the second floor; two bedrooms share a full bath and an optional fourth bedroom or reading area occupies the right side of the upper level.

plan# HPK1000113

STYLE: COLONIAL
FIRST FLOOR: 803 SQ. FT.
SECOND FLOOR: 1,053 SQ. FT.
TOTAL: 1,856 SQ. FT.
BEDROOMS: 3
BATHROOMS: 2
WIDTH: 32' - 4"
DEPTH: 34' - 0"
FOUNDATION: UNFINISHED BASEMENT

SEARCH ONLINE @ EPLANS.COM

4,20 x 3,10
14'-0" x 10'-4"

3,30 x 3,30
11'-0" x 11'-0"

3,50 x 5,80
11'-8" x 19'-4"

4,50 x 5,80
15'-0" x 19'-4"

FIRST FLOOR

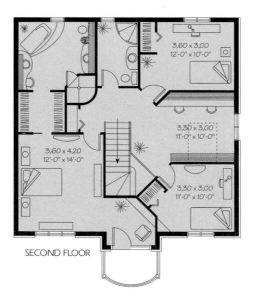

3,60 x 3,00
12'-0" x 10'-0"

3,60 x 4,20
12'-0" x 14'-0"

3,30 x 3,00
11'-0" x 10'-0"

3,30 x 3,00
11'-0" x 10'-0"

SECOND FLOOR

plan# HPK1000114

STYLE: NW CONTEMPORARY
SQUARE FOOTAGE 1,484
BEDROOMS: 3
BATHROOMS: 2
WIDTH: 38' - 0"
DEPTH: 70' - 0"
FOUNDATION: CRAWLSPACE

SEARCH ONLINE @ EPLANS.COM

Ideal for narrow lots, this fine bungalow is full of amenities. The entry is just off a covered front porch and leads to a living room complete with a fireplace. The formal dining room is nearby and works well with the L-shaped kitchen. The breakfast nook opens onto a rear patio. Sleeping quarters consist of a master suite with a walk-in closet and private bath, as well as two family bedrooms sharing a full bath. An unfinished attic waits future development; a two-car garage easily shelters the family vehicles.

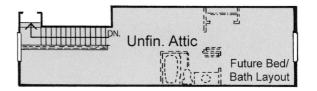

Unfin. Attic

Future Bed/
Bath Layout

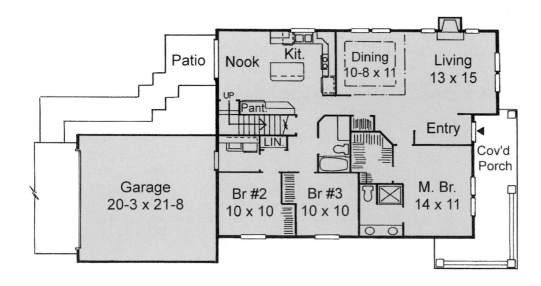

Patio

Nook

Kit.

Dining
10-8 x 11

Living
13 x 15

UP

Pant.

LIN.

Entry

Cov'd
Porch

Garage
20-3 x 21-8

Br #2
10 x 10

Br #3
10 x 10

M. Br.
14 x 11

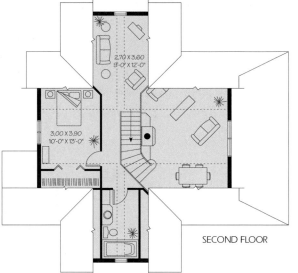

2,70 X 3,60
9'-0" X 12'-0"

3,00 X 3,90
10'-0" X 13'-0"

SECOND FLOOR

plan# HPK1000115

STYLE: CAPE COD
FIRST FLOOR: 1,024 SQ. FT.
SECOND FLOOR: 456 SQ. FT.
TOTAL: 1,480 SQ. FT.
BEDROOMS: 2
BATHROOMS: 2
WIDTH: 32' - 0"
DEPTH: 40' - 0"
FOUNDATION: FINISHED
WALKOUT BASEMENT

SEARCH ONLINE @ EPLANS.COM

Pillars, a large front porch, and plenty of win-dow views lend a classic feel to this lovely country cottage. Inside, the entry room has a coat closet and an interior entry door to elimi-nate drafts. The light-filled L-shaped kitchen lies conveniently near the entrance. A large room adjacent to the kitchen serves as a din-ing and living area where a fireplace adds warmth. A master suite boasts a walk-in closet and full bath. The second floor holds a loft, a second bedroom, and a full bath.

4,40 X 3,60
14'-8" X 12'-0"

4,20 X 6,80
14'-0" X 22'-8"

4,40 X 3,60
14'-8" X 12'-0"

FIRST FLOOR

plan# HPK1000116

STYLE: TRADITIONAL
FIRST FLOOR: 881 SQ. FT.
SECOND FLOOR: 933 SQ. FT.
TOTAL: 1,814 SQ. FT.
BEDROOMS: 3
BATHROOMS: 1½
WIDTH: 32' - 0"
DEPTH: 40' - 0"
FOUNDATION: UNFINISHED
BASEMENT

SEARCH ONLINE @ EPLANS.COM

This simple country design uses both siding and brick for a strong but uncomplicated exterior. The porch leads to an entry chamber with a coat closet and internal door. The living space includes the living room, dining room, and eat-in kitchen with a walk-in pantry. The second floor is home to the sleeping quarters. One option has a master bedroom with a sitting bay and two family bedrooms, all sharing a large bath. Another option includes a private master bath and a separate bath for the family bedrooms.

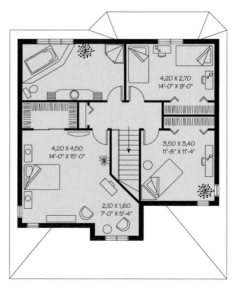

SECOND FLOOR

FIRST FLOOR

Rustic details such as a stone fireplace work well for a country cottage such as this. A floor-to-ceiling window wall accents the living and dining rooms and provides an expansive view past a wide deck. Twin sliding glass doors access the deck from the living space. The U-shaped kitchen offers roomy counters and is open to the dining room. Behind it is a laundry room and then a full bath serving the master bedroom. An additional bedroom sits on the second floor and may be used as a studio.

plan# HPK1000117

STYLE: VACATION
FIRST FLOOR: 616 SQ. FT.
SECOND FLOOR: 300 SQ. FT.
TOTAL: 916 SQ. FT.
BEDROOMS: 2
BATHROOMS: 1
WIDTH: 22' - 0"
DEPTH: 28' - 0"
FOUNDATION: CRAWLSPACE

SEARCH ONLINE @ EPLANS.COM

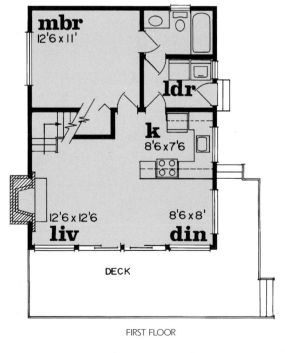

FIRST FLOOR

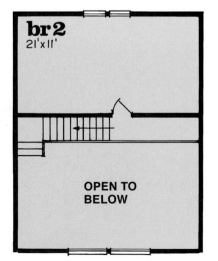

SECOND FLOOR

plan# HPK1000118

STYLE: RANCH
SQUARE FOOTAGE: 1,408
BEDROOMS: 3
BATHROOMS: 2
WIDTH: 70' - 0"
DEPTH: 34' - 0"
FOUNDATION: UNFINISHED
BASEMENT, CRAWLSPACE

SEARCH ONLINE @ EPLANS.COM

An eyebrow dormer and a large veranda give guests a warm country greeting outside; inside, vaulted ceilings lend a sense of spaciousness to this three-bedroom home. A bright country kitchen boasts an abundance of counter space and cupboards. The front entry is sheltered by a broad veranda. Built-in amenities adorn the interior, including a pot shelf over the entry coat closet, an art niche, a skylight, and a walk-in pantry and island workstation in the kitchen. A box-bay window and a spa-style tub highlight the master suite. The two-car garage provides a workshop area.

OPTIONAL LAYOUT

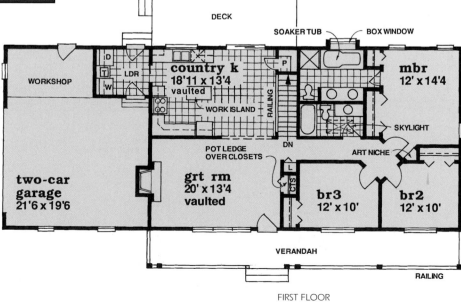

FIRST FLOOR

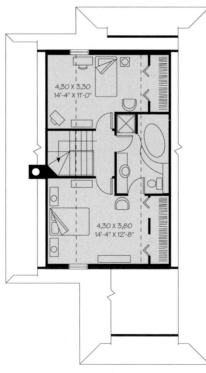

SECOND FLOOR

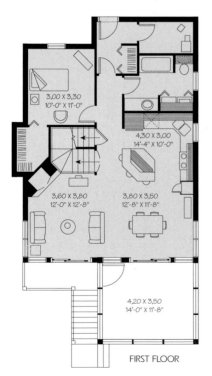

FIRST FLOOR

plan# HPK1000119

STYLE: CAPE COD
FIRST FLOOR: 908 SQ. FT.
SECOND FLOOR: 576 SQ. FT.
TOTAL: 1,484 SQ. FT.
BEDROOMS: 3
BATHROOMS: 2
WIDTH: 26' - 0"
DEPTH: 36' - 0"
FOUNDATION: FINISHED
WALKOUT BASEMENT

SEARCH ONLINE @ EPLANS.COM

Here's a favorite waterfront home with plenty of space to kick back and relax. A lovely sunroom opens from the dining room and allows great views. An angled hearth warms the living and dining areas. Three lovely windows brighten the dining space, which leads out to a stunning sunporch. The gourmet kitchen has an island counter with a snack bar. The first-floor master bedroom enjoys a walk-in closet and a nearby bath. Upstairs, a spacious bath with a whirlpool tub is thoughtfully placed between two bedrooms. A daylight basement allows a lower-level portico.

plan# HPK1000120

STYLE: TRANSITIONAL
FIRST FLOOR: 1,530 SQ. FT.
SECOND FLOOR: 469 SQ. FT.
TOTAL: 1,999 SQ. FT.
BEDROOMS: 3
BATHROOMS: 2½
WIDTH: 59' - 6"
DEPTH: 53' - 0"
FOUNDATION: UNFINISHED
BASEMENT, SLAB, CRAWLSPACE

SEARCH ONLINE @ EPLANS.COM

Stone porch supports and wide pillars lend a Craftsman look to this design. A truly elegant floor plan awaits within—an octagonal home office is just to the left of the entry, and a formal dining room sits to the right. The central living room offers a fireplace and a wall of windows that overlooks the deck; the nearby island kitchen includes a walk-in pantry and adjoins the breakfast bay. Access the greenhouse from the expansive side deck. Double doors open to the master bedroom, which provides a private bath with an angled soaking tub; two family bedrooms are found upstairs, where a balcony overlooks the two-story living room.

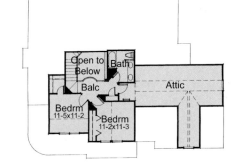

SECOND FLOOR

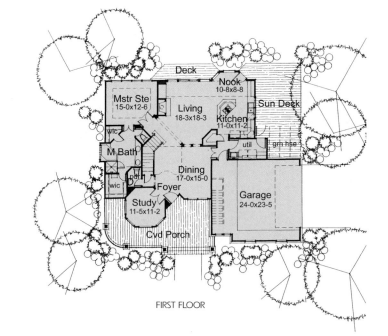

FIRST FLOOR

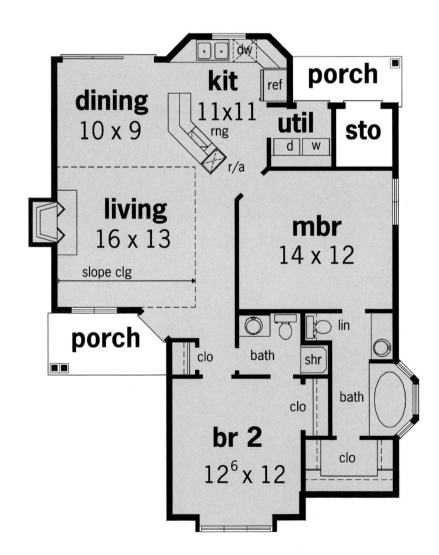

dining
10 x 9

kit
11x11
rng

ref

porch

util
d w

sto

living
16 x 13

slope clg

mbr
14 x 12

porch

clo

bath

shr

lin

bath

clo

clo

br 2
12⁶ x 12

plan# HPK1000121

STYLE: COUNTRY COTTAGE
SQUARE FOOTAGE: 984
BEDROOMS: 2
BATHROOMS: 2
WIDTH: 33' - 9"
DEPTH: 43' - 0"
FOUNDATION: CRAWLSPACE,
SLAB

SEARCH ONLINE @ EPLANS.COM

This snug home uses space efficiently, with no wasted square footage. Brightened by a clerestory window, the living room features a sloped ceiling and a warming fireplace. A spacious master suite enjoys a walk-in closet and a lavish bath with a garden tub set in a bay. The secondary bedroom has access to the hall bath. Wood trim and eye-catching windows make this home charming as well as practical.

plan # HPK1000122

STYLE: TRADITIONAL
FIRST FLOOR: 911 SQ. FT.
SECOND FLOOR: 1,029 SQ. FT.
TOTAL: 1,940 SQ. FT.
BEDROOMS: 3
BATHROOMS: 2½
WIDTH: 20' - 10"
DEPTH: 75' - 10"
FOUNDATION: CRAWLSPACE

SEARCH ONLINE @ EPLANS.COM

With irresistible charm and quiet curb appeal, this enchanting cottage conceals a sophisticated interior that's prepared for busy lifestyles. Built-in cabinetry in the great room frames a massive fireplace, which warms the area and complements the natural views. An open kitchen provides an island with a double sink and snack counter. Planned events are easily served in the formal dining room with French doors that lead to the veranda. On the upper level, a central hall with linen storage connects the sleeping quarters. The master suite boasts a walk-in closet and a roomy bath with a dual-sink vanity. Each of two secondary bedrooms has plenty of wardrobe space. Bedroom 3 leads out to the upper-level deck.

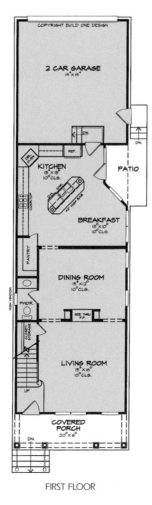

FIRST FLOOR

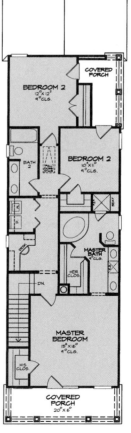

SECOND FLOOR

DECK

BREAKFAST
11'-4" X 8'-6"

BEDROOM NO. 3
11'-6" X 11'-0"

GREAT ROOM
14'-0" X 17'-6"

KITCHEN
11'-4" X 10'-0"

MASTER
BEDROOM
12'-4" X 15'-6"

BATH

DN

HIS

FOYER
6'-6" X 6'-6"

DINING ROOM
11'-4" X 10'-6"

PWDR.

MASTER
BATH

BEDROOM NO. 2
11'-0" X 14'-8"

LAUNDRY

HERS

TWO-CAR GARAGE
20'-4" X 19'-4"

plan # HPK1000123

STYLE: TRADITIONAL
SQUARE FOOTAGE: 1,733
BEDROOMS: 3
BATHROOMS: 2½
WIDTH: 55' - 6"
DEPTH: 57' - 6"
FOUNDATION: FINISHED
WALKOUT BASEMENT

SEARCH ONLINE @ EPLANS.COM

Delightfully different, this brick one-story home has everything for the active family. The foyer opens to a formal dining room, accented with four columns, and a great room with a fireplace and French doors to the rear deck. The efficient kitchen has an attached light-filled breakfast nook. The master bath features a tray ceiling, His and Hers walk-in closets, a double-sink vanity, and a huge garden tub. The two-car garage is accessed through the laundry room.

plan # HPK1000124

STYLE: VACATION
FIRST FLOOR: 1,042 SQ. FT.
SECOND FLOOR: 456 SQ. FT.
TOTAL: 1,498 SQ. FT.
BEDROOMS: 3
BATHROOMS: 2
WIDTH: 36' - 0"
DEPTH: 35' - 8"
FOUNDATION: CRAWLSPACE,
UNFINISHED BASEMENT

SEARCH ONLINE @ EPLANS.COM

With a deck to the front, this vacation home won't miss out on any outdoor fun. The living and dining rooms are dominated by a window wall that takes advantage of the view. A high vaulted ceiling and wood-burning fireplace create a warm atmosphere. The U-shaped kitchen, with an adjoining laundry room, is open to the dining room with a pass-through counter. Note the deck beyond the kitchen and the full wall closet by the laundry. The master bedroom to the rear utilizes a full bath with a large linen closet. Two family bedrooms upstairs share a full bath that includes a skylight.

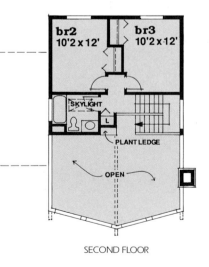

SECOND FLOOR

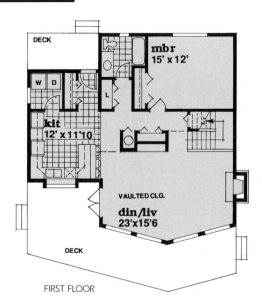

FIRST FLOOR

This chalet plan is enhanced by a steep gable roof, scalloped fascia boards, and fieldstone chimney detail. The front-facing deck and covered balcony add to outdoor living spaces. The fireplace is the main focus in the living room. The bedroom on the first floor enjoys access to a full hall bath. A storage/mudroom at the back of the plan is perfect for keeping skis and boots. Two additional bedrooms and a half-bath occupy the second floor. The master bedroom provides a walk-in closet. Three storage areas are also found on the second floor.

plan# HPK1000125

STYLE: COUNTRY COTTAGE
FIRST FLOOR: 672 SQ. FT.
SECOND FLOOR: 401 SQ. FT.
TOTAL: 1,073 SQ. FT.
BEDROOMS: 3
BATHROOMS: 1½
WIDTH: 24' - 0"
DEPTH: 36' - 0"
FOUNDATION: CRAWLSPACE,
UNFINISHED BASEMENT

SEARCH ONLINE @ EPLANS.COM

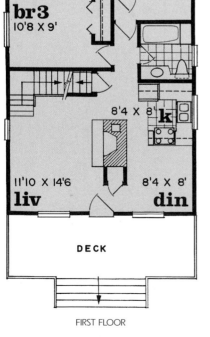

FIRST FLOOR

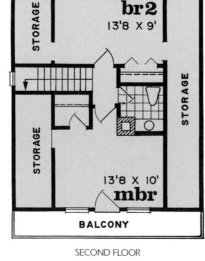

SECOND FLOOR

plan# HPK1000126

STYLE: COUNTRY COTTAGE
SQUARE FOOTAGE: 1,845
BONUS SPACE: 409 SQ. FT.
BEDROOMS: 3
BATHROOMS: 2½
WIDTH: 56' - 0"
DEPTH: 60' - 0"
FOUNDATION: CRAWLSPACE,
SLAB, UNFINISHED WALKOUT
BASEMENT

SEARCH ONLINE @ EPLANS.COM

The stucco exterior and combination rooflines give a stately appearance to this traditional home. Inside, the well-lit foyer leads to an elegant living room with a vaulted ceiling, fireplace, radius window, and French door that opens to the rear property. Two family bedrooms share a full bath on the right side of the home; an impressive master suite resides to the left for privacy. A formal dining room and an open kitchen with plenty of counter space complete the plan.

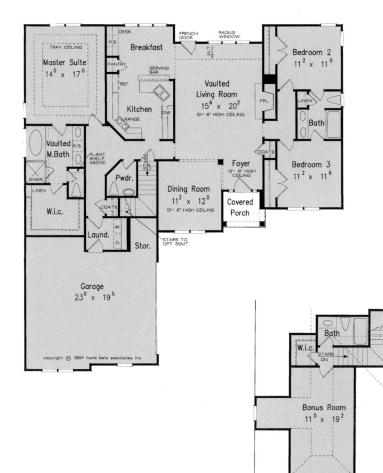

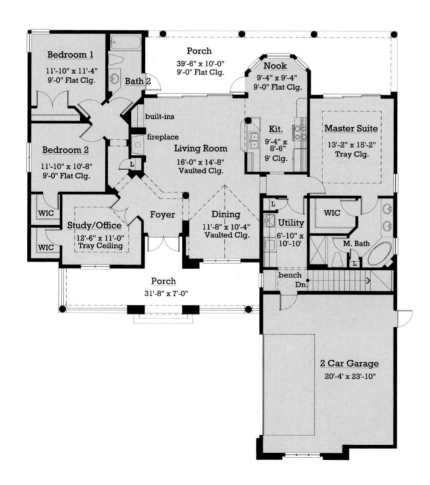

plan# HPK1000127

STYLE: FARMHOUSE
SQUARE FOOTAGE: 1,822
BEDROOMS: 3
BATHROOMS: 2
WIDTH: 58' - 0"
DEPTH: 67' - 2"
FOUNDATION: UNFINISHED
BASEMENT, FINISHED
BASEMENT

SEARCH ONLINE @ EPLANS.COM

Stone bays and wood siding make up the exterior facade on this one-story home. The interior revolves around the living room with an attached dining room and the galley kitchen with a breakfast room. The master suite has a fine bath and a walk-in closet. One of three family bedrooms on the left side of the plan could be used as a home office.

plan # HPK1000128

STYLE: EUROPEAN COTTAGE
SQUARE FOOTAGE: 1,823
BEDROOMS: 3
BATHROOMS: 2
WIDTH: 38' - 10"
DEPTH: 94' - 10"
FOUNDATION: SLAB

SEARCH ONLINE @ EPLANS.COM

This home's long, narrow footprint is ideal for a slim lot. A beautiful facade using stucco, brick, shuttered windows and steepled rooftops is as inviting as the floor plan. A courtyard entrance is flanked by the open dining and family spaces. Two family bedrooms are split from the master suite, which fosters privacy. The master bedroom, at the rear of the home, enjoys simple luxuries in the dual-vanity bath.

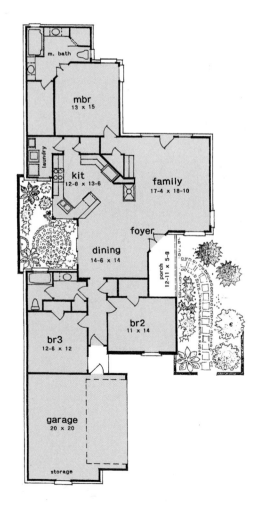

A grand brick facade, this home boasts muntin windows, multilevel rooflines, cut-brick jack arches, and a beautifully arched entry. A cathedral-ceilinged living room, complete with fireplace, and a family dining room flank the 20-foot-high entry. Relax in the family room, mix a drink from the wet bar, and look out through multiple windows to the covered veranda. A luxurious master suite includes a windowed sitting area looking over the rear view, private patio, full bath boasting a 10-foot ceiling, and a spacious walk-in closet On the second level, the three high-ceilinged bedrooms share two full baths and a study area with a built-in desk.

plan⊕ HPK1000127

STYLE: NW CONTEMPORARY
FIRST FLOOR: 1,157 SQ. FT.
SECOND FLOOR: 638 SQ. FT.
TOTAL: 1,795 SQ. FT.
BEDROOMS: 3
BATHROOMS: 2½
WIDTH: 36' - 0"
DEPTH: 40' - 0"

SEARCH ONLINE @ EPLANS.COM

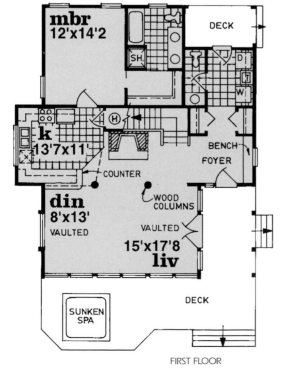

FIRST FLOOR

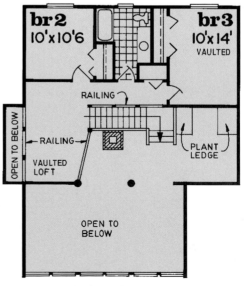

SECOND FLOOR

plan# HPK1000130

STYLE: FRENCH
FIRST FLOOR: 1,182 SQ. FT.
SECOND FLOOR: 716 SQ. FT.
TOTAL: 1,898 SQ. FT.
BEDROOMS: 4
BATHROOMS: 2½
WIDTH: 68' - 5"
DEPTH: 33' - 5"
FOUNDATION: UNFINISHED
BASEMENT

SEARCH ONLINE @ EPLANS.COM

Architectural elements borrowed from English Tudor style combine with French Country details to make this eclectic creation a picture-perfect European cottage. The entry contains a wood-railing staircase and opens to the formal bow-windowed dining room. To the right, a galley kitchen and its adjacent breakfast area lead to a morning patio. The great room features a partially vaulted ceiling and a fireplace flanked by built-in bookshelves. The master suite enjoys a relaxing master bath and twin walk-in closets.

FIRST FLOOR

SECOND FLOOR

Steep, soaring gables embellished with band-sawn ornamentation heighten the drama of this Gothic Revival gem. Adorned with gingerbread trim and swathed in cedar board-and-batten siding, this romantic house will be the envy of the neighborhood. The heavy carved brackets on the front porch invite the curious into the entry foyer complete with a half-bath, guest closet, and bay window with a window seat. The living room features a fireplace and plenty of light that filters through the casement windows. For effortless entertaining, the kitchen opens to the dining room. Upstairs, there are two spacious bedrooms and a full bath. The master bedroom features a vaulted ceiling and tie beams.

plan# HPK1000131

STYLE: TRADITIONAL
FIRST FLOOR: 688 SQ. FT.
SECOND FLOOR: 559 SQ. FT.
TOTAL: 1,247 SQ. FT.
BEDROOMS: 2
BATHROOMS: 1½
WIDTH: 27' - 8"
DEPTH: 30' - 8"
FOUNDATION: CRAWLSPACE

SEARCH ONLINE @ EPLANS.COM

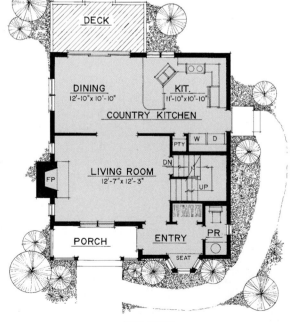

FIRST FLOOR

SECOND FLOOR

plan # HPK1000132

STYLE: COUNTRY COTTAGE
SQUARE FOOTAGE 1,509
BEDROOMS: 3
BATHROOMS: 2
WIDTH: 49' - 0"
DEPTH: 34' - 4"
FOUNDATION: UNFINISHED
WALKOUT BASEMENT

SEARCH ONLINE @ EPLANS.COM

Inside this well-planned traditional home, an elegant sunlit foyer leads up a short flight of stairs to an immense vaulted great room with a fireplace. Arched openings lead to the open bayed breakfast area and kitchen. The master suite is tucked to one side with plenty of amenities—entrance to a private covered porch, plenty of storage, and decorative built-in plant shelves. Two family bedrooms occupy the opposite side of the home and share a full bath and more closet space. An unfinished basement provides for future lifestyle needs.

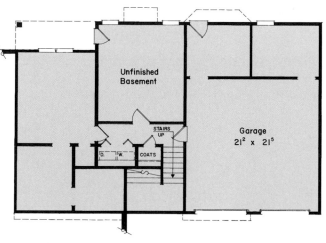

BASEMENT

SECOND FLOOR

With woodsy charm and cozy livability, this cottage plan offers comfortable living space in a smaller footprint. The exterior is geared for outdoor fun, with two flagstone patios connected by a two-way fireplace and graced by a built-in barbecue. French doors on two sides lead into the large play room, which features a kitchen area, washer and dryer space, and a bath with corner sink and shower. Take the L-shaped stairway to the bunk room upstairs, where there is space for sleeping and relaxing.

plan # HPK1000133

STYLE: EUROPEAN COTTAGE
FIRST FLOOR: 665 SQ. FT.
SECOND FLOOR: 395 SQ. FT.
TOTAL: 1,060 SQ. FT.
BEDROOMS: 1
BATHROOMS: 1
WIDTH: 34' - 3"
DEPTH: 32' - 5"
FOUNDATION: SLAB

SEARCH ONLINE @ EPLANS.COM

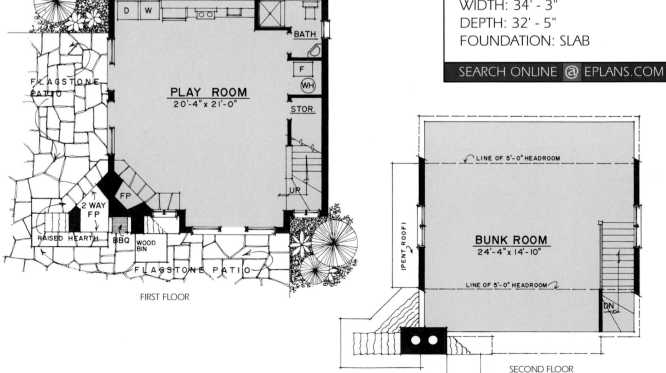

plan # HPK1000134

STYLE: COUNTRY COTTAGE
FIRST FLOOR: 728 SQ. FT.
SECOND FLOOR: 420 SQ. FT.
TOTAL: 1,148 SQ. FT.
BEDROOMS: 1
BATHROOMS: 1½
WIDTH: 28' - 0"
DEPTH: 26' - 0"
FOUNDATION: UNFINISHED
BASEMENT

SEARCH ONLINE @ EPLANS.COM

This stunning contemporary cottage has a heart of gold, with plenty of windows to bring in a wealth of natural light. Open planning allows the first-floor living and dining room to share the wide views of the outdoors. Glass doors frame the fireplace and open to the deck. A second-floor mezzanine enjoys an overlook to the living area and leads to a generous master suite with a walk-in closet, private bath, and a sitting area.

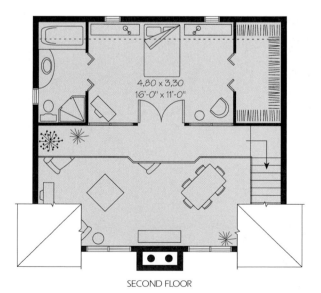

SECOND FLOOR

FIRST FLOOR

This absolutely charming Victorian-style ranch home is warm and inviting, yet the interior is decidedly up-to-date. An assemblage of beautiful windows surrounds the main entry, flooding the entrance foyer and adjoining great room with an abundance of shaded light. An elegant 10-foot stepped ceiling is featured in the great room, as is a corner fireplace and rear wall of French-style sliding doors. The beautiful multisided breakfast room features a 16-foot ceiling adorned with high clerestory windows, which become the exterior "turret." A private master suite includes a compartmented bath, dressing alcove, very large walk-in closet, 10-foot stepped ceiling, and beautiful bay window overlooking the rear.

plan# HPK1000135

STYLE: FARMHOUSE
SQUARE FOOTAGE: 1,466
BEDROOMS: 3
BATHROOMS: 2
WIDTH: 60' - 0"
DEPTH: 39' - 10"
FOUNDATION: UNFINISHED BASEMENT, SLAB, CRAWLSPACE

SEARCH ONLINE @ EPLANS.COM

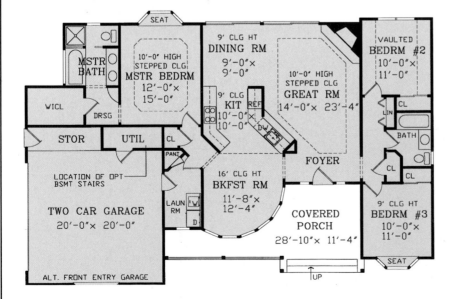

plan # HPK1000136

STYLE: VACATION
FIRST FLOOR: 725 SQ. FT.
SECOND FLOOR: 561 SQ. FT.
TOTAL: 1,286 SQ. FT.
BEDROOMS: 3
BATHROOMS: 2
WIDTH: 25' - 0"
DEPTH: 36' - 6"
FOUNDATION: CRAWLSPACE

SEARCH ONLINE @ EPLANS.COM

This cozy chalet design begins with a railed veranda opening to a living room with a warm fireplace and a dining room with a snack-bar counter through to the kitchen. The kitchen itself is U-shaped and has a sink with window over. A full bath and large storage area sit just beyond the kitchen. One bedroom with a roomy wall closet is on the first floor. The second floor holds two additional bedrooms—one a master bedroom with a private balcony—and a full bath. Additional storage is found on the second floor, as well.

FIRST FLOOR

SECOND FLOOR

The stone facade and woodwork detail give this home a Craftsman appeal. The foyer opens to a staircase up to the vaulted great room, which features a fireplace flanked by built-ins and French-door access to the rear covered porch. The open dining room with a tray ceiling offers convenience to the spacious kitchen. Two family bedrooms share a bath and enjoy private porches. An overlook to the great room below is a perfect introduction to the master suite. The second level spreads out the luxury of the master suite with a spacious walk-in closet, a private porch, and a glorious master bath with a garden tub, dual vanities, and a compartmented toilet.

plan # HPK1000137

STYLE: BUNGALOW
FIRST FLOOR: 1,383 SQ. FT.
SECOND FLOOR: 595 SQ. FT.
TOTAL: 1,978 SQ. FT.
BEDROOMS: 3
BATHROOMS: 2
WIDTH: 48' - 0"
DEPTH: 48' - 8"
FOUNDATION: UNFINISHED
WALKOUT BASEMENT

SEARCH ONLINE @ EPLANS.COM

BASEMENT

FIRST FLOOR

SECOND FLOOR

plan# HPK1000138

STYLE: FARMHOUSE
SQUARE FOOTAGE: 1,541
BEDROOMS: 3
BATHROOMS: 2
WIDTH: 87' - 0"
DEPTH: 44' - 0"
FOUNDATION: CRAWLSPACE,
UNFINISHED BASEMENT

SEARCH ONLINE @ EPLANS.COM

This popular design begins with a wraparound covered porch made even more charming with turned-wood spindles. The entry opens directly to the great room, which is warmed by a wood stove. The adjoining dining room offers access to a screened porch for outdoor after-dinner leisure. A country kitchen features a center island and a breakfast bay for casual meals. Family bedrooms share a full bath that features a soaking tub. The two-car garage connects to the plan via the screened porch.

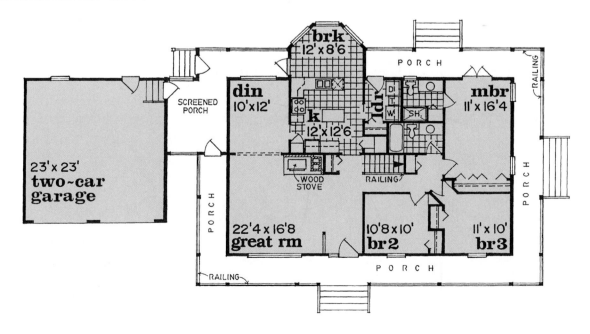

This down-home, one-story plan has all the comforts and necessities for solid family living. The vaulted family room, along with the adjoining country-style kitchen and breakfast nook, is at the center of the plan. The extended hearth fireplace flanked by radius windows will make this a cozy focus for family get-togethers and entertaining visitors. A formal dining room is marked off by decorative columns. The resplendent master suite assumes the entire right wing, where it is separated from two bedrooms located on the other side of the home. Built-in plant shelves in the master bath create a garden-like environment. Additional space is available for building another bedroom or study.

plan # HPK1000139

STYLE: CRAFTSMAN
SQUARE FOOTAGE: 1,724
BONUS SPACE: 375 SQ. FT.
BEDROOMS: 3
BATHROOMS: 2
WIDTH: 53' - 6"
DEPTH: 58' - 6"
FOUNDATION: CRAWLSPACE, UNFINISHED WALKOUT BASEMENT

SEARCH ONLINE @ EPLANS.COM

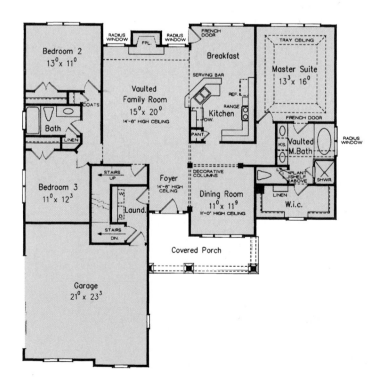

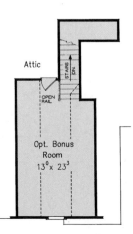

plan # HPK1000140

STYLE: TRADITIONAL
FIRST FLOOR: 716 SQ. FT.
SECOND FLOOR: 784 SQ. FT.
TOTAL: 1,500 SQ. FT.
BEDROOMS: 3
BATHROOMS: 2½
WIDTH: 36' - 0"
DEPTH: 44' - 0"
FOUNDATION: CRAWLSPACE

SEARCH ONLINE @ EPLANS.COM

A traditional neighborhood look is accented by stone and decorative arches on this stylish new design. Simplicity is the hallmark of this plan, giving the interior great flow and openness. The foyer, with a coat closet, leads directly into the two-story great room with abundant natural light and a warming fireplace. The island kitchen and dining area are to the left and enjoy rear-porch access. Upstairs, a vaulted master suite with a private bath joins two additional bedrooms to complete the plan.

FIRST FLOOR

SECOND FLOOR

You'll love the floor plan of this traditional family home, designed both for elegant entertaining and kick-your-shoes-off relaxation. The two-story entry leads guests into a combined living room and dining room, defining this area for formal occasions. A snack bar in the angled kitchen makes serving the bayed breakfast nook a snap, and it overlooks the hearth room's cozy fireplace. The master suite is on the far right with a 10-foot ceiling and an indulgent private bath. Upstairs, two bedrooms share a full bath, with an option for a fourth-bedroom addition.

plan# HPK1000141

STYLE: TRADITIONAL
FIRST FLOOR: 1,233 SQ. FT.
SECOND FLOOR: 433 SQ. FT.
TOTAL: 1,666 SQ. FT.
BEDROOMS: 3
BATHROOMS: 2½
WIDTH: 49' - 0"
DEPTH: 47' - 4"
FOUNDATION: CRAWLSPACE, SLAB, UNFINISHED BASEMENT

SEARCH ONLINE @ EPLANS.COM

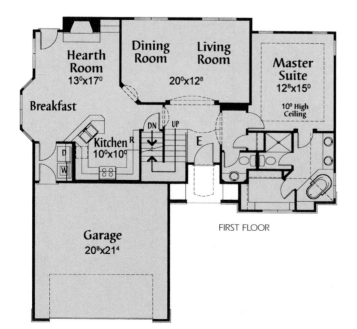

FIRST FLOOR

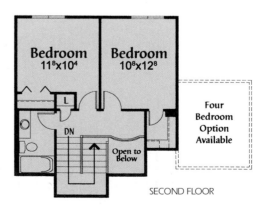

SECOND FLOOR

plan# HPK1000142

STYLE: COUNTRY COTTAGE
SQUARE FOOTAGE: 1,725
BONUS SPACE: 256 SQ. FT.
BEDROOMS: 3
BATHROOMS: 2
WIDTH: 58' - 0"
DEPTH: 54' - 6"
FOUNDATION: CRAWLSPACE,
UNFINISHED WALKOUT
BASEMENT

SEARCH ONLINE @ EPLANS.COM

This inviting Colonial-style home will capture your heart with a lovely facade and flowing floor plan. From the foyer and beyond, raised ceilings visually expand spaces. A vaulted great room is warmed by a cozy hearth and opens to the bayed breakfast nook. A serving-bar kitchen helps chefs prepare marvelous meals for any occasion and easily accesses the columned dining room. Tucked to the rear, the vaulted master suite enjoys light from radius windows and the comforts of a pampering spa bath. Two additional bedrooms are located to the far right, near a full bath and laundry room. Bonus space is available for an extra bedroom, study, or playroom—whatever your family desires.

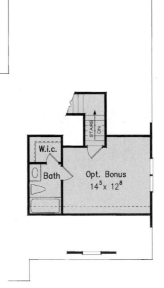

This plan combines a traditional, stately exterior with an updated floor plan to create a house that will please the entire family. The heart of the plan is surely the wide-open living space consisting of the vaulted family room, breakfast area, and gourmet kitchen. Highlights here are a full-length fireplace, a French door to the rear yard, and an island cooktop. The master suite has a tray ceiling and a vaulted master bath with a garden tub and walk-in closet. The family sleeping area on the upper level gives the option of two bedrooms and a loft overlooking the family room or three bedrooms.

plan# HPK1000143

STYLE: COUNTRY COTTAGE
FIRST FLOOR: 1,320 SQ. FT.
SECOND FLOOR: 554 SQ. FT.
TOTAL: 1,874 SQ. FT.
BONUS SPACE: 155 SQ. FT.
BEDROOMS: 4
BATHROOMS: 2½
WIDTH: 54' - 6"
DEPTH: 42' - 4"
FOUNDATION: CRAWLSPACE, UNFINISHED WALKOUT BASEMENT

SEARCH ONLINE @ EPLANS.COM

FIRST FLOOR

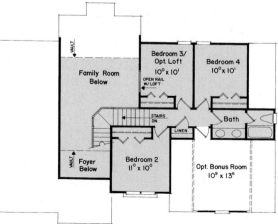

SECOND FLOOR

ptan# HPK1000144

STYLE: TRADITIONAL
SQUARE FOOTAGE: 2,018
BEDROOMS: 3
BATHROOMS: 2
WIDTH: 74' - 11"
DEPTH: 49' - 2"
FOUNDATION: CRAWLSPACE,
SLAB, UNFINISHED BASEMENT

SEARCH ONLINE @ EPLANS.COM

A Palladian window set into a front-facing gable highlights this country home. The dining room, on the right, includes accent columns and convenient kitchen service. The great room offers twin sets of French doors that access the rear porch. Meal preparation will be easy in the kitchen with a work island and cheerful light streaming in from the bay-windowed breakfast nook. The master suite is set to the rear and features a walk-in closet made for two, dual vanities, and a compartmented toilet. Two family bedrooms near the front of the plan share a full bath.

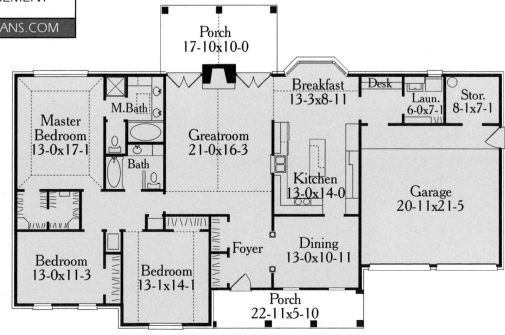

Porch
17-10x10-0

Breakfast
13-3x8-11

Desk

Laun.
6-0x7-1

Stor.
8-1x7-1

M.Bath

Master
Bedroom
13-0x17-1

Greatroom
21-0x16-3

Bath

Kitchen
13-0x14-0

Garage
20-11x21-5

Bedroom
13-0x11-3

Bedroom
13-1x14-1

Foyer

Dining
13-0x10-11

Porch
22-11x5-10

This design takes inspiration from the casual fishing cabins of the Pacific Northwest and interprets it for modern livability. It offers three options for a main entrance. One door opens to a mud porch, where a small hall leads to a galley kitchen and the vaulted great room. Two French doors on the side porch open into a dining room with bay-window seating. Another porch entrance opens directly into the great room, which is centered around a massive stone fireplace and accented with a wall of windows. The secluded master bedroom features a bath with a clawfoot tub and twin pedestal sinks, as well as a separate shower and walk-in closet. Two more bedrooms share a bath. An unfinished loft looks over the great room.

ptan# HPK1000145

STYLE: VACATION
SQUARE FOOTAGE: 2,019
BEDROOMS: 3
BATHROOMS: 2
WIDTH: 56' - 0"
DEPTH: 56' - 3"
FOUNDATION: CRAWLSPACE

SEARCH ONLINE @ EPLANS.COM

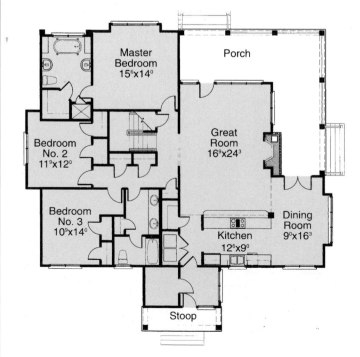

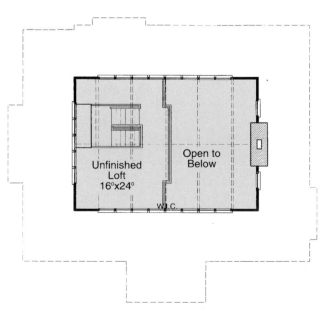

plan# HPK1000146

STYLE: TRADITIONAL
SQUARE FOOTAGE: 2,029
BEDROOMS: 3
BATHROOMS: 2
WIDTH: 61' - 0"
DEPTH: 51' - 0"
FOUNDATION: UNFINISHED BASEMENT

SEARCH ONLINE @ EPLANS.COM

Stonework, gables, a roof dormer, and double porches create a country flavor in this home that fits hand-in-glove with many types of landscapes. The kitchen enjoys extravagant cabinetry and counter space in a bay, an island snack bar, a built-in pantry, and a cheery dining area. The large entry showcases beautiful wood columns and is also open to the vaulted great room, which features a corner fireplace. The master bedroom boasts His and Hers walk-in closets and double doors that lead to an opulent master bath and private porch. Two family bedrooms enjoy walk-in closets and share a full bath.

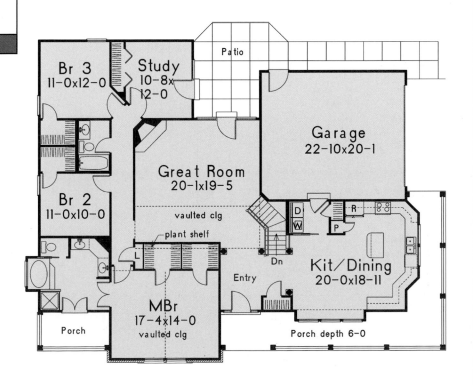

Victorian styling can come in an affordable size, as this home shows. A sitting area inside the front hall connects with the family room for handling large parties. An enclosed room off the sitting area can be used as a study or extra bedroom. A combination half-bath and laundry is just inside the rear entrance for quick cleanup; the covered rear porch is accessed from a door just beyond the laundry area. For easy upkeep, the three bedrooms on the second floor share a full bath that includes a corner tub. One of the bedrooms offers access to a private balcony.

plan# HPK1000147

STYLE: VICTORIAN
FIRST FLOOR: 1,070 SQ. FT.
SECOND FLOOR: 970 SQ. FT.
TOTAL: 2,040 SQ. FT.
BEDROOMS: 3
BATHROOMS: 1½
WIDTH: 36' - 0"
DEPTH: 40' - 8"
FOUNDATION: UNFINISHED BASEMENT

SEARCH ONLINE @ EPLANS.COM

FIRST FLOOR

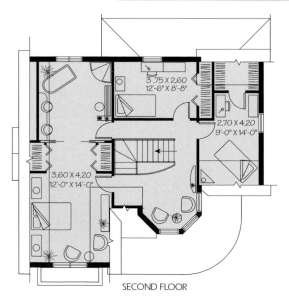

SECOND FLOOR

plan# HPK1000148

STYLE: SW CONTEMPORARY
SQUARE FOOTAGE: 2,086
BEDROOMS: 3
BATHROOMS: 2
WIDTH: 82' - 0"
DEPTH: 58' - 4"
FOUNDATION: SLAB

SEARCH ONLINE @ EPLANS.COM

A majestic facade makes this home pleasing to view. This home provides dual-use space in the wonderful sunken sitting room and media area. The kitchen has a breakfast bay and overlooks the snack bar to the sunken family area. A few steps from the kitchen is the formal dining room, which functions well with the upper patio. Two family bedrooms share a full bath. The private master suite includes a sitting area and French doors that open to a private covered patio.

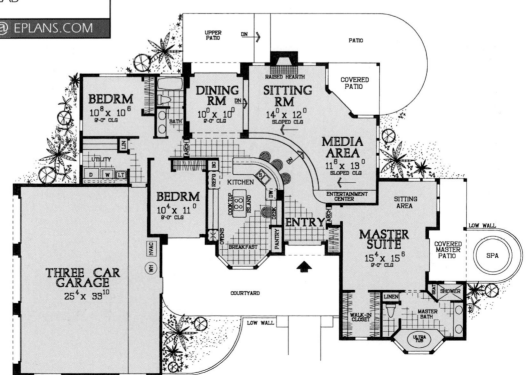

This enchanting farmhouse looks great in the country, on the waterfront, or on your street! Inside, the foyer is accented by a barrel arch and opens on the right to a formal dining room. An 11-foot ceiling in the living room expands the space, as a warming fireplace makes it feel cozy. The step-saving kitchen easily serves the bayed breakfast nook. In the sumptuous master suite, a sitting area is bathed in natural light, and the walk-in closet is equipped with a built-in dresser. The luxurious bath features dual vanities and a spa tub. Three upstairs bedrooms, one with a private bath, access optional future space, designed to meet your family's needs.

plan# HPK1000149

STYLE: FARMHOUSE
FIRST FLOOR: 1,383 SQ. FT.
SECOND FLOOR: 703 SQ. FT.
TOTAL: 2,086 SQ. FT.
BONUS SPACE: 342 SQ. FT.
BEDROOMS: 4
BATHROOMS: 3½
WIDTH: 49' - 0"
DEPTH: 50' - 0"

SEARCH ONLINE @ EPLANS.COM

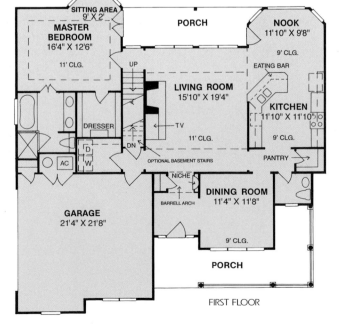

FIRST FLOOR

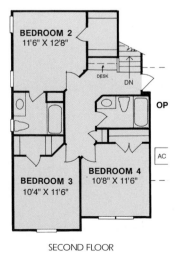

SECOND FLOOR

© William E. Poole Designs, Inc.

plan # HPK1000150

STYLE: COUNTRY COTTAGE
SQUARE FOOTAGE: 2,096
BONUS SPACE: 374 SQ. FT.
BEDROOMS: 3
BATHROOMS: 2
WIDTH: 64' - 8"
DEPTH: 60' - 0"
FOUNDATION: CRAWLSPACE,
UNFINISHED BASEMENT

SEARCH ONLINE @ EPLANS.COM

Brick-and-siding, a long covered porch, and three petite dormers combine to give this home plenty of curb appeal. Inside, the layout is equally delightful. The formal dining room is defined from the foyer by graceful columns, and the great room features a fireplace, built-ins, and French doors to the backyard. The efficient kitchen offers a pantry, a corner sink, and a bayed breakfast area. Two family bedrooms and a full bath are located to the right side of the plan, and the master suite provides privacy, a walk-in closet, and a pampering bath off to the left.

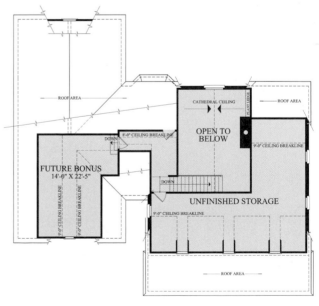

An exterior with a rich, solid look and an exciting roofline is very important to the discriminating buyer. An octagonal and vaulted master bedroom and a sunken great room with a balcony above provide this home with all the amenities. The island kitchen is easily accessible to both the breakfast area and the bayed dining area. The tapered staircase leads to two family bedrooms, each with its own access to a full dual-vanity bath. Both bedrooms have a vast closet area with double doors.

plan(#) HPK1000151

STYLE: CAPE COD
FIRST FLOOR: 1,626 SQ. FT.
SECOND FLOOR: 475 SQ. FT.
TOTAL: 2,101 SQ. FT.
BEDROOMS: 3
BATHROOMS: 2½
WIDTH: 59' - 0"
DEPTH: 60' - 8"
FOUNDATION: UNFINISHED BASEMENT

SEARCH ONLINE @ EPLANS.COM

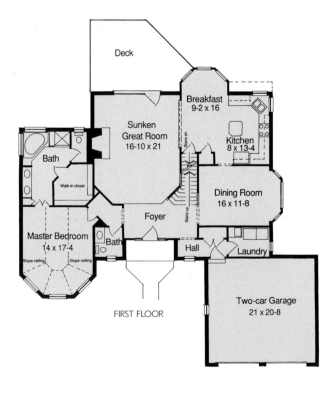

FIRST FLOOR

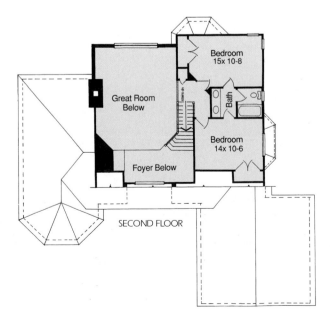

SECOND FLOOR

plan # HPK1000152

STYLE: FARMHOUSE
FIRST FLOOR: 1,082 SQ. FT.
SECOND FLOOR: 1,021 SQ. FT.
TOTAL: 2,103 SQ. FT.
BEDROOMS: 4
BATHROOMS: 2½
WIDTH: 50' - 0"
DEPTH: 40' - 0"

SEARCH ONLINE @ EPLANS.COM

A covered porch invites you into this country-style home. Handsome bookcases frame the fireplace in the spacious family room. Double doors off the entry provide the family room with added privacy. The kitchen features an island, a lazy Susan, and easy access to a walk-in laundry. The master bedroom features a boxed ceiling and separate entries to a walk-in closet and a pampering bath. The upstairs hall bath is compartmented, allowing maximum usage for today's busy family.

SECOND FLOOR

FIRST FLOOR

Behind the gables and arched windows of this fine traditional home lies a great floor plan. The two-story foyer leads past a formal dining room defined by decorative pillars to a vaulted family room with a fireplace. The L-shaped kitchen is open to the sunny breakfast nook and provides access to the rear property. The lavish master suite is separated from the two upper-level bedrooms. Optional bonus space on the second floor invites the possibility of a recreation room, exercise room, or media room.

plan# HPK1000153

STYLE: COUNTRY COTTAGE
FIRST FLOOR: 1,581 SQ. FT.
SECOND FLOOR: 534 SQ. FT.
TOTAL: 2,115 SQ. FT.
BONUS SPACE: 250 SQ. FT.
BEDROOMS: 3
BATHROOMS: 2½
WIDTH: 53' - 0"
DEPTH: 43' - 4"
FOUNDATION: CRAWLSPACE, UNFINISHED WALKOUT BASEMENT

SEARCH ONLINE @ EPLANS.COM

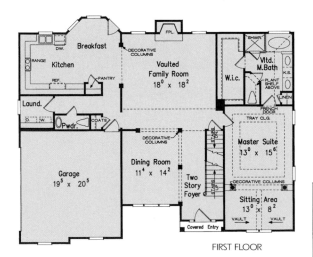

FIRST FLOOR

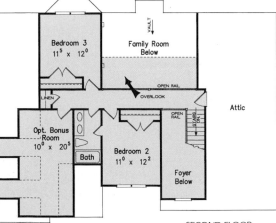

SECOND FLOOR

plan # HPK1000154

STYLE: RANCH
FIRST FLOOR: 1,501 SQ. FT.
SECOND FLOOR: 631 SQ. FT.
TOTAL: 2,132 SQ. FT.
BEDROOMS: 3
BATHROOMS: 2½
WIDTH: 76' - 0"
DEPTH: 48' - 4"
FOUNDATION: SLAB,
UNFINISHED BASEMENT,
CRAWLSPACE

SEARCH ONLINE @ EPLANS.COM

This home reveals its rustic charm with a metal roof, dormers, and exposed-column rafters. The full-length porch is an invitation to comfortable living inside. The great room shares a fireplace with the spacious dining room that has rear-porch access. The kitchen is this home's focus, with plenty of counter and cabinet space, a window sink, and an open layout. The first-floor master suite features two walk-in closets and a grand bath. Two family bedrooms and a playroom reside on the second floor.

SECOND FLOOR

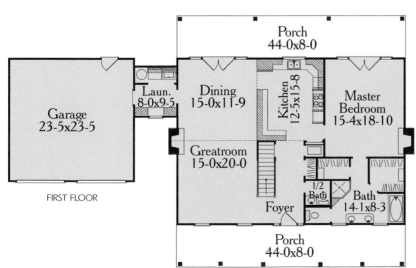

FIRST FLOOR

This home draws its inspiration from both French and English Country homes. The great room and dining room combine to form an impressive gathering space, with the dining area subtly defined by columns and a large triple window. The kitchen, with its work island, adjoins the breakfast area and keeping room with a fireplace. The home is completed by a master suite with a bay window and a garden tub. Space on the lower level can be developed later.

plan# HPK1000155

STYLE: FRENCH
SQUARE FOOTAGE: 2,150
BEDROOMS: 3
BATHROOMS: 2½
WIDTH: 64' - 0"
DEPTH: 60' - 4"
FOUNDATION: FINISHED
WALKOUT BASEMENT

SEARCH ONLINE @ EPLANS.COM

plan⊕# HPK1000156

STYLE: TRADITIONAL
SQUARE FOOTAGE: 2,160
BEDROOMS: 3
BATHROOMS: 2
WIDTH: 68' - 0"
DEPTH: 64' - 0"
FOUNDATION: CRAWLSPACE, SLAB

SEARCH ONLINE @ EPLANS.COM

Steep rooflines and columns make this home one to remember. Starburst windows align along the exterior and offer a nice touch of sophistication. Extra amenities run rampant through this one-story home. The sunroom can be enjoyed during every season. An eating nook right off the kitchen brightens the rear of the home. Utility and storage areas are also found at the rear of the home. A cozy study privately accesses the side porch. The master bedroom is complete with dual vanities and His and Hers closets. Two family bedrooms reside to the left of the plan.

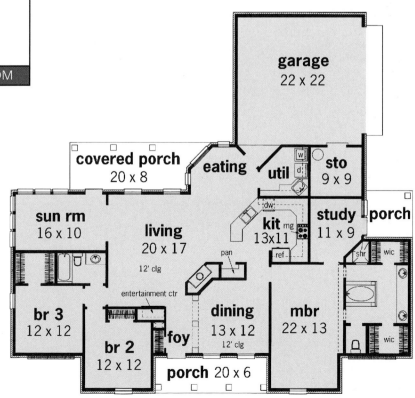

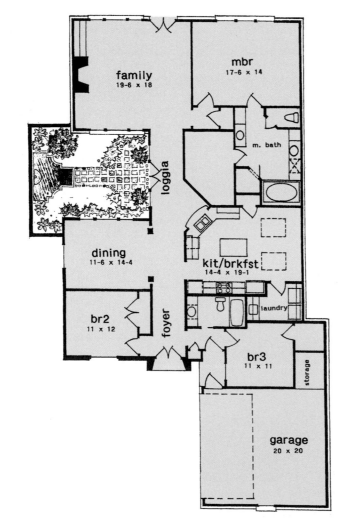

plan# HPK1000157

STYLE: EUROPEAN COTTAGE
SQUARE FOOTAGE: 2,163
BEDROOMS: 3
BATHROOMS: 2
WIDTH: 44' - 0"
DEPTH: 83' - 0"
FOUNDATION: SLAB

SEARCH ONLINE @ EPLANS.COM

This cozy stucco design fits a shady lane in town or takes advantage of the views in the country. French doors open from an arched entryway with a transom window to the foyer. Two family bedrooms flank the foyer, and a hallway opens to the dining room. Across the hall, the kitchen and breakfast room serve up casual and formal meals. A loggia, just before the family room, accesses a garden courtyard. The family room sports a fireplace, built-ins, and French doors to the rear yard. The master suite features a spacious walk-in closet and an amenity-filled bath.

plan# HPK1000158

STYLE: TRADITIONAL
FIRST FLOOR: 832 SQ. FT.
SECOND FLOOR: 1,331 SQ. FT.
TOTAL: 2,163 SQ. FT.
BEDROOMS: 3
BATHROOMS: 2½
WIDTH: 37' - 6"
DEPTH: 48' - 4"
FOUNDATION: UNFINISHED BASEMENT

SEARCH ONLINE @ EPLANS.COM

This home offers two stories, with a twist! The living spaces are on the second floor and include a living/dining room combination with a deck and fireplace. The family room also has a fireplace, plus a built-in entertainment center, and is open to the skylit kitchen. The master bedroom is also on this level and features a private bath. Family bedrooms, a full bath, and a cozy den reside on the first level.

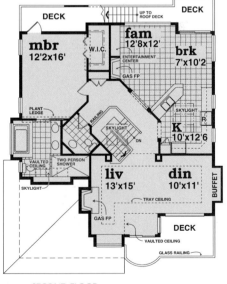

SECOND FLOOR

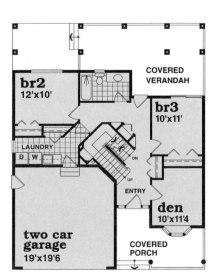

FIRST FLOOR

The simplicity of the ranch lifestyle is indicated in every detail of this charming country design. Front and rear verandas along with earthy materials combine to give the exterior of this home a true land-lover's look. A central fireplace warms the cathedral-enhanced space of the formal great room. The casual kitchen area features an island workstation overlooking the rear veranda. The master suite is a sumptuous retreat with a sitting area, private bath, and walk-in closet. Two additional bedrooms share a full hall bath.

plan# HPK1000159

STYLE: FARMHOUSE
SQUARE FOOTAGE: 2,172
BEDROOMS: 3
BATHROOMS: 2
WIDTH: 79' - 0"
DEPTH: 47' - 0"
FOUNDATION: CRAWLSPACE, SLAB

SEARCH ONLINE @ EPLANS.COM

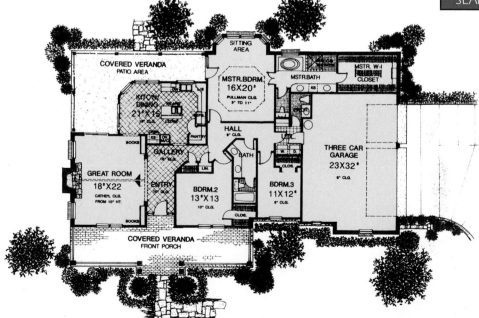

plan # HPK1000160

STYLE: TRADITIONAL
FIRST FLOOR: 1,580 SQ. FT.
SECOND FLOOR: 595 SQ. FT.
TOTAL: 2,175 SQ. FT.
BEDROOMS: 3
BATHROOMS: 2½
WIDTH: 50' - 2"
DEPTH: 70' - 11"
FOUNDATION: FINISHED
WALKOUT BASEMENT

SEARCH ONLINE @ EPLANS.COM

This home is a true Southern original. Inside, the spacious foyer leads directly to a large vaulted great room with its handsome fireplace. The dining room, just off the foyer, features a dramatic vaulted ceiling. The spacious kitchen offers both storage and large work areas opening up to the breakfast room. At the rear of the home you will find the master suite with its garden bath, His and Hers vanities, and an oversize closet. The second floor provides two additional bedrooms with a shared bath and a balcony overlook to the foyer below.

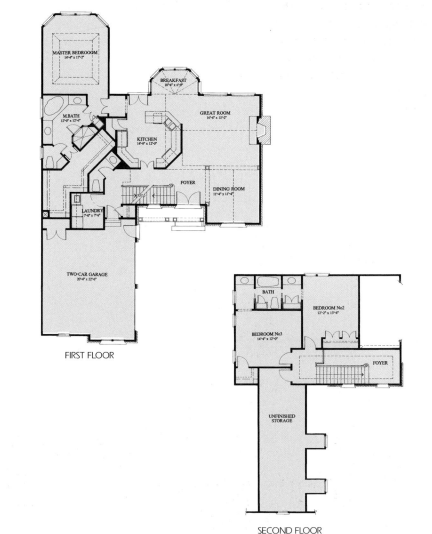

FIRST FLOOR

SECOND FLOOR

© The Sater Design Collection, Inc.

Perfect for a corner lot, this Mediterranean villa is a beautiful addition to any neighborhood. Low and unassuming on the outside, this plan brings modern amenities and classic stylings together for a great family home. The study and two-story dining room border the foyer; an elongated gallery introduces the great room. Here, a rustic beamed ceiling, fireplace, and art niche are thoughtful touches. The step-saving U-shaped kitchen flows into a sunny bayed breakfast nook. To the far right, two bedrooms share a full bath. The master suite is separated for privacy, situated to the far left. French-door access to the veranda and a sumptuous bath make this a pleasurable retreat.

plan# HPK1000161

STYLE: ITALIANATE
SQUARE FOOTAGE: 2,191
BEDROOMS: 3
BATHROOMS: 2½
WIDTH: 62' - 10"
DEPTH: 73' - 6"
FOUNDATION: SLAB

SEARCH ONLINE @ EPLANS.COM

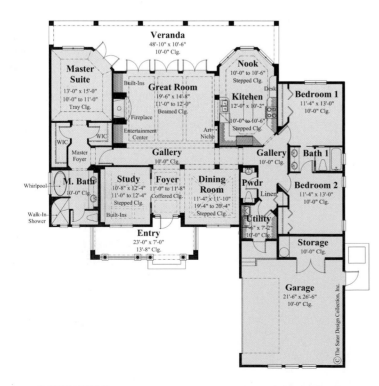

plan# HPK1000162

STYLE: TRADITIONAL
SQUARE FOOTAGE: 2,193
BONUS SPACE: 400 SQ. FT.
BEDROOMS: 4
BATHROOMS: 2
WIDTH: 64' - 6"
DEPTH: 59' - 0"
FOUNDATION: SLAB,
UNFINISHED WALKOUT
BASEMENT, CRAWLSPACE

SEARCH ONLINE @ EPLANS.COM

From the hipped and gabled roof to the gracious entryway, style is a common element in the makeup of this home. Inside, the foyer is flanked by a formal living room (or make it a guest bedroom) and a formal dining room, defined by columns. Directly ahead lies the spacious family room, offering a warming fireplace. The sleeping quarters are separated for privacy. The master suite has a lavish bath and tray ceiling.

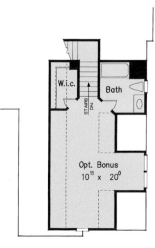

Graceful details combine with a covered entryway to welcome friends and family to come on in. The canted bay sitting area in the master suite provides sunny respite and quiet solitude. To be the center of attention, invite everyone to party in the vaulted great room, which spills over into the big, airy kitchen. Guests can make use of the optional study/bedroom. Upstairs, secondary bedrooms share a full bath and a balcony overlook. A spacious central hall leads to a bonus room that provides wardrobe space.

plan# HPK1000163

STYLE: COUNTRY COTTAGE
FIRST FLOOR: 1,688 SQ. FT.
SECOND FLOOR: 558 SQ. FT.
TOTAL: 2,246 SQ. FT.
BONUS SPACE: 269 SQ. FT.
BEDROOMS: 4
BATHROOMS: 3
WIDTH: 54' - 0"
DEPTH: 48' - 0"
FOUNDATION: CRAWLSPACE, SLAB, UNFINISHED WALKOUT BASEMENT

SEARCH ONLINE @ EPLANS.COM

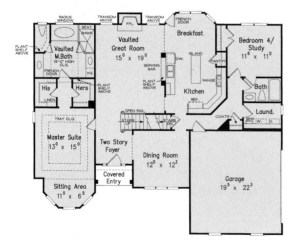

FIRST FLOOR

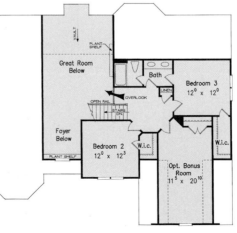

SECOND FLOOR

plan# HPK1000164

STYLE: EUROPEAN COTTAGE
SQUARE FOOTAGE: 2,260
BEDROOMS: 3
BATHROOMS: 2½
WIDTH: 65' - 0"
DEPTH: 57' - 10"
FOUNDATION: CRAWLSPACE,
SLAB

SEARCH ONLINE @ EPLANS.COM

This home is reminiscent of those found in the French countryside with its hipped roof, keystone arches, and rustic stone detailing. Inside, the floor plan offers all the modern conveniences. The family dining room is just steps from the kitchen which adjoins the sunny breakfast nook. The living room boasts a cathedral ceiling, fireplace, and built-in entertainment center. A study to the left of the entry offers a quiet place to retreat, as does the lavish master suite.

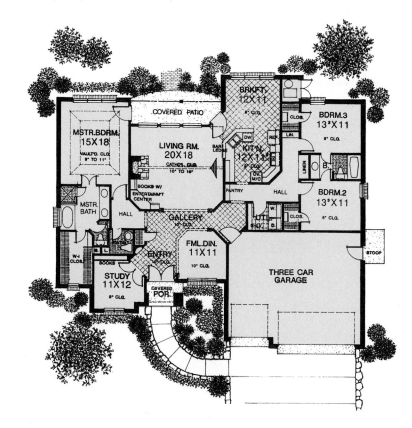

Shingles, stone, and gables are all elements of fine Craftsman styling, beautifully demonstrated on this three-bedroom home. The foyer is flanked by a formal dining room and a cozy den. A galley kitchen is open to the spacious gathering room and sunny, bayed nook. Upstairs, the secondary bedrooms share a hall bath. The master suite is full of amenities, including a sitting area with a private balcony, and a luxurious bath. A bonus room is located above the garage, perfect for a playroom, home office, or guest room.

plan# HPK1000165

STYLE: NW CONTEMPORARY
FIRST FLOOR: 1,170 SQ. FT.
SECOND FLOOR: 1,091 SQ. FT.
TOTAL: 2,261 SQ. FT.
BONUS SPACE: 240 SQ. FT.
BEDROOMS: 3
BATHROOMS: 2½
WIDTH: 66' - 0"
DEPTH: 46' - 0"
FOUNDATION: CRAWLSPACE

SEARCH ONLINE @ EPLANS.COM

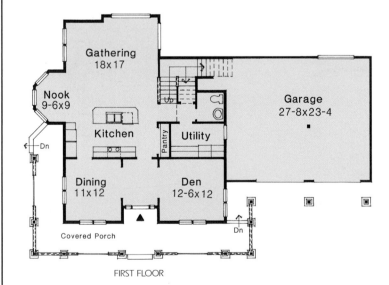

FIRST FLOOR

SECOND FLOOR

© William E. Poole Designs, Inc.

plan# HPK1000166

STYLE: COUNTRY COTTAGE
FIRST FLOOR: 1,981 SQ. FT.
SECOND FLOOR: 291 SQ. FT.
TOTAL: 2,272 SQ. FT.
BONUS SPACE: 412 SQ. FT.
BEDROOMS: 4
BATHROOMS: 3½
WIDTH: 58' - 0"
DEPTH: 53' - 0"
FOUNDATION: CRAWLSPACE

SEARCH ONLINE @ EPLANS.COM

With three dormers and a welcoming front door accented by sidelights and a sunburst, this country cottage is sure to please. The dining room, immediately to the right from the foyer, is defined by decorative columns. In the great room, a volume ceiling heightens the space and showcases a fireplace and built-in bookshelves. The kitchen has plenty of work space and flows into the bayed breakfast nook. A considerate split-bedroom design places the plush master suite to the far left and two family bedrooms to the far right. A fourth bedroom and future space upstairs allow room to grow.

SECOND FLOOR

FIRST FLOOR

Fine architectural details make this home a showplace with its large windows, intricate brickwork, fine woodwork, and trim. The stunning two-story entry is decorated with an attractive wood railing and balustrades in the foyer. Conveniently, the wraparound kitchen features a window view and a planning center with a pantry. Upstairs, the master suite includes a sumptuous private bath and a walk-in closet. Three family bedrooms, one with a box-bay window, share a bath on this floor.

plan# HPK1000167

STYLE: TRADITIONAL
FIRST FLOOR: 1,283 SQ. FT.
SECOND FLOOR: 1,003 SQ. FT.
TOTAL: 2,286 SQ. FT.
BEDROOMS: 4
BATHROOMS: 2½
WIDTH: 64' - 0"
DEPTH: 34' - 0"
FOUNDATION: UNFINISHED
BASEMENT

SEARCH ONLINE @ EPLANS.COM

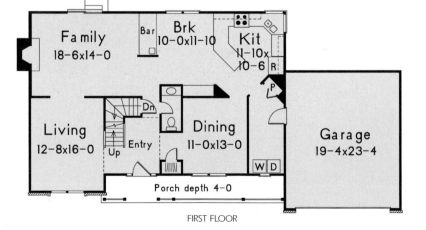

FIRST FLOOR

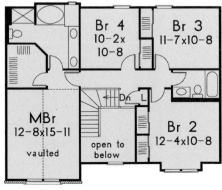

SECOND FLOOR

plan# HPK1000168

STYLE: INTERNATIONAL
SQUARE FOOTAGE: 2,293
BONUS SPACE: 509 SQ. FT.
BEDROOMS: 3
BATHROOMS: 2
WIDTH: 51' - 0"
DEPTH: 79' - 4"
FOUNDATION: SLAB

SEARCH ONLINE @ EPLANS.COM

Multiple rooflines, shutters, and a charming vaulted entry lend interest and depth to the exterior of this well-designed three-bedroom home. Inside, double doors to the left open to a cozy den. The dining room, open to the family room and foyer, features a stunning ceiling design. A fireplace and patio access and view adorn the family room. Two family bedrooms share a double-sink bathroom to the right, and the master bedroom resides to the left. Note the private patio access, two walk-in closets, and luxurious bath that ensure a restful retreat for the homeowner.

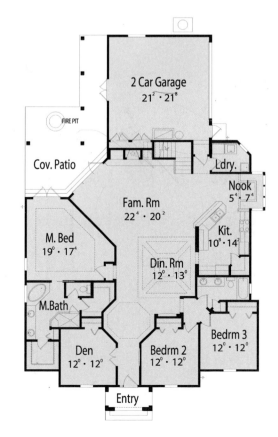

Special window detailing and a gazebo veranda highlight the exterior of this charming home. From the entry, French doors open to an elegant drawing room with a spider-beam ceiling. The dining room, with hutch space and bay window, suits entertaining needs. In the gathering room, three repeating arch windows, a fireplace, and two bookcases form a comfortable retreat. The island kitchen features two pantries, a planning desk, and wrapping counters. The curved staircase leads to upper-level sleeping quarters. The impressive master suite enjoys a tiered ceiling, a massive wardrobe and dressing area, and a private bath. Three family bedrooms—two with window seats—share a full bath.

plan# HPK1000169

STYLE: VICTORIAN
FIRST FLOOR: 1,249 SQ. FT.
SECOND FLOOR: 1,075 SQ. FT.
TOTAL: 2,324 SQ. FT.
BEDROOMS: 4
BATHROOMS: 2½
WIDTH: 56' - 0"
DEPTH: 46' - 0"

SEARCH ONLINE @ EPLANS.COM

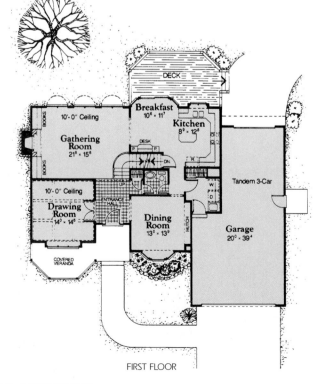

FIRST FLOOR

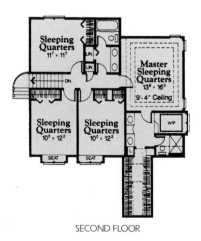

SECOND FLOOR

plan # HPK1000170

STYLE: BUNGALOW
FIRST FLOOR: 1,205 SQ. FT.
SECOND FLOOR: 1,123 SQ. FT.
TOTAL: 2,328 SQ. FT.
BEDROOMS: 4
BATHROOMS: 2½
WIDTH: 57' - 2"
DEPTH: 58' - 7"
FOUNDATION: UNFINISHED
BASEMENT, CRAWLSPACE

SEARCH ONLINE @ EPLANS.COM

With Craftsman details and modern amenities, this design offers an attractive lay-out. The long foyer opens to the dining and living rooms, which enjoy a flowing space. To the rear, a family room features a corner fireplace and access to the rear grounds. The breakfast nook sports French doors, which liven up the nearby island kitchen with natural light. Upstairs, the master bedroom is luxurious with a spa tub, shower, dual-basin vanity, compartmented toilet, and walk-in closet. Three family bedrooms share a full hall bath.

SECOND FLOOR

FIRST FLOOR

Decorative arches and quoins give this home wonderful curb appeal that matches its comfortable interior. The two-story foyer is bathed in natural light as it leads to the formal dining room and beyond to the counter-filled kitchen and the vaulted breakfast nook. A den, or possible fourth bedroom, is tucked away at the rear for privacy and includes a full bath. A spacious master suite with a luxurious private bath is located on the first floor. Two family bedrooms and a full bath reside on the second floor, as well as a balcony that looks down to the family room and the foyer. An optional bonus room is available for expanding at a later date.

plan# HPK1000173

STYLE: COUNTRY COTTAGE
FIRST FLOOR: 1,761 SQ. FT.
SECOND FLOOR: 580 SQ. FT.
TOTAL: 2,341 SQ. FT.
BONUS SPACE: 276 SQ. FT.
BEDROOMS: 4
BATHROOMS: 3
WIDTH: 56' - 0"
DEPTH: 47' - 6"
FOUNDATION: CRAWLSPACE,
UNFINISHED WALKOUT
BASEMENT, SLAB

SEARCH ONLINE @ EPLANS.COM

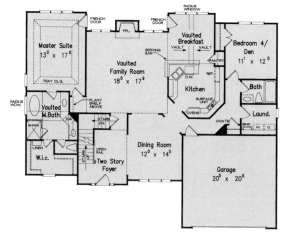

FIRST FLOOR

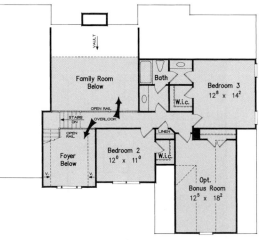

SECOND FLOOR

plan # HPK1000174

STYLE: COUNTRY COTTAGE
FIRST FLOOR: 1,279 SQ. FT.
SECOND FLOOR: 1,071 SQ. FT.
TOTAL: 2,350 SQ. FT.
BEDROOMS: 4
BATHROOMS: 3
WIDTH: 50' - 0"
DEPTH: 42' - 6"
FOUNDATION: CRAWLSPACE,
UNFINISHED WALKOUT
BASEMENT

SEARCH ONLINE @ EPLANS.COM

Rustic details complement brick and siding on the exterior of this home. The interior features vaulted living and family rooms and a convenient kitchen separating the dining and breakfast rooms. The living room provides a fireplace flanked by radius windows, and a French door in the breakfast room opens to the rear property. A bedroom to the back could be used as a study. Second-floor bedrooms include a master suite with a sitting area.

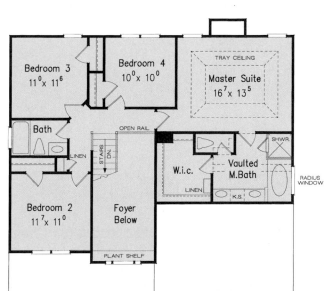

SECOND FLOOR

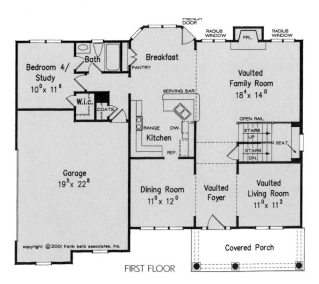

FIRST FLOOR

Santa Fe styling creates interesting angles in this one-story home. A grand entrance leads through a courtyard into the foyer with a circular skylight, closet space, niches, and a convenient powder room. Fireplaces in the living room, dining room, and on the covered porch create a warming heart of the home. Make note of the island range in the kitchen and the cozy breakfast room adjacent. The master suite has a privacy wall on the covered porch, a deluxe bath, and a study close at hand. Two more family bedrooms are placed quietly in the far wing of the house near a segmented family room. Indoor/outdoor relationships are wonderful, with every room having access to the outdoors. The three-car garage offers extra storage.

plan# HPK1000175

STYLE: SANTA FE
SQUARE FOOTAGE: 2,350
BEDROOMS: 3
BATHROOMS: 2½
WIDTH: 92' - 7"
DEPTH: 79' - 0"
FOUNDATION: SLAB

SEARCH ONLINE @ EPLANS.COM

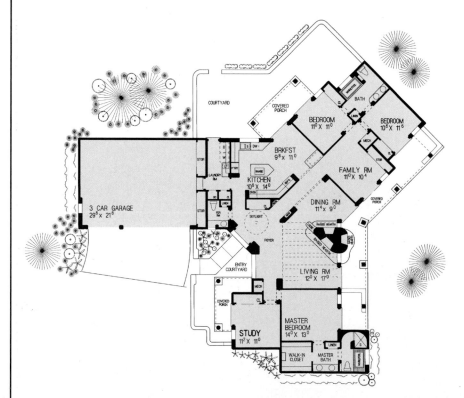

plan ⊞ HPK1000176

STYLE: PRAIRIE
FIRST FLOOR: 1,893 SQ. FT.
SECOND FLOOR: 501 SQ. FT.
TOTAL: 2,394 SQ. FT.
BEDROOMS: 3
BATHROOMS: 2½
WIDTH: 76' - 0"
DEPTH: 49' - 4"
FOUNDATION: CRAWLSPACE,
SLAB, UNFINISHED BASEMENT

SEARCH ONLINE @ EPLANS.COM

This unique, contemporary design is high-lighted by an unusual exterior that encloses an amenity-filled layout. A two-sided fire-place warms the formal living room and family room. The gourmet island kitchen connects to a nook warmed by a second fireplace. The master suite is enhanced by twin walk-in closets and a private bath. The rear outdoor patio encourages entertaining al fresco. A useful utility room is placed just outside of the two-car garage. Two additional bedrooms share a full bath upstairs.

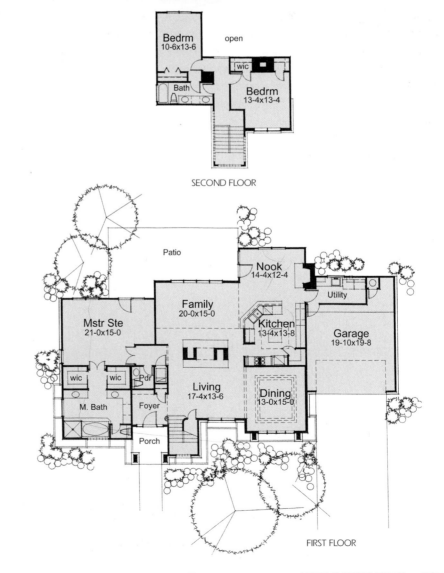

SECOND FLOOR

FIRST FLOOR

Asymmetrical gables, pediments, and tall, arch-top windows accent a European-style exterior; inside, an unrestrained floor plan expresses its independence. A spider-beam ceiling and a centered fireplace framed by shelves redraw the open space of the family room to cozy dimensions. The vaulted breakfast nook enjoys a radius window and a French door that leads outside. Split sleeping quarters lend privacy to the luxurious master suite.

plan# HPK1000177

STYLE: COUNTRY COTTAGE
SQUARE FOOTAGE: 2,403
BONUS SPACE: 285 SQ. FT.
BEDROOMS: 3
BATHROOMS: 2½
WIDTH: 60' - 0"
DEPTH: 67' - 0"
FOUNDATION: CRAWLSPACE, SLAB, UNFINISHED WALKOUT BASEMENT

SEARCH ONLINE @ EPLANS.COM

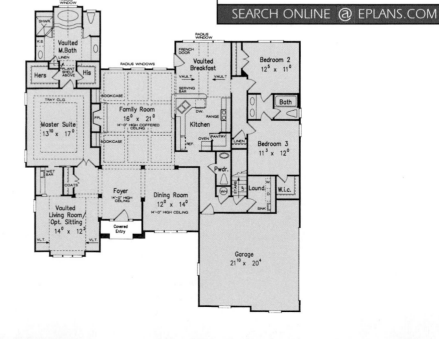

© William E. Poole Designs, Inc.

plan # HPK1000178

STYLE: COUNTRY COTTAGE
FIRST FLOOR: 1,627 SQ. FT.
SECOND FLOOR: 783 SQ. FT.
TOTAL: 2,410 SQ. FT.
BONUS SPACE: 418 SQ. FT.
BEDROOMS: 4
BATHROOMS: 2½
WIDTH: 46' - 0"
DEPTH: 58' - 6"
FOUNDATION: CRAWLSPACE

SEARCH ONLINE @ EPLANS.COM

This "little jewel" of a home emanates a warmth and joy not soon forgotten. The two-story foyer leads to the formal living room, defined by graceful columns. A formal dining room opens off from the living room, making entertaining a breeze. A family room at the back features a fireplace and works well with the kitchen and breakfast areas. A lavish master suite is secluded on the first floor; three family bedrooms reside upstairs.

SECOND FLOOR

FIRST FLOOR

This gorgeous design would easily accommodate a sloping lot. With windows and glass panels to take in the view, this design would make an exquisite seaside resort. A grand great room sets the tone inside, with an elegant tray ceiling and French doors to a private front balcony. The formal dining room is off the center of the plan for quiet elegance and is served by a nearby gourmet kitchen. Three steps up from the foyer, the sleeping level includes a spacious master suite with a sizable private bath. The two additional bedrooms access a shared bath with two vanities.

plan# HPK1000179

STYLE: NW CONTEMPORARY
SQUARE FOOTAGE: 2,412
BEDROOMS: 3
BATHROOMS: 2½
WIDTH: 60' - 0"
DEPTH: 59' - 0"
FOUNDATION: SLAB

SEARCH ONLINE @ EPLANS.COM

FIRST FLOOR

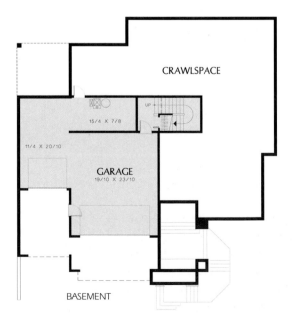

BASEMENT

plan# HPK1000180

STYLE: TRADITIONAL
FIRST FLOOR: 2,348 SQ. FT.
SECOND FLOOR: 80 SQ. FT.
TOTAL: 2,428 SQ. FT.
BONUS SPACE: 860 SQ. FT.
BEDROOMS: 3
BATHROOMS: 2½
WIDTH: 70' - 10"
DEPTH: 65' - 4"
FOUNDATION: CRAWLSPACE,
SLAB, UNFINISHED BASEMENT

SEARCH ONLINE @ EPLANS.COM

Traditional charm complements a contemporary interior. The foyer allows direct access to the central great room and the formal dining room. The great room enjoys a large warming fireplace; high ceilings increase the spacious feeling. A casual breakfast area is adjacent to the amenity-filled kitchen. The opposite side of the plan is dedicated to sleeping chambers. The opulent master suite includes an enormous private bath with His and Hers walk-in closets, dual vanities, and a separate shower. Two family bedrooms that share a full bath occupy the remainder of the sleeping wing.

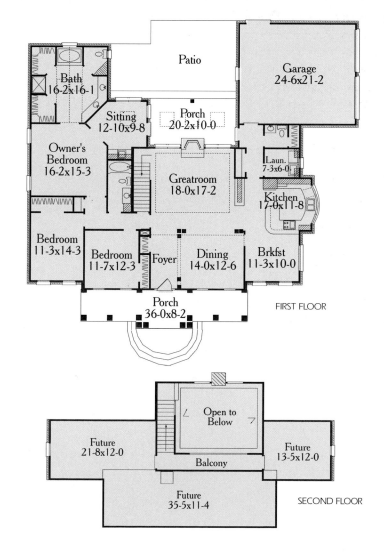

FIRST FLOOR

SECOND FLOOR

This striking design is reminiscent of the grand homes of the past century. Its wood siding and covered porch are complemented by shuttered windows and a glass-paneled entry. Historic design is updated in the floor plan to include a vaulted living room, a two-story family room, and a den that doubles as a guest suite on the first floor. Second-floor bedrooms feature a master suite with tray ceiling and vaulted bath. An optional loft on the second floor may be finished as a study area.

plan# HPK1000181

STYLE: VICTORIAN
FIRST FLOOR: 1,415 SQ. FT.
SECOND FLOOR: 1,015 SQ. FT.
TOTAL: 2,430 SQ. FT.
BONUS SPACE: 169 SQ. FT.
BEDROOMS: 4
BATHROOMS: 3½
WIDTH: 54' - 0"
DEPTH: 43' - 4"
FOUNDATION: UNFINISHED WALKOUT BASEMENT, CRAWLSPACE

SEARCH ONLINE @ EPLANS.COM

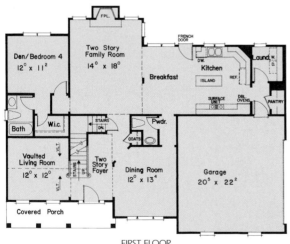

FIRST FLOOR

SECOND FLOOR

plan # HPK1000182

STYLE: COUNTRY COTTAGE
FIRST FLOOR: 1,704 SQ. FT.
SECOND FLOOR: 734 SQ. FT.
TOTAL: 2,438 SQ. FT.
BONUS SPACE: 479 SQ. FT.
BEDROOMS: 3
BATHROOMS: 3½
WIDTH: 50' - 0"
DEPTH: 82' - 6"
FOUNDATION: CRAWLSPACE

SEARCH ONLINE @ EPLANS.COM

Elegant country—that's one way to describe this attractive three-bedroom home. Inside, comfort is evidently the theme, with the formal dining room flowing into the U-shaped kitchen and casual dining taking place in the sunny breakfast area. The spacious, vaulted great room offers a fireplace and built-ins. The first-floor master suite is complete with a walk-in closet, a whirlpool tub, and a separate shower. Upstairs, the sleeping quartersinclude two family bedrooms with private baths and walk-in closets.

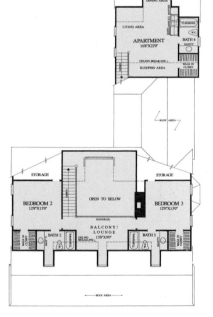

SECOND FLOOR

FIRST FLOOR

Brick detailing, shingles, and siding come together to create a refined exterior on this country farmhouse. The foyer is flanked by a dining room and a living room. At the rear of the house is the two-story family room, which is graced with a central fireplace and rear-door access to a sun deck. The kitchen blends into the breakfast area and is provided with backyard views. Storage space, a powder room, and a computer station complete the first floor of this plan. The sleeping quarters upstairs include a lavish master suite—with a full bath and sitting area—three vaulted family bedrooms, another full bath and a laundry area.

plan# HPK1000183

STYLE: FARMHOUSE
FIRST FLOOR: 1,160 SQ. FT.
SECOND FLOOR: 1,316 SQ. FT.
TOTAL: 2,476 SQ. FT.
BEDROOMS: 4
BATHROOMS: 2½
WIDTH: 52' - 0"
DEPTH: 44' - 0"
FOUNDATION: UNFINISHED
WALKOUT BASEMENT

SEARCH ONLINE @ EPLANS.COM

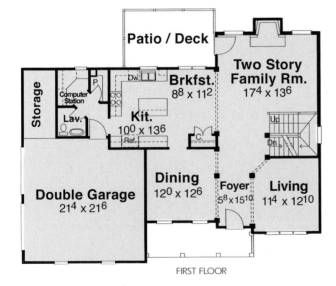

FIRST FLOOR

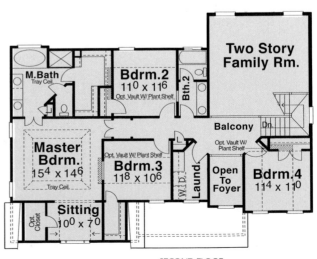

SECOND FLOOR

plan# HPK1000184

STYLE: BUNGALOW
SQUARE FOOTAGE: 2,489
BEDROOMS: 3
BATHROOMS: 2½
WIDTH: 68' - 3"
DEPTH: 62' - 0"
FOUNDATION: FINISHED
WALKOUT BASEMENT

SEARCH ONLINE @ EPLANS.COM

This fine bungalow, with its multiple gables, rafter tails, and pillared front porch, will be the envy of any neighborhood. A beam-ceilinged great room is further enhanced by a through-fireplace and French doors to the rear terrace. The U-shaped kitchen features a cooktop island with a snack bar and offers a beam-ceilinged breakfast/keeping room that shares the through-fireplace with the great room. Two secondary bedrooms share a full bath; the master suite is designed to pamper. Here, the homeowner will be pleased with a walk-in closet, a separate shower, and access to the terrace. The two-car garage has a side entrance and will easily shelter the family fleet.

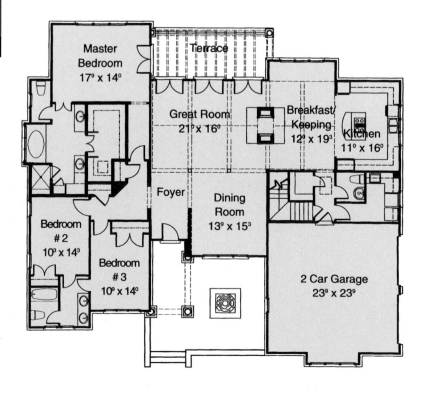

The hipped roof, gable accents, and side-entry garage make this a striking home. The vaulted family room features a central fireplace for maximum comfort. The kitchen is open to the breakfast area and the vaulted keeping room. The master suite features a tray ceiling and a vaulted bath with an oval tub under a radius window. Two family bedrooms and an optional bonus room are located on the second level.

plan# HPK1000185

STYLE: TRADITIONAL
FIRST FLOOR: 1,946 SQ. FT.
SECOND FLOOR: 562 SQ. FT.
TOTAL: 2,508 SQ. FT.
BONUS SPACE: 366 SQ. FT.
BEDROOMS: 4
BATHROOMS: 3½
WIDTH: 54' - 0"
DEPTH: 63' - 4"
FOUNDATION: CRAWLSPACE, UNFINISHED WALKOUT BASEMENT

SEARCH ONLINE @ EPLANS.COM

FIRST FLOOR

SECOND FLOOR

ptan# HPK1000186

STYLE: EUROPEAN COTTAGE
FIRST FLOOR: 1,152 SQ. FT.
SECOND FLOOR: 1,434 SQ. FT.
TOTAL: 2,586 SQ. FT.
BEDROOMS: 4
BATHROOMS: 3
WIDTH: 44' - 0"
DEPTH: 44' - 0"
FOUNDATION: UNFINISHED
BASEMENT

SEARCH ONLINE @ EPLANS.COM

Tall, robust columns flank the impressive two-story entry of this European-style home. Views can be had in the living room—in the turret—and with the open dining area just steps away, entertaining will be a splendid affair. The kitchen features a breakfast bar and adjoining sun room. Upstairs, the master suite is enhanced by a large sitting area, bumped-out bay window, and a relaxing bath. Three family bedrooms and a full bath complete this level.

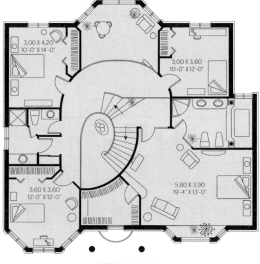

SECOND FLOOR

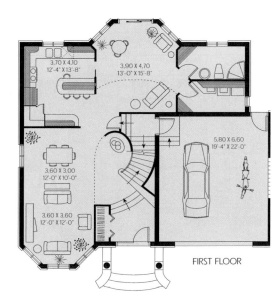

FIRST FLOOR

For sheer comfort and satisfaction of a wide spectrum of needs, this stately two-story home can't be beat. An outstanding grand room and elegant formal dining room will host many enjoyable get-togethers. To the left of the two-story foyer, the library is perfect for cordial conversations with friends or quiet reading time. The rear keeping room, just off the well-equipped kitchen, will draw family members together for informal meals, games, and discussions. A gorgeous master suite is also found on this level, and upstairs, three more bedrooms allow ample sleeping space for family members or guests. A good-size media room and lots of storage space are also on the second floor.

plan# HPK1000189

STYLE: NORMAN
FIRST FLOOR: 1,932 SQ. FT.
SECOND FLOOR: 1,052 SQ. FT.
TOTAL: 2,984 SQ. FT.
BEDROOMS: 4
BATHROOMS: 3½
WIDTH: 50' - 0"
DEPTH: 51' - 0"
FOUNDATION: SLAB, FINISHED WALKOUT BASEMENT

SEARCH ONLINE @ EPLANS.COM

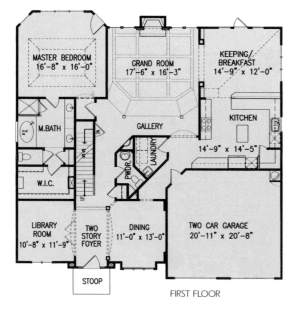

FIRST FLOOR

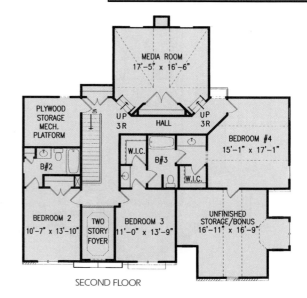

SECOND FLOOR

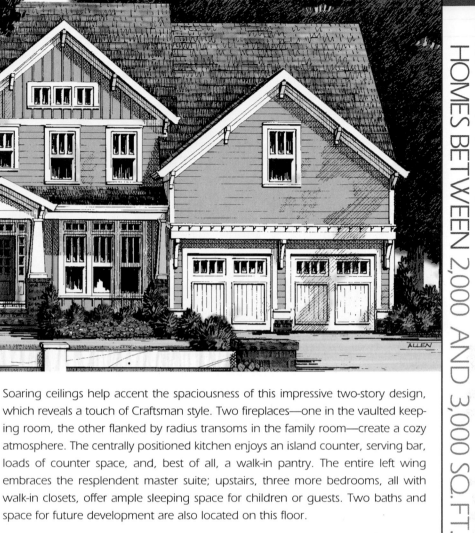

plan # HPK1000190

STYLE: CRAFTSMAN
FIRST FLOOR: 1,909 SQ. FT.
SECOND FLOOR: 835 SQ. FT.
TOTAL: 2,744 SQ. FT.
BONUS SPACE: 165 SQ. FT.
BEDROOMS: 4
BATHROOMS: 3½
WIDTH: 56' - 0"
DEPTH: 51' - 4"
FOUNDATION: CRAWLSPACE,
UNFINISHED WALKOUT
BASEMENT

SEARCH ONLINE @ EPLANS.COM

Soaring ceilings help accent the spaciousness of this impressive two-story design, which reveals a touch of Craftsman style. Two fireplaces—one in the vaulted keeping room, the other flanked by radius transoms in the family room—create a cozy atmosphere. The centrally positioned kitchen enjoys an island counter, serving bar, loads of counter space, and, best of all, a walk-in pantry. The entire left wing embraces the resplendent master suite; upstairs, three more bedrooms, all with walk-in closets, offer ample sleeping space for children or guests. Two baths and space for future development are also located on this floor.

SECOND FLOOR

FIRST FLOOR

Arch-top and multipane window treatments give the elevation of this four bedroom, two-story home an unmistakable elegance. Inside, the floor plan is equally appealing. Note the bay windows in the formal dining room and living area, visible from the entrance foyer. The large family room has a fireplace and opens to the food preparation area via an angled breakfast bar. A spacious, sunlit breakfast area adjoins the kitchen which features a nearby walk-in pantry and internal access to the garage. The second-floor master suite is highlighted by a tray ceiling, walk-in closet, and luxurious master bath including a large tub, shower, and dual vanities. A separate bedroom suite and two family bedrooms sharing a full bath complete the second-floor with a conveniently placed laundry.

plan# HPK1000191

STYLE: TRADITIONAL
FIRST FLOOR: 1,230 SQ. FT.
SECOND FLOOR: 1,496 SQ. FT.
TOTAL: 2,726 SQ. FT.
BEDROOMS: 4
BATHROOMS: 3½
WIDTH: 60' - 0"
DEPTH: 34' - 6"
FOUNDATION: CRAWLSPACE,
SLAB, UNFINISHED BASEMENT

SEARCH ONLINE @ EPLANS.COM

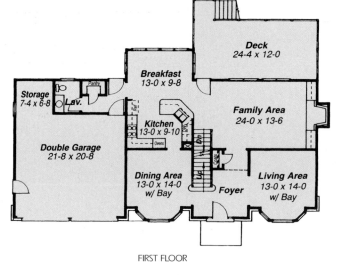

FIRST FLOOR

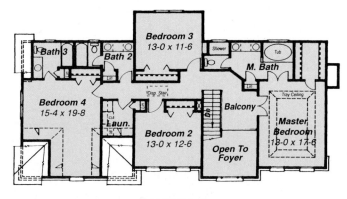

SECOND FLOOR

© William E. Poole Designs, Inc.

plan# HPK1000192

STYLE: SOUTHERN COLONIAL
FIRST FLOOR: 1,273 SQ. FT.
SECOND FLOOR: 1,358 SQ. FT.
TOTAL: 2,631 SQ. FT.
BEDROOMS: 4
BATHROOMS: 3½
WIDTH: 54' - 10"
DEPTH: 48' - 6"
FOUNDATION: CRAWLSPACE

SEARCH ONLINE @ EPLANS.COM

This two-story home suits the needs of each household member. Family gatherings won't be crowded in the spacious family room, which is adjacent to the kitchen and the breakfast area. Just beyond the foyer, the dining and living rooms view the front yard. The master suite features its own full bath with dual vanities, a whirlpool tub, and separate shower. Three family bedrooms—one with a walk-in closet—and two full hall baths are available upstairs. Extra storage space is found in the two-car garage.

SECOND FLOOR

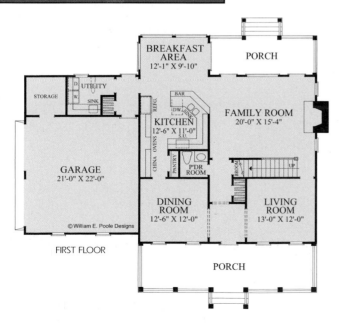

FIRST FLOOR

The use of stone and stucco has created a very pleasant exterior that would fit in well with a traditional environment. The double-door entry, which leads to the foyer, welcomes guests to a formal living and dining room area. Upon entering the master suite through double doors, the master bed wall becomes the focal point. A stepped ceiling treatment adds excitement, with floor-length windows framing the bed. The sitting area created by the bayed door wall further enhances the opulence of the suite. The master bath comes complete with His and Hers walk-in closets, dual vanities with a makeup area, and a soaking tub balanced by the large shower and private toilet chamber.

plan# HPK1000193

STYLE: FLORIDIAN
SQUARE FOOTAGE: 2,755
BONUS SPACE: 440 SQ. FT.
BEDROOMS: 4
BATHROOMS: 3
WIDTH: 73' - 0"
DEPTH: 82' - 8"
FOUNDATION: SLAB

SEARCH ONLINE @ EPLANS.COM

plan# HPK1000194

STYLE: TRADITIONAL
SQUARE FOOTAGE: 2,046
BEDROOMS: 3
BATHROOMS: 2½
WIDTH: 68' - 2"
DEPTH: 57' - 4"
FOUNDATION: CRAWLSPACE,
SLAB, UNFINISHED BASEMENT

SEARCH ONLINE @ EPLANS.COM

A six-panel door with an arched transom makes an impressive entry. Upon entering the foyer, the formal dining room resides to the right. The great room comes complete with a cozy fireplace and built-ins. On the far left of the home, two bedrooms share a full bath and a linen closet. The kitchen and breakfast room provide ample space for the family to enjoy meals together. The rear porch is also accessible from a rear bedroom and from an angled door between the great room and breakfast room. In the master bedroom, two walk-in closets provide plenty of space, and two separate vanities make dressing less crowded.

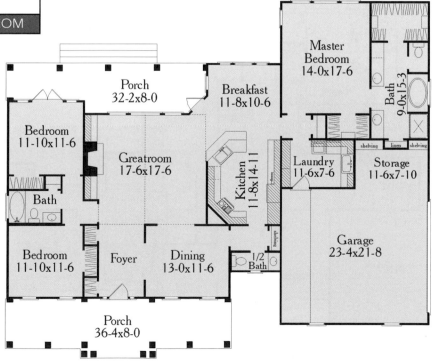

Step into the two-story foyer, where a living room will greet you on the right and a boxed dining room on the left. Further into the plan is a two-story family room with a corner fireplace. The kitchen looks over a bar into the bayed breakfast area, which has rear-door access to the sun deck. The first-floor master bedroom is situated at the rear of the plan for maximum privacy and includes many lavish amenities. The second level presents many unique additions for the whole family. A future media space is perfect for a home theater or perhaps an additional bedroom. Three family bedrooms and two full baths complete the sleeping quarters. A storage space, a loft, and overlooks to the two-story family room and foyer are included in this versatile design.

plan # HPK1000197

STYLE: FARMHOUSE
FIRST FLOOR: 1,771 SQ. FT.
SECOND FLOOR: 1,235 SQ. FT.
TOTAL: 3,006 SQ. FT.
BEDROOMS: 4
BATHROOMS: 3½
WIDTH: 61' - 4"
DEPTH: 54' - 0"
FOUNDATION: CRAWLSPACE, SLAB, UNFINISHED WALKOUT BASEMENT

SEARCH ONLINE @ EPLANS.COM

FIRST FLOOR

SECOND FLOOR

plan# HPK1000198

STYLE: GEORGIAN
FIRST FLOOR: 2,081 SQ. FT.
SECOND FLOOR: 940 SQ. FT.
TOTAL: 3,021 SQ. FT.
BEDROOMS: 4
BATHROOMS: 3½
WIDTH: 69' - 9"
DEPTH: 65' - 0"
FOUNDATION: FINISHED
WALKOUT BASEMENT

SEARCH ONLINE @ EPLANS.COM

This Georgian country-style home displays an impressive appearance. The front porch and columns frame the elegant elliptical entrance. Georgian symmetry balances the living room and dining room off the foyer. The first floor continues into the two-story great room, which offers built-in cabinetry, a fireplace, and a large bay window that overlooks the rear deck. A dramatic tray ceiling, a wall of glass, and access to the rear deck complete the master bedroom. To the left of the great room, a large kitchen opens to a breakfast area with walls of windows. Upstairs, each of three family bedrooms features ample closet space as well as direct access to a bathroom.

SECOND FLOOR

FIRST FLOOR

The wood-and-brick siding, muntin windows with shutters and keystones, and a covered front porch with columns on this traditional home will catch anyone's attention. The two-story foyer leads to a formal dining room with decorative columns and a vaulted living room to the opposite side. The grand room enjoys a vaulted ceiling, a fireplace, and radius windows. The gourmet kitchen features a serving bar and a large pantry. The master bedroom takes over the right wing of the home with its tray ceiling, a sitting room with a bay window, built-in art niche, and French doors leading to the private bath. This private bath includes a vaulted ceiling, an oversized garden tub, and a huge His and Hers walk-in closet. The second floor holds three additional family bedrooms along with an optional bonus room—note all bedrooms include a walk-in closet.

plan# HPK1000199

STYLE: FRENCH
FIRST FLOOR: 2,146 SQ. FT.
SECOND FLOOR: 878 SQ. FT.
TOTAL: 3,024 SQ. FT.
BONUS SPACE: 341 SQ. FT.
BEDROOMS: 4
BATHROOMS: 3½
WIDTH: 61' - 0"
DEPTH: 60' - 4"
FOUNDATION: CRAWLSPACE, UNFINISHED WALKOUT BASEMENT

SEARCH ONLINE @ EPLANS.COM

FIRST FLOOR

SECOND FLOOR

plan ⊕ HPK1000200

STYLE: EUROPEAN COTTAGE
FIRST FLOOR: 1,982 SQ. FT.
SECOND FLOOR: 1,071 SQ. FT.
TOTAL: 3,053 SQ. FT.
BEDROOMS: 3
BATHROOMS: 3½
WIDTH: 48' - 4"
DEPTH: 69' - 6"
FOUNDATION: CRAWLSPACE

SEARCH ONLINE @ EPLANS.COM

A unique collection of windows really draws attention to this European-style home. The private and luxurious master suite is hidden behind the circular staircase of the foyer. A turret in the master bedroom and a bow window in the private bath will fill this suite with an abundance of natural light. A fireplace in the two-story gathering room and another in the keeping room add warmth and charm. Two bedrooms, two baths, and a study complete the second level, which has a balcony overlooking the two-story dining room.

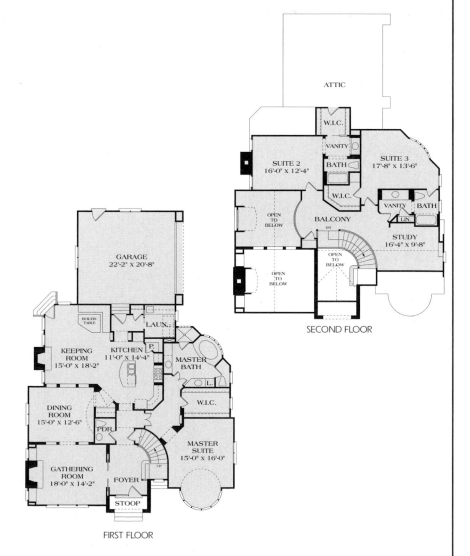

SECOND FLOOR

FIRST FLOOR

The individual charm and natural beauty of this sensational home reside in its pure symmetry and perfect blend of past and future. A steeply pitched roof caps a collection of Prairie-style windows and elegant columns. The portico leads to a midlevel foyer, which rises to the grand salon. A wide-open leisure room hosts a corner fireplace that's ultra cozy. The master wing sprawls from the front portico to the rear covered porch, rich with luxury amenities and plenty of secluded space.

plan# HPK1000201

STYLE: TIDEWATER
SQUARE FOOTAGE: 3,074
BEDROOMS: 3
BATHROOMS: 3½
WIDTH: 77' - 0"
DEPTH: 66' - 8"
FOUNDATION: ISLAND BASEMENT

SEARCH ONLINE @ EPLANS.COM

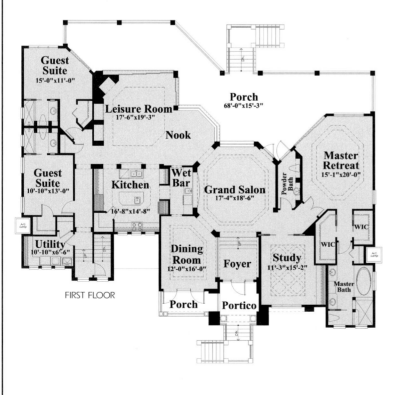

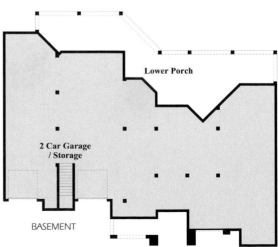

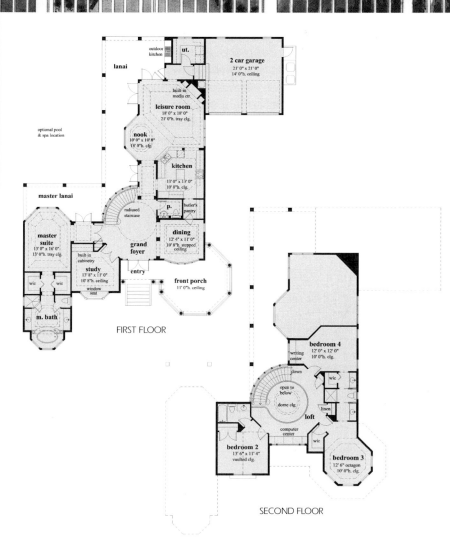

plan# HPK1000202

STYLE: TIDEWATER
FIRST FLOOR: 2,083 SQ. FT.
SECOND FLOOR: 1,013 SQ. FT.
TOTAL: 3,096 SQ. FT.
BEDROOMS: 4
BATHROOMS: 3½
WIDTH: 74' - 0"
DEPTH: 88' - 0"
FOUNDATION: SLAB

SEARCH ONLINE @ EPLANS.COM

This beautiful design is accented by the circular front porch and the abundance of windows. The entry leads into a grand foyer, where a radius staircase presents itself. Most of the rooms in this house are graced with tray, stepped, or vaulted ceilings, adding a sense of spaciousness to the plan. The first-floor master suite boasts many amenities including a private lanai, His and Hers walk-in closets, a bayed tub area, and a separate shower. Other unique features on the first-floor include a study, with a window seat and built-in cabinetry, a breakfast nook, butler's pantry, utility room, and outdoor kitchen, among others. The upstairs houses three family bedrooms and two full baths. Bedroom 3 boasts an octagonal ceiling, and the ceiling of Bedroom 2 is vaulted. A computer center, linen area, and loft complete the second floor.

FIRST FLOOR

SECOND FLOOR

This Southwestern contemporary home offers a distinctive look for any neighborhood—both inside and out. The formal living areas are concentrated in the center of the plan, perfect for entertaining. To the right, the kitchen and family room function well together as a working and living area. The first-floor sleeping wing includes a guest suite and a master suite. Upstairs, two family bedrooms are reached by a balcony overlooking the living room. Each bedroom has a walk-in closet and a dressing area with a vanity; they share a compartmented bath that includes a linen closet.

plan# HPK1000205

STYLE: SW CONTEMPORARY
FIRST FLOOR: 2,422 SQ. FT.
SECOND FLOOR: 714 SQ. FT.
TOTAL: 3,136 SQ. FT.
BEDROOMS: 4
BATHROOMS: 4
WIDTH: 77' - 6"
DEPTH: 62' - 0"
FOUNDATION: SLAB

SEARCH ONLINE @ EPLANS.COM

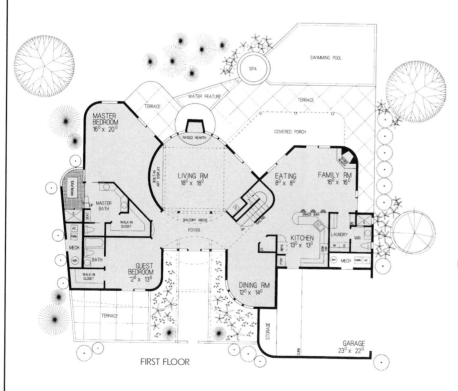

FIRST FLOOR

SECOND FLOOR

plan # HPK1000206

STYLE: VICTORIAN
FIRST FLOOR: 2,041 SQ. FT.
SECOND FLOOR: 1,098 SQ. FT.
TOTAL: 3,139 SQ. FT.
BONUS SPACE: 385 SQ. FT.
BEDROOMS: 4
BATHROOMS: 3½
WIDTH: 76' - 6"
DEPTH: 62' - 2"
FOUNDATION: SLAB

SEARCH ONLINE @ EPLANS.COM

The turret and the circular covered porch of this Victorian home make a great impression. The foyer carries you past a library and dining room to the hearth-warmed family room. A spacious kitchen with an island acts as a passageway to the nook and dining area. The master bedroom is located on the first floor and offers its own French doors to the rear covered porch. The master bath is designed to cater to both His and Her needs with two walk-in closets, separate vanities, a garden tub, and separate shower. The second-floor balcony looks to the family room below.

SECOND FLOOR

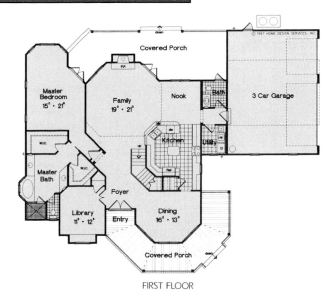

FIRST FLOOR

Designed for active lifestyles, this home caters to homeowners who enjoy dinner guests, privacy, luxurious surroundings, and open spaces. The foyer, parlor, and dining hall are defined by four sets of columns and share a gallery hall that runs through the center of the plan. The grand room opens to the deck/terrace, which is also accessed from the sitting area and morning room. The right wing of the plan contains the well-appointed kitchen. The left wing is dominated by the master suite with its sitting bay, fireplace, two walk-in closets, and compartmented bath.

plan # HPK1000209

STYLE: TRADITIONAL
FIRST FLOOR: 2,198 SQ. FT.
SECOND FLOOR: 1,028 SQ. FT.
TOTAL: 3,226 SQ. FT.
BONUS SPACE: 466 SQ. FT.
BEDROOMS: 4
BATHROOMS: 3½
WIDTH: 72' - 8"
DEPTH: 56' - 6"
FOUNDATION: CRAWLSPACE

SEARCH ONLINE @ EPLANS.COM

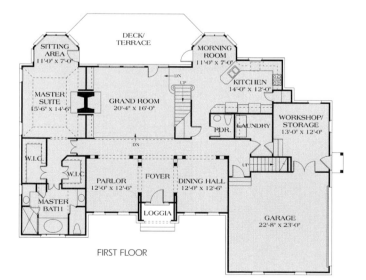

FIRST FLOOR

SECOND FLOOR

plan # HPK1000210

STYLE: FARMHOUSE
FIRST FLOOR: 2,642 SQ. FT.
SECOND FLOOR: 603 SQ. FT.
TOTAL: 3,245 SQ. FT.
BONUS SPACE: 255 SQ. FT.
BEDROOMS: 4
BATHROOMS: 3½
WIDTH: 80' - 0"
DEPTH: 61' - 0"
FOUNDATION: CRAWLSPACE

SEARCH ONLINE @ EPLANS.COM

In this four-bedroom design, the casual areas are free-flowing, open, and soaring, and the formal areas are secluded and well defined. The two-story foyer with a clerestory window leads to a quiet parlor with a vaulted ceiling and a Palladian window. The formal dining room opens from the foyer through decorative columns and is served by a spacious gourmet kitchen. The family room, defined by columns, has an angled corner hearth and is open to the kitchen and breakfast nook. The master suite is full of interesting angles, from the triangular bedroom and multi-angled walk-in closet to the corner tub in the sumptuous master bath. A nearby den has its own bathroom and could serve as a guest room. Upstairs, two additional bedrooms share a full bath and a balcony hall.

SECOND FLOOR

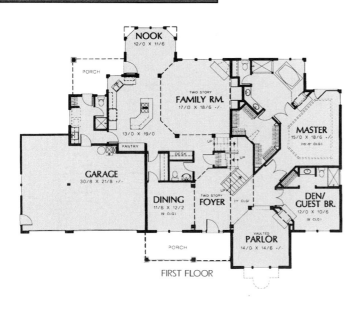

FIRST FLOOR

Wonderful rooflines top a brick exterior with cedar and stone accents and lots of English Country charm. The two-story entry reveals a graceful curving staircase and opens to the formal living and dining rooms. Fireplaces are found in the living room as well as the great room, which also boasts built-in bookcases and access to the rear patio. The kitchen and breakfast room add to the informal area and include a snack bar. A private patio is part of the master suite, which also offers a lavish bath, a large walk-in closet, and a nearby study. Three family bedrooms and a bonus room complete the second floor.

plan# HPK1000213

STYLE: COUNTRY COTTAGE
FIRST FLOOR: 2,438 SQ. FT.
SECOND FLOOR: 882 SQ. FT.
TOTAL: 3,320 SQ. FT.
BONUS SPACE: 230 SQ. FT.
BEDROOMS: 4
BATHROOMS: 4½
WIDTH: 70' - 0"
DEPTH: 63' - 2"
FOUNDATION: SLAB,
UNFINISHED BASEMENT

SEARCH ONLINE @ EPLANS.COM

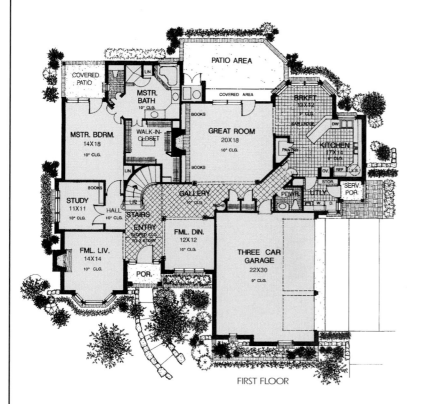

FIRST FLOOR

SECOND FLOOR

plan # HPK1000214

STYLE: MISSION
SQUARE FOOTAGE: 3,343
BEDROOMS: 3
BATHROOMS: 2½ + ½
WIDTH: 84' - 0"
DEPTH: 92' - 0"
FOUNDATION: SLAB

SEARCH ONLINE @ EPLANS.COM

This distinctive stucco home is reminiscent of early Mission-style architecture. Decorative vigas line the entry as double doors lead into an elongated columned foyer. A living/dining room combination ahead enjoys abundant light from three French doors, and the warmth of a Southwestern fireplace. An abbreviated hall leads either to the bedroom gallery or to the gourmet kitchen. A sunny nook and leisure room just beyond are bathed in natural light. A veranda grill is perfect in any season. Separated from the rest of the home for complete privacy, the master suite relishes a bay window, veranda access, and a lavish bath.

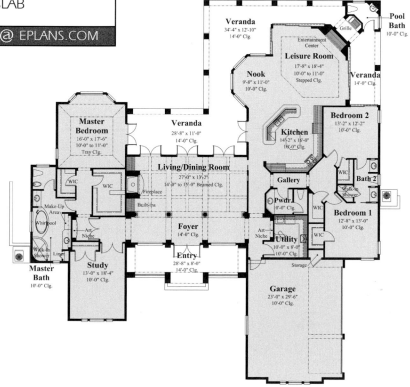

Rich with Old World elements, this English Country manor steps sweetly into the future with great rooms and splendid outdoor spaces. Varied window treatments define this elegant facade, enhanced by a massive stone turret. A leaded-glass paneled door with sidelights leads to a gallery-style foyer. Grand interior vistas are provided by a soaring triple window capped with an arch-top transom. The living area leads to the breakfast bay and gourmet kitchen. This culinary paradise features a food-preparation island and a peninsula snack counter. Double doors open to a quiet library with a turret-style bay window. The master retreat boasts views of the secluded side property.

plan # HPK1000215

STYLE: FRENCH
FIRST FLOOR: 2,479 SQ. FT.
SECOND FLOOR: 956 SQ. FT.
TOTAL: 3,435 SQ. FT.
BEDROOMS: 4
BATHROOMS: 3½
WIDTH: 67' - 6"
DEPTH: 75' - 6"
FOUNDATION: UNFINISHED
WALKOUT BASEMENT

SEARCH ONLINE @ EPLANS.COM

FIRST FLOOR

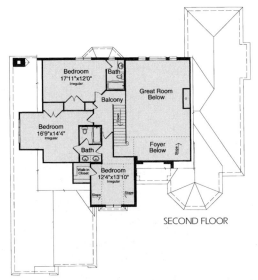

SECOND FLOOR

plan # HPK1000216

STYLE: FARMHOUSE
SQUARE FOOTAGE: 3,439
BONUS SPACE: 514 SQ. FT.
BEDROOMS: 4
BATHROOMS: 3½
WIDTH: 100' - 0"
DEPTH: 67' - 11"
FOUNDATION: CRAWLSPACE,
SLAB, UNFINISHED BASEMENT

SEARCH ONLINE @ EPLANS.COM

This gigantic country farmhouse is accented by exterior features that really stand out—a steep roof gable, shuttered muntin windows, stone siding, and the double-columned, covered front porch. Inside, the entry is flanked by the study/Bedroom 2 and the dining room. Across the tiled gallery, the great room provides an impressive fireplace and overlooks the rear veranda. The island kitchen opens to a bayed breakfast room. The right side of the home includes a utility room and a three-car garage, and two family bedrooms that share a bath. The master wing of the home enjoys a bayed sitting area, a sumptuous bath, and an enormous walk-in closet. The second-floor bonus room is cooled by a ceiling fan and is perfect for a guest suite.

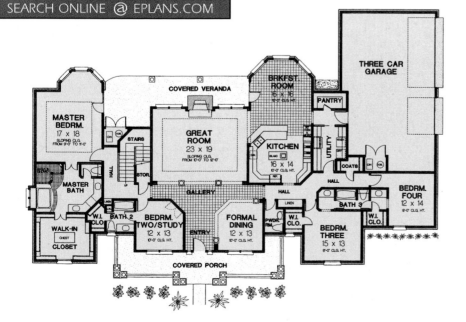

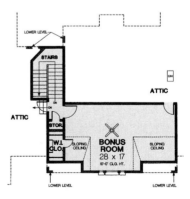

This traditional design fits well into a countryside setting and boasts an abundance of amenities. Inside, the great room and hearth room offer fireplaces. The kitchen features a snack bar and walk-in pantry. The master suite provides a sitting area, whirlpool bath, and walk-in closet. A den off the foyer easily flexes to a library or home office. Upstairs, each of three secondary bedrooms provides a walk-in closet.

plan# HPK1000217

STYLE: TRADITIONAL
FIRST FLOOR: 2,454 SQ. FT.
SECOND FLOOR: 986 SQ. FT.
TOTAL: 3,440 SQ. FT.
BEDROOMS: 4
BATHROOMS: 3½
WIDTH: 73' - 4"
DEPTH: 59' - 4"

SEARCH ONLINE @ EPLANS.COM

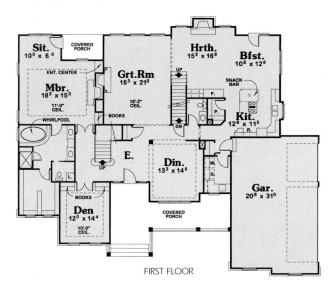

FIRST FLOOR

SECOND FLOOR

plan# HPK1000218

STYLE: COUNTRY COTTAGE
FIRST FLOOR: 2,660 SQ. FT.
SECOND FLOOR: 914 SQ. FT.
TOTAL: 3,574 SQ. FT.
BEDROOMS: 3
BATHROOMS: 4½
WIDTH: 114' - 8"
DEPTH: 75' - 10"
FOUNDATION: CRAWLSPACE

SEARCH ONLINE @ EPLANS.COM

Gently curved arches and dormers contrast with the straight lines of gables and wooden columns on this French-style stone exterior. Small-pane windows are enhanced by shutters; tall chimneys and a cupola add height. Inside, a spacious gathering room with an impressive fireplace opens to a cheery morning room. The kitchen is a delight, with a beam ceiling, triangular work island, walk-in pantry, and angular counter with a snack bar. The nearby laundry room includes a sink, a work area, and plenty of room for storage. The first-floor master suite boasts a bay-windowed sitting nook, a deluxe bath, and a handy study.

SECOND FLOOR

FIRST FLOOR

An eye-catching roofline and a gently arched entry draw attention to this home's exterior; the interior contains a wide variety of amenity-packed rooms. On the first floor, the central grand room overlooks both the rear screened porch and a side deck; a wet bar sits just outside the nearby dining room. The gourmet kitchen offers a walk-in pantry and adjoins a cozy "good morning" room, suitable for quiet family meals and open to a small dining deck. A library and gathering room round out the first-floor living space, and a luxurious master suite with a private lounge comprises the sleeping space. Three more family bedrooms—one with a private bath and deck—are found upstairs.

plan # HPK1000221

STYLE: TRADITIONAL
FIRST FLOOR: 2,345 SQ. FT.
SECOND FLOOR: 1,336 SQ. FT.
TOTAL: 3,681 SQ. FT.
BEDROOMS: 4
BATHROOMS: 3½
WIDTH: 65' - 0"
DEPTH: 66' - 0"
FOUNDATION: CRAWLSPACE

SEARCH ONLINE @ EPLANS.COM

FIRST FLOOR

SECOND FLOOR

© William E. Poole Designs, Inc.

plan # HPK1000222

STYLE: FARMHOUSE
FIRST FLOOR: 2,442 SQ. FT.
SECOND FLOOR: 1,286 SQ. FT.
TOTAL: 3,728 SQ. FT.
BONUS SPACE: 681 SQ. FT.
BEDROOMS: 4
BATHROOMS: 3½ + ½
WIDTH: 84' - 8"
DEPTH: 60' - 0"
FOUNDATION: CRAWLSPACE

SEARCH ONLINE @ EPLANS.COM

With a gazebo-style covered porch and careful exterior details, you can't help but imagine tea parties, porch swings, and lazy summer evenings. Inside, a living room/library will comfort with its fireplace and built-ins. The family room is graced with a fireplace and a curved, two-story ceiling with an overlook above. The master bedroom is a private retreat with a lovely bath, twin walk-in closets, and rear-porch access. Upstairs, three bedrooms with sizable closets—one bedroom would make an excellent guest suite or alternate master suite—share access to expandable space.

SECOND FLOOR

FIRST FLOOR

© The Sater Design Collection, Inc.

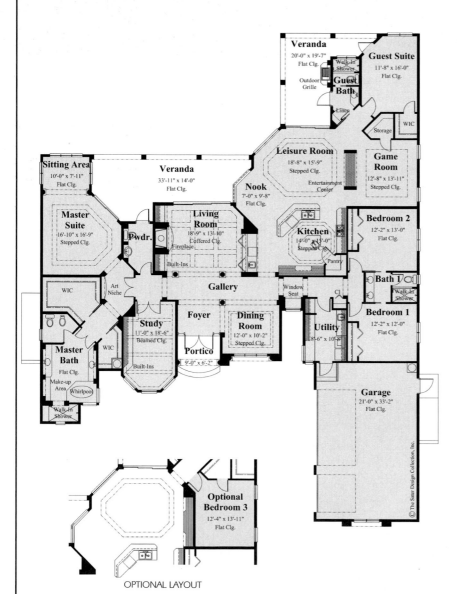

Veranda
20'-0" x 19'-7"
Flat Clg.

Guest Suite
11'-8" x 16'-0"
Flat Clg.

Walk-In Shower

Outdoor Grille

Guest Bath

Linen

Storage

WIC

Sitting Area
10'-0" x 7'-11"
Flat Clg.

Veranda
33'-11" x 14'-0"
Flat Clg.

Leisure Room
18'-8" x 15'-9"
Stepped Clg.

Game Room
12'-8" x 13'-11"
Stepped Clg.

Nook
7'-0" x 9'-8"
Flat Clg.

Entertainment Center

Master Suite
16'-10" x 16'-9"
Stepped Clg.

Pwdr.

Living Room
18'-9" x 13'-10"
Coffered Clg.

Fireplace

Kitchen
14'-0" x 13'-0"
Stepped Clg.

Pantry

Bedroom 2
12'-2" x 13'-0"
Flat Clg.

Built-Ins

Art Niche

WIC

Gallery

Window Seat

Bath 1

Walk-In Shower

Cl.

Bedroom 1
12'-2" x 12'-0"
Flat Clg.

Master Bath
Flat Clg.

WIC

Study
11'-0" x 18'-6"
Beamed Clg.

Foyer

Dining Room
12'-0" x 10'-2"
Stepped Clg.

Utility
8'-6" x 10'-8"

Make-up Area

Whirlpool

Built-Ins

Portico
9'-0" x 6'-2"

Walk-In Shower

Garage
21'-0" x 33'-2"
Flat Clg.

© The Sater Design Collection, Inc.

Optional Bedroom 3
12'-4" x 13'-11"
Flat Clg.

OPTIONAL LAYOUT

plan# HPK1000223

STYLE: ITALIANATE
SQUARE FOOTAGE: 3,743
BEDROOMS: 4
BATHROOMS: 3½
WIDTH: 80' - 0"
DEPTH: 103' - 8"
FOUNDATION: SLAB

SEARCH ONLINE @ EPLANS.COM

With California style and Mediterranean good looks, this striking stucco manor is sure to delight. The portico and foyer open to reveal a smart plan with convenience and flexibility in mind. The columned living room has a warming fireplace and access to the rear property. In the gourmet kitchen, an open design with an island and walk-in pantry will please any chef. From here, the elegant dining room and sunny nook are easily served. The leisure room is separated from the game room by a built-in entertainment center. The game area can also be finished off as a bedroom. To the rear, a guest room is perfect for frequent visitors or as an in-law suite. The master suite features a bright sitting area, oversized walk-in closets, and a pampering bath with a whirlpool tub. Extra features not to be missed: the outdoor grill, game-room storage, and gallery window seat.

plan # HPK1000224

STYLE: COUNTRY COTTAGE
FIRST FLOOR: 1,901 SQ. FT.
SECOND FLOOR: 1,874 SQ. FT.
TOTAL: 3,775 SQ. FT.
BEDROOMS: 4
BATHROOMS: 3½
WIDTH: 50' - 0"
DEPTH: 70' - 0"
FOUNDATION: PIER

SEARCH ONLINE @ EPLANS.COM

This elegant Charleston townhouse is enhanced by Southern grace and three levels of charming livability. Covered porches offer outdoor living space at every level. The first floor offers a living room warmed by a fireplace, an island kitchen serving a bayed nook, and a formal dining room. A first-floor guest bedroom is located at the front of the plan, along with a laundry and powder room. The second level offers a sumptuous master suite boasting a private balcony, a master bath, and enormous walk-in closet. Two other bedrooms sharing a Jack-and-Jill bath are also on this level. The basement level includes a three-car garage and game room warmed by a fireplace.

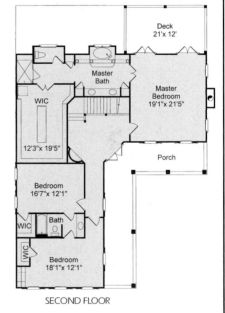

SECOND FLOOR

FIRST FLOOR

A covered, columned porch and symmetrically placed windows welcome you to this elegant brick home. The formal living room offers built-in bookshelves and one of two fireplaces, the other being found in the spacious family room. A gallery running between these rooms leads to the sumptuous master suite, which includes a sitting area, a private covered patio, and a bath with two walk-in closets, dual vanities, a large shower, and a garden tub. The step-saving kitchen features a work island and a snack bar. The breakfast and family rooms offer doors to the large covered veranda. Upstairs, you'll find three bedrooms and attic storage space. The three-car garage even has room for a golf cart.

plan# HPK1000225

STYLE: CHATEAU STYLE
FIRST FLOOR: 2,814 SQ. FT.
SECOND FLOOR: 979 SQ. FT.
TOTAL: 3,793 SQ. FT.
BEDROOMS: 4
BATHROOMS: 3½
WIDTH: 98' - 0"
DEPTH: 45' - 10"
FOUNDATION: SLAB, UNFINISHED BASEMENT

SEARCH ONLINE @ EPLANS.COM

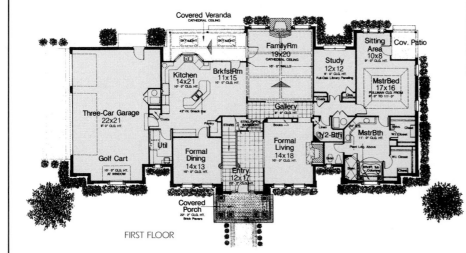

FIRST FLOOR

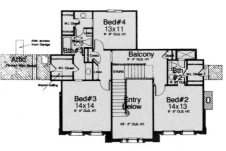

SECOND FLOOR

plan# HPK1000226

STYLE: SW CONTEMPORARY
SQUARE FOOTAGE: 3,838
BEDROOMS: 4
BATHROOMS: 3½
WIDTH: 127' - 6"
DEPTH: 60' - 10"
FOUNDATION: SLAB

SEARCH ONLINE @ EPLANS.COM

This diamond in the desert gives new meaning to old style. A courtyard leads to a covered porch with nooks for sitting and open-air dining. The gracious living room is highlighted by a corner fireplace; the formal dining room comes with an adjacent butler's pantry and access to the porch dining area. Two sleeping zones are luxurious with whirlpool tubs and separate showers. The master suite also boasts an exercise room and a nearby private office. A guest suite includes a private entrance and another corner fireplace.

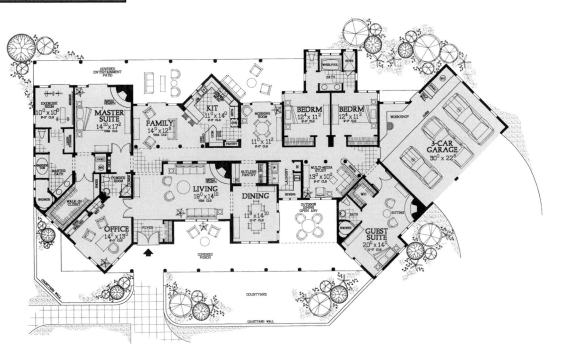

A grand brick facade, this home boasts muntin windows, multilevel rooflines, cut-brick jack arches, and a beautifully arched entry. A cathedral-ceilinged living room, complete with fireplace, and a family dining room flank the 20-foot-high entry. Relax in the family room, mix a drink from the wet bar, and look out through multiple windows to the covered veranda. A luxurious master suite includes a windowed sitting area looking over the rear view, private patio, full bath boasting a 10-foot ceiling, and a spacious walk-in closet. On the second level, the three high-ceilinged bedrooms share two full baths and a study area with a built-in desk.

ptan# HPK1000229

STYLE: TRADITIONAL
FIRST FLOOR: 2,751 SQ. FT.
SECOND FLOOR: 1,185 SQ. FT.
TOTAL: 3,936 SQ. FT.
BEDROOMS: 4
BATHROOMS: 3½
WIDTH: 79' - 0"
DEPTH: 66' - 4"
FOUNDATION: SLAB,
UNFINISHED BASEMENT

SEARCH ONLINE @ EPLANS.COM

FIRST FLOOR

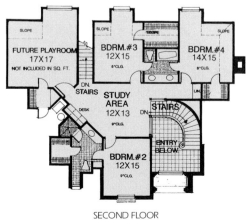

SECOND FLOOR

© The Sater Design Collection, Inc.

plan # HPK1000230

STYLE: ITALIANATE
SQUARE FOOTAGE: 3,942
BEDROOMS: 3
BATHROOMS: 4
WIDTH: 83' - 10"
DEPTH: 106' - 0"
FOUNDATION: SLAB

SEARCH ONLINE @ EPLANS.COM

Welcome home to a country manor with Renaissance flair. Full-length, squint-style windows and brick accents bring Old World charm to a modern plan. Designed for flexibility, the open foyer, living room, and dining room have infinite decor options. Down a gallery (with art niches), two bedroom suites enjoy private baths. The bon-vivant island kitchen is introduced with a wet bar and pool bath. In the leisure room, family and friends will revel in expansive views of the rear property. An outdoor kitchen on the lanai invites alfresco dining. Separated for ultimate privacy, the master suite is an exercise in luxurious living. Past the morning kitchen and into the grand bedroom, an octagonal sitting area is bathed in light. The bath is gracefully set in the turret, with a whirlpool tub and views of the master garden.

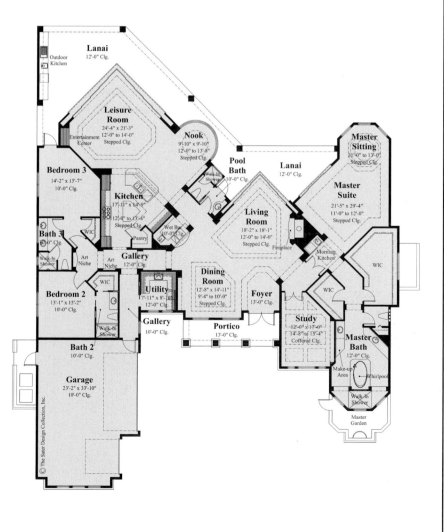

© The Sater Design Collection, Inc.

Mediterranean accents enhance the facade of this contemporary estate home. Two fanciful turret bays add a sense of grandeur to the exterior. Double doors open inside to a grand two-story foyer. A two-sided fireplace warms the study and living room, with a two-story coffered ceiling. To the right, the master suite includes a private bath, two walk-in closets, and double-door access to the sweeping rear veranda. Casual areas of the home include the gourmet island kitchen, breakfast nook, and leisure room warmed by a fireplace. A spiral staircase leads upstairs, where a second-floor balcony separates two family bedrooms from the luxurious guest suite.

plan # HPK1000231

STYLE: EUROPEAN COTTAGE
FIRST FLOOR: 2,834 SQ. FT.
SECOND FLOOR: 1,143 SQ. FT.
TOTAL: 3,977 SQ. FT.
BEDROOMS: 4
BATHROOMS: 3½
WIDTH: 85' - 0"
DEPTH: 76' - 8"
FOUNDATION: SLAB

SEARCH ONLINE @ EPLANS.COM

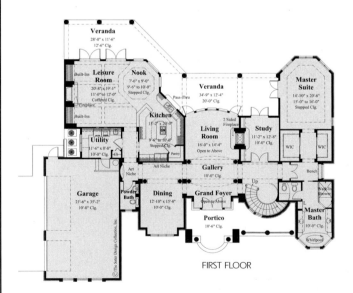

FIRST FLOOR

SECOND FLOOR

plan ⊛ HPK1000232

STYLE: CRAFTSMAN
MAIN LEVEL: 2,172 SQ. FT.
LOWER LEVEL: 1,813 SQ. FT.
TOTAL: 3,985 SQ. FT.
BEDROOMS: 4
BATHROOMS: 3½
WIDTH: 75' - 0"
DEPTH: 49' - 0"
FOUNDATION: FINISHED
WALKOUT BASEMENT

SEARCH ONLINE @ EPLANS.COM

With the Craftsman stylings of a mountain lodge, this rustic four-bedroom home is full of surprises. The foyer opens to the right to the great room, warmed by a stone hearth. A corner media center is convenient for entertaining. The dining room, with a furniture alcove, opens to the side terrace, inviting meals alfresco. An angled kitchen provides lots of room to move. The master suite is expansive, with French doors, a private bath, and spa tub. On the lower level, two bedrooms share a bath; a third enjoys a private suite. The games room includes a fireplace, media center, wet bar, and wine cellar. Don't miss the storage capacity and work area in the garage.

MAIN LEVEL

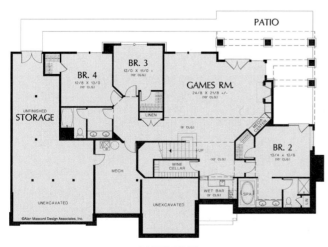

LOWER LEVEL

A distinctively French flair is the hallmark of this European design. Inside, the two-story foyer provides views to the huge great room beyond. A well-placed study off the foyer provides space for a home office. The kitchen, breakfast room, and sunroom are adjacent to lend a spacious feel. The great room is visible from this area through decorative arches. The master suite includes a roomy sitting area and a lovely bath with a centerpiece whirlpool tub flanked by half-columns. Upstairs, Bedrooms 2 and 3 share a bath that includes separate dressing areas.

plan # HPK1000233

STYLE: FRENCH
FIRST FLOOR: 2,608 SQ. FT.
SECOND FLOOR: 1,432 SQ. FT.
TOTAL: 4,040 SQ. FT.
BEDROOMS: 4
BATHROOMS: 3½
WIDTH: 89' - 10"
DEPTH: 63' - 8"
FOUNDATION: CRAWLSPACE, SLAB

SEARCH ONLINE @ EPLANS.COM

FIRST FLOOR

SECOND FLOOR

plan # HPK1000234

STYLE: FRENCH
FIRST FLOOR: 2,814 SQ. FT.
SECOND FLOOR: 1,231 SQ. FT.
TOTAL: 4,045 SQ. FT.
BEDROOMS: 5
BATHROOMS: 3½
WIDTH: 98' - 0"
DEPTH: 45' - 10"
FOUNDATION: SLAB,
UNFINISHED BASEMENT

SEARCH ONLINE @ EPLANS.COM

This very formal Georgian home was designed to be admired, but also to be lived in. It features handsome formal areas in a living room and formal dining room, but also an oversized family room with a focal fireplace. The master suite sits on the first floor, as is popluar with most homeowners today. Besides its wealth of amenities, it is located near a cozy study. Don't miss the private patio and sitting area with glass in the master bedroom. Upstairs, there are four family bedrooms with great closet space. A three-car garage contains space for a golf cart and a work bench.

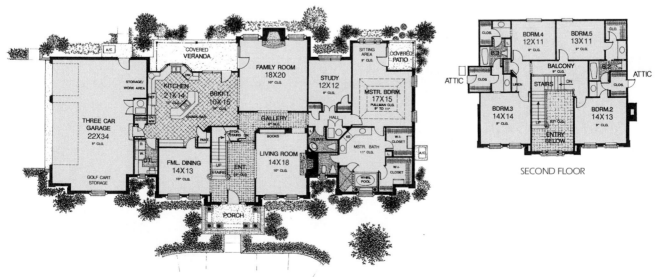

FIRST FLOOR

SECOND FLOOR

The inside of this design is just as majestic as the outside. The grand foyer opens to a two-story living room with a fireplace and magnificent views. Dining in the bayed formal dining room will be a memorable experience. A well-designed kitchen is near a sunny nook and a leisure room with a fireplace and outdoor access. The master wing includes a separate study and an elegant private bath. The second level features a guest suite with its own bath and deck, two family bedrooms (Bedroom 3 also has its own deck), and a gallery loft with views to the living room below.

plan# HPK1000235

STYLE: TRADITIONAL
FIRST FLOOR: 3,027 SQ. FT.
SECOND FLOOR: 1,079 SQ. FT.
TOTAL: 4,106 SQ. FT.
BEDROOMS: 4
BATHROOMS: 3½
WIDTH: 87' - 4"
DEPTH: 80' - 4"
FOUNDATION: UNFINISHED BASEMENT

SEARCH ONLINE @ EPLANS.COM

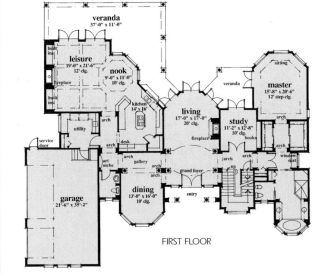

FIRST FLOOR

SECOND FLOOR

© William E. Poole Designs, Inc.

plan # HPK1000236

STYLE: COUNTRY COTTAGE
FIRST FLOOR: 2,891 SQ. FT.
SECOND FLOOR: 1,336 SQ. FT.
TOTAL: 4,227 SQ. FT.
BONUS SPACE: 380 SQ. FT.
BEDROOMS: 4
BATHROOMS: 3½ + ½
WIDTH: 90' - 8"
DEPTH: 56' - 4"
FOUNDATION: CRAWLSPACE,
UNFINISHED BASEMENT

SEARCH ONLINE @ EPLANS.COM

This Southern coastal cottage radiates charm and elegance. Step inside from the covered porch and discover a floor plan with practicality and architectural interest. The foyer has a raised ceiling and is partially open to above. The library and great room offer fireplaces and built-in shelves; the great room also provides rear-porch access. The kitchen, featuring an island with a separate sink, is adjacent to the breakfast room and a study with a built-in desk. On the far right, the master bedroom will amaze, with a sumptuous bath and enormous walk-in closet. Three upstairs bedrooms share a loft and recreation room. Convenient storage opportunities make organization easy.

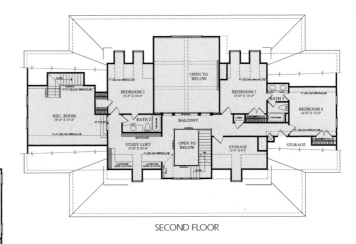

SECOND FLOOR

FIRST FLOOR

Finished with French Country adornments, this estate home is comfortable in just about any setting. Main living areas are sunk down just a bit from the entry foyer, providing them with soaring ceilings and sweeping views. The family room features a focal fireplace. A columned entry gains access to the master suite where separate sitting and sleeping areas are defined by a three-sided fireplace. There are three bedrooms upstairs; one has a private bath. The sunken media room on this level includes storage space. Note the second half bath under the staircase landing.

plan# HPK1000237

STYLE: FRENCH
FIRST FLOOR: 2,899 SQ. FT.
SECOND FLOOR: 1,472 SQ. FT.
TOTAL: 4,371 SQ. FT.
BEDROOMS: 4
BATHROOMS: 3½ + ½
WIDTH: 69' - 4"
DEPTH: 76' - 8"
FOUNDATION: SLAB

SEARCH ONLINE @ EPLANS.COM

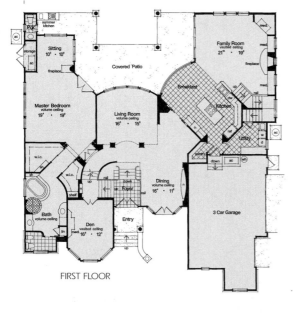

FIRST FLOOR

SECOND FLOOR

OPTIONAL LAYOUT

plan # HPK1000238

STYLE: FRENCH
FIRST FLOOR: 2,899 SQ. FT.
SECOND FLOOR: 1,472 SQ. FT.
TOTAL: 4,371 SQ. FT.
BEDROOMS: 4
BATHROOMS: 3 1/2 + 1/2
WIDTH: 69' - 4"
DEPTH: 76' - 8"
FOUNDATION: SLAB

SEARCH ONLINE @ EPLANS.COM

Arch-topped windows, graceful details, and a stunning stucco facade give this manor plenty of appeal. Inside, the foyer is flanked by a cozy drawing room and the formal dining room. Entertaining will be a breeze with the huge keeping room near the efficient kitchen, and the grand room; both rooms have fireplaces and access to the covered rear terrace. A guest suite provides privacy for visitors. The lavish master suite features a walk-in closet, deluxe bath, covered balcony, and fireplace. Upstairs, two amenity-filled suites are separated by a balcony. The basement-level of the home expands its livability greatly, with a spacious exercise room (complete with a full bath), a summer kitchen, a gathering room (includes a fireplace and bar), and a suite for future needs. Note the studio apartment over the main garage.

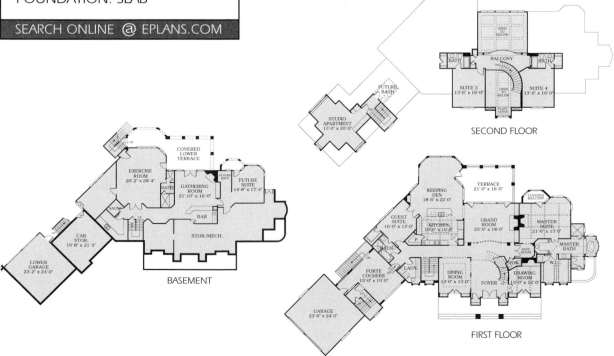

© William E. Poole Designs, Inc.

The paired double-end chimneys, reminiscent of the Georgian style of architecture, set this design apart from the rest. The covered entry opens to the columned foyer with the dining room on the left and the living room on the right, each enjoying the warmth and charm of a fireplace. Beyond the grand staircase, the family room delights with a third fireplace and a window wall that opens to the terrace. The expansive kitchen and breakfast area sit on the far left; the master suite is secluded on the the right with its pampering private bath. The second floor holds three additional bedrooms (including a second master bedroom), three full baths, a computer room, and the future recreation room.

plan# HPK1000239

STYLE: SOUTHERN COLONIAL
FIRST FLOOR: 2,998 SQ. FT.
SECOND FLOOR: 1,556 SQ. FT.
TOTAL: 4,554 SQ. FT.
BONUS SPACE: 741 SQ. FT.
BEDROOMS: 4
BATHROOMS: 4½
WIDTH: 75' - 6"
DEPTH: 91' - 2"
FOUNDATION: CRAWLSPACE

SEARCH ONLINE @ EPLANS.COM

FIRST FLOOR

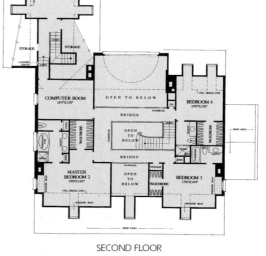

SECOND FLOOR

plan # HPK1000240

STYLE: TRADITIONAL
FIRST FLOOR: 3,297 SQ. FT.
SECOND FLOOR: 1,453 SQ. FT.
TOTAL: 4,750 SQ. FT.
BEDROOMS: 5
BATHROOMS: 4½
WIDTH: 80' - 10"
DEPTH: 85' - 6"
FOUNDATION: SLAB

SEARCH ONLINE @ EPLANS.COM

This elegant home combines a traditional exterior with a contemporary interior and provides a delightful setting for both entertaining and individual solitude. A living room and bay-windowed dining room provide an open area for formal entertaining, which can spill outside to the entertainment terrace or to the nearby gathering room with its dramatic fireplace. On the opposite side of the house, French doors make it possible for the study/guest room to be closed off from the rest of the first floor. The master suite is also a private retreat, offering a fireplace as well as an abundance of natural light, and a bath designed to pamper. The entire family will enjoy the second-floor media loft from which a balcony overlooks the two-story gathering room below.

FIRST FLOOR

SECOND FLOOR

This grand home offers an elegant, welcoming residence with a Mediterranean flair. Beyond the grand foyer, the spacious living room provides views of the rear grounds and opens to the veranda and rear yard through three pairs of French doors. An arched galley hall leads past the formal dining room to the family areas. Here, an ample gourmet kitchen easily serves the nook and the leisure room. The master wing includes a study or home office. Upstairs, each of three secondary bedrooms features a walk-in closet, and two bedrooms offer private balconies.

plan# HPK1000241

STYLE: TRADITIONAL
FIRST FLOOR: 3,546 SQ. FT.
SECOND FLOOR: 1,213 SQ. FT.
TOTAL: 4,759 SQ. FT.
BEDROOMS: 4
BATHROOMS: 3½
WIDTH: 96' - 0"
DEPTH: 83' - 0"
FOUNDATION: UNFINISHED BASEMENT

SEARCH ONLINE @ EPLANS.COM

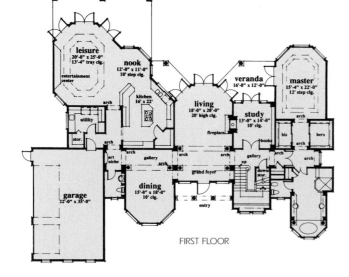

FIRST FLOOR

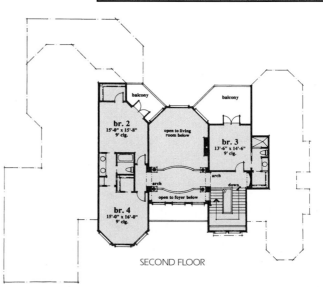

SECOND FLOOR

plan # HPK1000242

STYLE: MEDITERRANEAN
FIRST FLOOR: 3,307 SQ. FT.
SECOND FLOOR: 1,642 SQ. FT.
TOTAL: 4,949 SQ. FT.
BONUS SPACE: 373 SQ. FT.
BEDROOMS: 5
BATHROOMS: 4½ + ½
WIDTH: 143' - 3"
DEPTH: 71' - 2"
FOUNDATION: CRAWLSPACE

SEARCH ONLINE @ EPLANS.COM

You'll be amazed at what this estate has to offer. A study/parlor and a formal dining room announce a grand foyer. Ahead, the living room offers a wet bar and French doors to the rear property. The kitchen is dazzling, with an enormous pantry, oversized cooktop island... even a pizza oven! The gathering room has a corner fireplace and accesses the covered veranda. To the far right, the master suite is a delicious retreat from the world. A bowed window lets in light and a romantic fireplace makes chilly nights cozy. The luxurious bath is awe-inspiring, with a Roman tub and separate compartmented toilet areas—one with a bidet. Upstairs, three family bedrooms share a generous bonus room. A separate pool house is available, which includes a fireplace, full bath, and dressing area.

SECOND FLOOR

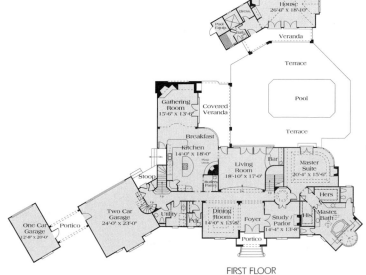

FIRST FLOOR

This magnificent estate is detailed with exterior charm: a porte cochere connecting the detached garage to the house, a covered terrace, and oval windows. The first floor consists of a lavish master suite, a cozy library with a fireplace, a grand room/solarium combination, and an elegant formal dining room with another fireplace. Three bedrooms dominate the second floor—each features a walk-in closet. For the kids, there is a playroom, and, up another flight of stairs, is a room for future expansion into a deluxe studio with a fireplace. Over the three-car garage, there is space for a future mother-in-law or maid's suite.

plan# HPK1000243

STYLE: FRENCH
FIRST FLOOR: 3,703 SQ. FT.
SECOND FLOOR: 1,427 SQ. FT.
TOTAL: 5,130 SQ. FT.
BONUS SPACE: 1,399 SQ. FT.
BEDROOMS: 4
BATHROOMS: 3½ + ½
WIDTH: 125' - 2"
DEPTH: 58' - 10"
FOUNDATION: FINISHED
WALKOUT BASEMENT

SEARCH ONLINE @ EPLANS.COM

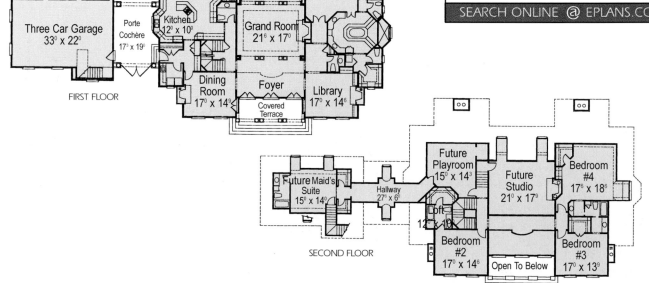

plan # HPK1000244

STYLE: GEORGIAN
FIRST FLOOR: 3,599 SQ. FT.
SECOND FLOOR: 1,621 SQ. FT.
TOTAL: 5,220 SQ. FT.
BONUS SPACE: 537 SQ. FT.
BEDROOMS: 4
BATHROOMS: 5½
WIDTH: 108' - 10"
DEPTH: 53' - 10"
FOUNDATION: SLAB,
UNFINISHED BASEMENT

SEARCH ONLINE @ EPLANS.COM

A grand facade detailed with brick corner quoins, stucco flourishes, arched windows, and an elegant entrance presents this home. A spacious foyer is accented by curving stairs and flanked by a formal living room and a formal dining room. For cozy times, a through-fireplace is located between a large family room and a quiet study. The master bedroom is designed to pamper, with two walk-in closets, a two-sided fireplace, a bayed sitting area, and a lavish private bath. Upstairs, three secondary bedrooms each have a private bath and a walk-in closet. Also on this level is a spacious recreation room, perfect for a game room or children's playroom.

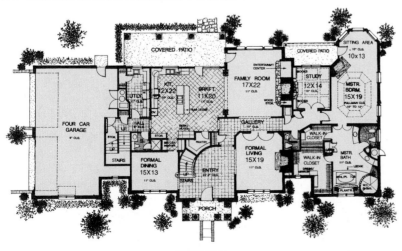

FIRST FLOOR

SECOND FLOOR

plan# HPK1000245

STYLE: EUROPEAN COTTAGE
FIRST FLOOR: 2,620 SQ. FT.
SECOND FLOOR: 2,001 SQ. FT.
THIRD FLOOR: 684 SQ. FT.
TOTAL: 5,305 SQ. FT.
BEDROOMS: 4
BATHROOMS: 5½ + ½
WIDTH: 67' - 0"
DEPTH: 103' - 8"
FOUNDATION: CRAWLSPACE

SEARCH ONLINE @ EPLANS.COM

FIRST FLOOR

GARAGE
23'-0" x 35'-8"

SECOND FLOOR

THIRD FLOOR

With unique angles, brick detailing, and double chimneys, this home is as sophisticated as it is comfortable. The foyer enters into a refined gallery, which runs past a dining room, complete with French doors opening to the front covered porch. The gallery also passes the grand room, which boasts a fireplace and three sets of French doors to the rear covered veranda. On the right, the master retreat provides its own private fireplace and access to the veranda. The kitchen and breakfast area is situated on the left side of the plan. Follow the steps up and an abundance of rooms will greet you. The recreation room directly accesses a small covered veranda. Two additional family suites flank the rec room, and each accesses a full bath. An apartment—perfect for renters or parents—and an office complete this floor.

plan # HPK1000246

STYLE: PLANTATION
FIRST FLOOR: 2,732 SQ. FT.
SECOND FLOOR: 2,734 SQ. FT.
TOTAL: 5,466 SQ. FT.
BEDROOMS: 5
BATHROOMS: 5½ + ½
WIDTH: 85' - 0"
DEPTH: 85' - 6"
FOUNDATION: CRAWLSPACE,
SLAB, UNFINISHED WALKOUT
BASEMENT

SEARCH ONLINE @ EPLANS.COM

A wraparound covered porch adds plenty of outdoor space to this already impressive home. Built-in cabinets flank the fireplace in the grand room; a fireplace also warms the hearth room. The gourmet kitchen includes an island counter, large walk-in pantry, and serving bar. A secluded home office, with a separate entrance nearby, provides a quiet work place. A front parlor provides even more room for entertaining or relaxing. The master suite dominates the second floor, offering a spacious sitting area with an elegant tray ceiling, a dressing area, and a luxurious bath with two walk-in closets, double vanities, and a raised garden tub. The second floor is also home to an enormous exercise room and three additional bedrooms.

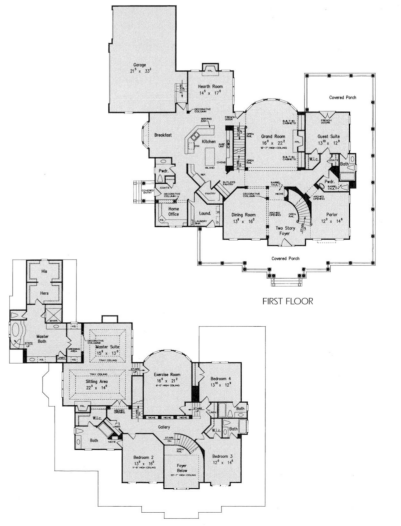

FIRST FLOOR

SECOND FLOOR

Soaring ceiling heights allow full walls of glass for gorgeous views within this estate home. The grand salon, library and foyer all have two-story ceilings that expand on their already expansive areas. More intimate in ambience, the keeping room and attached morning room are designed for casual gatherings—and found near the kitchen for convenience. The kitchen features a curved work counter, a walk-in pantry and a built-in desk. Sharing a through-fireplace with the grand salon, the formal library is tucked away beyond gathering spaces. Sitting-room space complements the master suite where you will also find an exquisite bath and His and Hers walk-in closets. Twin staircases lead to four staterooms upstairs—each has a private bath.

plan# HPK1000247

STYLE: FRENCH
FIRST FLOOR: 4,463 SQ. FT.
SECOND FLOOR: 2,507 SQ. FT.
TOTAL: 6,970 SQ. FT.
BEDROOMS: 5
BATHROOMS: 5½
WIDTH: 131' - 0"
DEPTH: 73' - 0"
FOUNDATION: UNFINISHED BASEMENT

SEARCH ONLINE @ EPLANS.COM

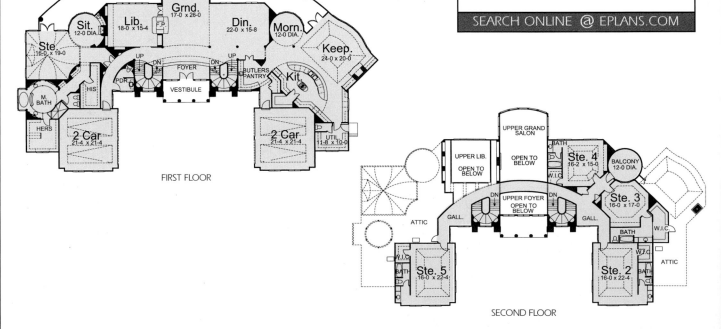

FIRST FLOOR

SECOND FLOOR

plan # HPK1000248

STYLE: TRADITIONAL
FIRST FLOOR: 2,450 SQ. FT.
SECOND FLOOR: 787 SQ. FT.
TOTAL: 3,237 SQ. FT.
BEDROOMS: 4
BATHROOMS: 3½
WIDTH: 68' - 10"
DEPTH: 64' - 7"
FOUNDATION: UNFINISHED
BASEMENT

SEARCH ONLINE @ EPLANS.COM

Striking gable rooflines and intriguing multipane windows of diverse shapes and sizes emphatically announce that this is an enchanting place to call "home." The mammoth country kitchen opens to a keeping room with a vault ceiling and fireplace and a cozy breakfast alcove with windows on five sides. The congenial formal dining room is easily served by the kitchen and opens conveniently to the dazzling and aptly named grand room. The front study, a quiet retreat, also enjoys a vault ceiling. An especially attractive feature of the first-floor master suite is a sitting room that opens to the rear yard. A bedroom with a private bath and sitting room shares the second level with two family bedrooms. Unfinished space on this floor can be used as you want. A three-car garage will ably protect the family's vehicles.

FIRST FLOOR

SECOND FLOOR

Stucco corner quoins, multiple gables, and graceful columns all combine to give this European manor plenty of appeal. Inside, a gallery entry presents a formal dining room on the right, defined by elegant columns, while the formal living room awaits just ahead. The highly efficient kitchen features a worktop island, pantry, and a serving bar to the nearby octagonal breakfast area. The family room offers a built-in entertainment center, a fireplace, and its own covered patio. The left side of the first floor is dedicated to the master suite. Here, the homeowner is pampered with an octagonal study, huge walk-in closet, lavish bath, and a very convenient nursery. The second floor contains two family bedrooms, each with a walk-in closet, and a media area with built-in bookshelves.

plan# HPK1000249

STYLE: FRENCH
FIRST FLOOR: 3,168 SQ. FT.
SECOND FLOOR: 998 SQ. FT.
TOTAL: 4,166 SQ. FT.
BONUS SPACE: 210 SQ. FT.
BEDROOMS: 4
BATHROOMS: 3½
WIDTH: 90' - 0"
DEPTH: 63' - 5"
FOUNDATION: SLAB,
UNFINISHED BASEMENT,
CRAWLSPACE

SEARCH ONLINE @ EPLANS.COM

FIRST FLOOR

SECOND FLOOR

plan # HPK1000250

STYLE: NW CONTEMPORARY
FIRST FLOOR: 3,162 SQ. FT.
SECOND FLOOR: 1,595 SQ. FT.
TOTAL: 4,757 SQ. FT.
BEDROOMS: 3
BATHROOMS: 3 + 3 HALF
BATHS
WIDTH: 110' - 2"
DEPTH: 68' - 11"
FOUNDATION: SLAB, FINISHED
BASEMENT

SEARCH ONLINE @ EPLANS.COM

Victorian and Craftsman styles blend and create an inviting and detailed home. A two-story turret houses a second-floor reading room and first-floor master sitting bay. The dining and living areas are open and convenient to the rear porch and gourmet kitchen. An interior fountain divides the breakfast area and the spacious family room. The first-floor master suite features a corner fireplace and private bath. Family quarters, including two bedrooms and a large library, can be found on the second floor. Storage for holiday items and large keepsakes is also provided. On the lower level, a magnificent auto gallery, complete with a special car elevator, is perfect for the auto enthusiast in the family.

SECOND FLOOR

FIRST FLOOR

BASEMENT

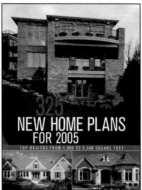

1001 ALL TIME BEST SELLING HOME PLANS
ISBN 1-881955-67-2

$12.95 (704 PAGES)

The largest compendium available, with complete blueprints available for every style of home—from Tudor to Southwestern or Contemporary to Victorian, this book has it all.

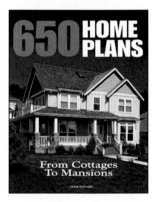

650 HOME PLANS
ISBN 1-931131-04-X

$8.95 (464 PAGES)

Tons of illustrations highlight 650 different plans covering all housing styles, from cottages to mansions.

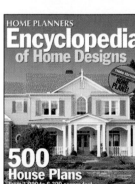

ENCYCLOPEDIA OF HOME DESIGNS, 3RD ED.

ISBN 1-931131-12-0

$9.95 (528 PAGES)

Already in its 3rd edition, this best-selling volume offers over 500 house plans ranging from 1,000 to 6,300 sq. feet.

With over 2,500 home plans, finding the right new home to fit

▶ Your style
▶ Your budget
▶ Your life

...has never been easier.

HANLEY WOOD CONSUMER GROUP
One Thomas Circle, NW, Suite 600, Washington, DC 20005

YCH1

With more than 50 years of experience in the industry and millions of blueprints sold, Hanley Wood is a trusted source of high-quality, high-value pre-drawn home plans.

Using pre-drawn home plans is a **reliable, cost-effective way** to build your dream home, and our vast selection of plans is second-to-none. The nation's finest designers craft these plans that builders know they can trust. Meanwhile, our friendly, knowledgeable customer service representatives can help you every step of the way.

WHAT YOU'LL GET WITH YOUR ORDER

The contents of each designer's blueprint package is unique, but all contain detailed, high-quality working drawings. You can expect to find the following standard elements in most sets of plans:

1. FRONT PERSPECTIVE

This artist's sketch of the exterior of the house gives you an idea of how the house will look when built and landscaped.

2. FOUNDATION AND BASEMENT PLANS

This sheet shows the foundation layout including concrete walls, footings, pads, posts, beams, bearing walls, and foundation notes. If the home features a basement, the first-floor framing details may also be included on this plan. If your plan features slab construction rather than a basement, the plan shows footings and details for a monolithic slab. This page, or another in the set, may include a sample plot plan for locating your house on a building site. Additional sheets focus on foundation cross-sections and other details.

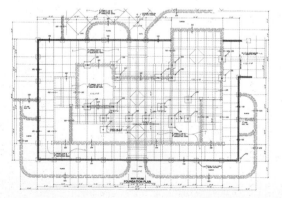

3. DETAILED FLOOR PLANS

These plans show the layout of each floor of the house. Rooms and interior spaces are carefully dimensioned, doors and windows located, and keys are given for cross-section details provided elsewhere in the plans.

4. HOUSE AND DETAIL CROSS-SECTIONS

Large-scale views show sections or cutaways of the foundation, interior walls, exterior walls, floors, stairways, and roof details. Additional cross-sections may show important changes in floor, ceiling, or roof heights, or the relationship of one level to another. These sections show exactly how the various parts of the house fit together and are extremely valuable during construction. Additional sheets may include enlarged wall, floor, and roof construction details.

5. ROOF AND FLOOR STRUCTURAL SUPPORTS

The roof and floor framing plans provide detail for these crucial elements of your home. Each includes floor joist, ceiling joist, rafter and roof joist size, spacing, direction, span, and specifications. Beam and window headers, along with necessary details for framing connections, stairways, skylights, or dormers are also included.

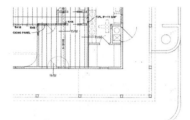

6. ELECTRICAL PLAN

The electrical plan offers a detailed outline of all wiring for your home, with notes for all lighting, outlets, switches, and circuits. A layout is provided for each level, as well as basements, garages, or other structures.

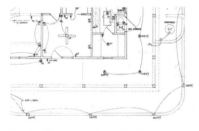

7. EXTERIOR ELEVATIONS

In addition to the front exterior, your blueprint set will include drawings of the rear and sides of your house as well. These drawings give notes on exterior materials and finishes. Particular attention is given to cornice detail, brick and stone accents, or other finish items that make your home unique.

BEFORE YOU CALL

You are making a terrific decision to use a pre-drawn house plan—it is one you can make with confidence, knowing that your blueprints are crafted by national-award-winning certified residential designers and architects, and trusted by builders.

Once you've selected the plan you want—or even if you have questions along the way—our experienced customer service representatives are available 24 hours a day, seven days a week to help you navigate the home-building process. To help them provide you with even better service, please consider the following questions before you call:

■ Have you chosen or purchased your lot?
If so, please review the building setback requirements of your local building authority before you call. You don't need to have a lot before ordering plans, but if you own land already, please have the width and depth dimensions handy when you call.

■ Have you chosen a builder?
Involving your builder in the plan selection and evaluation process may be beneficial. Luckily, builders know they can have confidence with pre-drawn plans because they've been designed for livability, functionality, and typically are builder-proven at successful home sites across the country.

■ Do you need a construction loan?
Construction loans are unique because they involve determining the value of something that is not yet constructed. Several lenders offer convenient contstruction-to-permanent loans. It is important to choose a good lending partner—one who will help guide you through the application and appraisal process. Most will even help you evaluate your contractor to ensure reliability and credit worthiness. Our partnership with IndyMac Bank, a nationwide leader in construction loans, can help you save on your loan if needed.

■ How many sets of plans do you need?
Building a home can typically require a number of sets of blueprints—one for yourself, two or three for the builder and subcontractors, two for the local building department, and one or more for your lender. For this reason, we offer 5- and 8-set plan packages, but your best value is the Reproducible Plan Package. Reproducible plans are accompanied by a license to make modifications and typically up to 12 duplicates of the plan so you have enough copies of the plan for everyone involved in the financing and construction of your home.

■ Do you want to make any changes to the plan?
We understand that it is difficult to find blueprints for a home that will meet all of your needs. That is why Hanley Wood is glad to offer plan Customization Services. We will work with you to design the modifications you'd like to see and to adjust your blueprint plans accordingly—anything from changing the foundation; adding square footage, redesigning baths, kitchens, or bedrooms; or most other modifications. This simple, cost-effective service saves you from hiring an outside architect to make alterations. Modifications may only be made to Reproducible Plan Packages that include the license to modify.

■ Do you have to make any changes to meet local building codes?
While all of our plans are drawn to meet national building codes at the time they were created, many areas required that plans be stamped by a local engineer to certify that they meet local building codes. Building codes are updated frequently and can vary by state, county, city, or municipality. Contact your local building inspection department, office of planning and zoning, or department of permits to determine how your local codes will affect your construction project. The best way to assure that you can make changes to your plan, if necessary, is to purchase a Reproducible Plan Package.

■ Has everyone—from family members to contractors—been involved in selecting the plan?
Building a new home is an exciting process, and using pre-drawn plans is a great way to realize your dreams. Make sure that everyone involved has had an opportunity to review the plan you've selected. While Hanley Wood is the only plans provider with an exchange policy, it's best to be sure all parties agree on your selection before you buy.

CALL TOLL-FREE 1-800-521-6797

Source Key
HPK10

CUSTOMIZE YOUR PLAN –
HANLEY WOOD CUSTOMIZATION SERVICES

Creating custom home plans has never been easier and more directly accessible. Using state-of-the-art technology and top-performing architectural expertise, Hanley Wood delivers on a long-standing customer commitment to provide world-class home-plans and customization services. Our valued customers—professional home builders and individual home owners—appreciate the convenience and accessibility of this interactive, consultative service.

With the Hanley Wood Customization Service you can:

■ Save valuable time by avoiding drawn-out and frequently repetitive face-to-face design meetings

■ Communicate design and home-plan changes faster and more efficiently
■ Speed-up project turn-around time
■ Build on a budget without sacrificing quality
■ Transform master home plans to suit your design needs and unique personal style

All of our design options and prices are impressively affordable. A detailed quote is available for a $50 consultation fee. Plan modification is an interactive service. Our skilled team of designers will guide you through the customization process from start to finish making recommendations, offering ideas, and determining the feasibility of your changes. This level of service is offered to ensure the final modified plan meets your expectations. If you use our service the $50 fee will be applied to the cost of the modifications.

You may purchase the customization consultation before or after purchasing a plan. In either case, it is necessary to purchase the Reproducible Plan Package and complete the accompanying license to modify the plan before we can begin customization.

Customization Consultation **$50**

TOOLS TO WORK WITH YOUR BUILDER

Two Reverse Options For Your Convenience –
Mirror and Right-Reading Reverse (as available)
Mirror reverse plans simply flip the design 180 degrees—keep in mind, the text will also be flipped. For a minimal fee you can have one or all of your plans shipped mirror reverse, although we recommend having at least one regular set handy. Right-reading reverse plans show the design flipped 180 degrees but the text reads normally. When you choose this option, we ship each set of purchased blueprints in this format.

Mirror Reverse Fee (indicate the number of sets when ordering)....$55
Right Reading Reverse Fee (all sets are reversed)................$175

A Shopping List Exclusively for Your Home – Materials List
A customized Materials List helps you plan and estimate the cost of your new home, outlining the quantity, type, and size of materials needed to build your house (with the exception of mechanical system items). Included are framing lumber, windows and doors, kitchen and bath cabinetry, rough and finished hardware, and much more.

Materials List...$75 each
Additional Materials Lists (at original time of purchase)..$20 each

Plan Your Home-
Building Process – Specification Outline
Work with your builder on this step-by-step chronicle of 166 stages or items crucial to the building process. It provides a comprehensive review of the construction process and helps you choose materials.
Specification Outline......................................$10 each

Get Accurate Cost Estimates for Your Home –
Quote One® Cost Reports
The Summary Cost Report, the first element in the Quote One® package, breaks down the cost of your home into various categories based on building materials, labor, and installation, and includes three grades of construction: Budget, Standard, and Custom. Make even more informed decisions about your project with the second element of our package, the Material Cost Report. The material and installation cost is shown for each of more than 1,000 line items provided in the standard-grade Materials List, which is included with this tool. Additional space is included for estimates from contractors and subcontractors, such as for mechanical materials, which are not included in our packages.

Quote One® Summary Cost Report................................$35
Quote One® Detailed Material Cost Report......................$140*
***Detailed material cost report includes the Materials List**

Learn the Basics of Building – Electrical, Plumbing, Mechanical, Construction Detail Sheets
If you want to know more about building techniques—and deal more confidently with your subcontractors—we offer four useful detail sheets. These sheets provide non-plan-specific general information, but are excellent tools that will add to your understanding of Plumbing Details, Electrical Details, Construction Details, and Mechanical Details.

Electrical Detail Sheet..$14.95
Plumbing Detail Sheet...$14.95
Mechanical Detail Sheet.......................................$14.95
Construction Detail Sheet.....................................$14.95
SUPER VALUE SETS:
Buy any 2: $26.95; Buy any 3: $34.95;

Best Value

MAKE YOUR HOME TECH-READY – HOME AUTOMATION UPGRADE

Building a new home provides a unique opportunity to wire it with a plan for future needs. A Home Automation-Ready (HA-Ready) home contains the wiring substructure of tomorrow's connected home. It means that every room—from the front porch to the backyard, and from the attic to the basement—is wired for security, lighting, telecommunications, climate control, home computer networking, whole-house audio, home theater, shade control, video surveillance, entry access control, and yes, video gaming electronic solutions.

Along with the conveniences HA-Ready homes provide, they also have a higher resale value. The Consumer Electronics Association (CEA), in conjunction with the Custom Electronic Design and Installation Association (CEDIA), have developed a TechHome™ Rating system that quantifies the value of HA-Ready homes. The rating system is gaining widespread recognition in the real estate industry.

Developed by CEDIA-certified installers, our Home Automation Upgrade package includes everything you need to work with an installer during the construction of your home. It provides a short explanation of the various subsystems, a wiring floor plan for each level of your home, a detailed materials list with estimated costs, and a list of CEDIA-certified installers in your local area.

Home Automation Upgrade $250

GET YOUR HOME PLANS PAID FOR!

IndyMac Bank, in partnership with Hanley Wood, will reimburse you up to $600 toward the cost of your home plans simply by financing the construction of your new home with IndyMac Bank Home Construction Lending.

IndyMac's construction and permanent loan is a one-time close loan, meaning that one application—and one set of closing fees—provides all the financing you need.

Apply today at www.indymacbank.com, call toll free at 1-866-237-3478, or ask a Hanley Wood customer service representative for details.

DESIGN YOUR HOME – INTERIOR AND EXTERIOR FINISHING TOUCHES

Be Your Own Interior Designer! – Home Furniture Planner

Effectively plan the space in your home using our Hands-On Home Furniture Planner. It's fun and easy—no more moving heavy pieces of furniture to see how the room will go together. The kit includes reusable peel-and-stick furniture templates that fit on a 12"x18" laminated layout board—enough space to lay out every room in your house.

Home Furniture Planning Kit **$15.95**

Enjoy the Outdoors! – Deck Plans

Many of our homes have a corresponding deck plan, sold separately, which includes a Deck Plan Frontal Sheet, Deck Framing and Floor Plans, Deck Elevations, and a Deck Materials List. A Standard Deck Details Package, also available, provides all the how-to information necessary for building any deck. Get both the Deck Plan and the Standard Deck Details Package for one low price in our Complete Deck Building Package. See the price tier chart below and call for deck plan availability.

Deck Details (only) **$14.95**
Deck Building Package . . . . **Plan price + $14.95**

Create a Professionally Designed Landscape – Landscape Plans

Many of our homes have a front-yard Landscape Plan that is complementary in design to the house plan. These comprehensive Landscape Blueprint Packages include a Frontal Sheet, Plan View, Regionalized Plant & Materials List, a sheet on Planting and Maintaining Your Landscape, Zone Maps,  and a Plant Size and Description Guide. Each set of blueprints is a full 18" x 24" with clear, complete instructions in easy-to-read type. Our Landscape Plans are available with a Plant & Materials List adapted by horticultural experts to eight regions of the country. Please specify your region when ordering your plan—see region map below. Call for more information about landscape plan availability and applicable regions.

LANDSCAPE & DECK PRICE SCHEDULE

PRICE TIERS	1-SET STUDY PACKAGE	5-SET BUILDING PACKAGE	8-SET BUILDING PACKAGE	1-SET REPRODUCIBLE*
P1	$25	$55	$95	$145
P2	$45	$75	$115	$165
P3	$75	$105	$145	$195
P4	$105	$135	$175	$225
P5	$145	$175	$215	$275
P6	$185	$215	$255	$315

PRICES SUBJECT TO CHANGE   * REQUIRES A FAX NUMBER

TERMS & CONDITIONS

OUR EXCHANGE POLICY

Hanley Wood is committed to ensuring your satisfaction with your blueprint order, which is why we're the only provider of pre-drawn house plans to offer an exchange policy. With the exception of Reproducible Plan Package orders, we will exchange your entire first order for an equal or greater number of blueprints from our plan collection within 90 days of the original order. The entire content of your original order must be returned before an exchange will be processed. Please call our customer service department at 1-888-690-1116 for your return authorization number and shipping instructions. If the returned blueprints look used, redlined, or copied, we will not honor your exchange. Fees for exchanging your blueprints are as follows: 20% of the amount of the original order, plus the difference in cost if exchanging for a design in a higher price bracket or less the difference in cost if exchanging for a design in a lower price bracket. (Because they can be copied, Reproducible blueprints are not exchangeable or refundable.) Please call for current postage and handling prices. Shipping and handling charges are not refundable.

ARCHITECTURAL AND ENGINEERING SEALS

Some cities and states now require that a licensed architect or engineer review and "seal" a blueprint, or officially approve it, prior to construction. Prior to application for a building permit or the start of actual construction, we strongly advise that you consult your local building official who can tell you if such a review is required.

LOCAL BUILDING CODES AND ZONING REQUIREMENTS

Each plan was designed to meet or exceed the requirements of a nationally recognized model building code in effect at the time and place the plan was drawn. Typically plans designed after the year 2000 conform to the International Residential Building Code (IRC 2000 or 2003). The IRC is comprised of portions of the three major codes below. Plans drawn before 2000 conform to one of the three recognized building codes in effect at the time: Building Officials and Code Administrators (BOCA) International, Inc.; the Southern Building Code Congress International, (SBCCI) Inc.; the International Conference of Building Officials (ICBO); or the Council of American Building Officials (CABO).

Because of the great differences in geography and climate throughout the United States and Canada, each state, county, and municipality has its own building codes, zone requirements, ordinances, and building regulations. Your plan may need to be modified to comply with local requirements. In addition, you may need to obtain permits or inspections from local governments before and in the course of construction. We authorize the use of the blueprints on the express condition that you consult a local licensed architect or engineer of your choice prior to beginning construction and strictly comply with all local building codes, zoning requirements, and other applicable laws, regulations, ordinances, and requirements. Notice: Plans for homes to be built in Nevada must be redrawn by a Nevada-registered professional. Consult your local building official for more information on this subject.

TERMS AND CONDITIONS

These designs are protected under the terms of United States Copyright Law and may not be copied or reproduced in any way, by any means, unless you have purchased a Reproducible Plan Package and signed the accompanying license to modify and copy the plan, which clearly indicates your right to modify, copy, or reproduce. We authorize the use of your chosen design as an aid in the construction of ONE (1) single- or multifamily home only. You may not use this design to build a second dwelling or multiple dwellings without purchasing another blueprint or blueprints or paying additional design fees. Multi-use fees vary by designer—please call one of experienced sales representatives for a quote.

DISCLAIMER

The designers we work with have put substantial care and effort into the creation of their blueprints. However, because we cannot provide on-site consultation, supervision, and control over actual construction, and because of the great variance in local building requirements, building practices, and soil, seismic, weather, and other conditions, WE MAKE NO WARRANTY OF ANY KIND, EXPRESS OR IMPLIED, WITH RESPECT TO THE CONTENT OR USE OF THE BLUEPRINTS, INCLUDING BUT NOT LIMITED TO ANY WARRANTY OF MERCHANTABILITY OR OF FITNESS FOR A PARTICULAR PURPOSE. ITEMS, PRICES, TERMS, AND CONDITIONS ARE SUBJECT TO CHANGE WITHOUT NOTICE.

CALL TOLL-FREE
1-866-473-4052
OR VISIT
EPLANS.COM

IMPORTANT COPYRIGHT NOTICE

From the Council of Publishing Home Designers

Blueprints for residential construction (or working drawings, as they are often called in the industry) are copyrighted intellectual property, protected under the terms of the United States Copyright Law and, therefore, cannot be copied legally for use in building. The following are some guidelines to help you get what you need to build your home, without violating copyright law:

1. HOME PLANS ARE COPYRIGHTED

Just like books, movies, and songs, home plans receive protection under the federal copyright laws. The copyright laws prevent anyone, other than the copyright owner, from reproducing, modifying, or reusing the plans or design without permission of the copyright owner.

2. DO NOT COPY DESIGNS OR FLOOR PLANS FROM ANY PUBLICATION, ELECTRONIC MEDIA, OR EXISTING HOME

It is illegal to copy, change, or redraw home designs found in a plan book, CDROM or on the Internet. The right to modify plans is one of the exclusive rights of copyright. It is also illegal to copy or redraw a constructed home that is protected by copyright, even if you have never seen the plans for the home. If you find a plan or home that you like, you must purchase a set of plans from an authorized source. The plans may not be lent, given away, or sold by the purchaser.

3. DO NOT USE PLANS TO BUILD MORE THAN ONE HOUSE

The original purchaser of house plans is typically licensed to build a single home from the plans. Building more than one home from the plans without permission is an infringement of the home designer's copyright. The purchase of a multiple-set package of plans is for the construction of a single home only. The purchase of additional sets of plans does not grant the right to construct more than one home.

4. HOUSE PLANS IN THE FORM OF BLUEPRINTS OR BLACKLINES CANNOT BE COPIED OR REPRODUCED

Plans, blueprints, or blacklines, unless they are reproducibles, cannot be copied or reproduced without prior written consent of the copyright owner. Copy shops and blueprinters are prohibited from making copies of these plans without the copyright release letter you receive with reproducible plans.

5. HOUSE PLANS IN THE FORM OF BLUEPRINTS OR BLACKLINES CANNOT BE REDRAWN

Plans cannot be modified or redrawn without first obtaining the copyright owner's permission. With your purchase of plans, you are licensed to make non-structural changes by "red-lining" the purchased plans. If you need to make structural changes or need to redraw the plans for any reason, you must purchase a reproducible set of plans (see topic 6) which includes a license to modify the plans. Blueprints do not come with a license to make structural changes or to redraw the plans. You may not reuse or sell the modified design.

6. REPRODUCIBILE HOME PLANS

Reproducible plans (for example sepias, mylars, CAD files, electronic files, and vellums) come with a license to make modifications to the plans. Once modified, the plans can be taken to a local copy shop or blueprinter to make up to 10 or 12 copies of the plans to use in the construction of a single home. Only one home can be constructed from any single purchased set of reproducible plans either in original form or as modified. The license to modify and copy must be completed and returned before the plan will be shipped.

7. MODIFIED DESIGNS CANNOT BE REUSED

Even if you are licensed to make modifica-tions to a copyrighted design, the modified design is not free from the original designer's copyright. The sale or reuse of the modified design is prohibited. Also, be aware that any modification to plans relieves the original designer from liability for design defects and voids all warranties expressed or implied.

8. WHO IS RESPONSIBLE FOR COPYRIGHT INFRINGEMENT?

Any party who participates in a copyright violation may be responsible including the purchaser, designers, architects, engineers, drafters, homeowners, builders, contractors, sub-contractors, copy shops, blueprinters, developers, and real estate agencies. It does not matter whether or not the individual knows that a violation is being committed. Ignorance of the law is not a valid defense.

9. PLEASE RESPECT HOME DESIGN COPYRIGHTS

In the event of any suspected violation of a copyright, or if there is any uncertainty about the plans purchased, the publisher, architect, designer, or the Council of Publishing Home Designers (www.cphd.org) should be contacted before proceeding. Awards are sometimes offered for information about home design copyright infringement.

10. PENALTIES FOR INFRINGEMENT

Penalties for violating a copyright may be severe. The responsible parties are required to pay actual damages caused by the infringement (which may be substantial), plus any profits made by the infringer commissions to include all profits from the sale of any home built from an infringing design. The copyright law also allows for the recovery of statutory damages, which may be as high as $150,000 for each infringement. Finally, the infringer may be required to pay legal fees which often exceed the damages.

BLUEPRINT PRICE SCHEDULE

PRICE TIERS	1-SET STUDY PACKAGE	5-SET BUILDING PACKAGE	8-SET BUILDING PACKAGE	1-SET REPRODUCIBLE*
A1	$450	$500	$555	$675
A2	$490	$545	$595	$735
A3	$540	$605	$665	$820
A4	$590	$660	$725	$895
C1	$640	$715	$775	$950
C2	$690	$760	$820	$1025
C3	$735	$810	$875	$1100
C4	$785	$860	$925	$1175
L1	$895	$990	$1075	$1335
L2	$970	$1065	$1150	$1455
L3	$1075	$1175	$1270	$1600
L4	$1185	$1295	$1385	$1775
SQ1				.40/SQ. FT.
SQ3				.55/SQ. FT.
SQ5				.80/SQ. FT.

PRICES SUBJECT TO CHANGE

* REQUIRES A FAX NUMBER

PLAN #	PRICE TIER	PAGE	MATERIALS LIST	QUOTE ONE®	DECK	DECK PRICE	LANDSCAPE	LANDSCAPE PRICE	REGIONS
HPK1000001	C2	15							
HPK1000005	SQ3	22							
HPK1000006	C2	10							
HPK1000008	SQ3	25	Y						
HPK1000009	A3	34							
HPK1000010	A3	35							
HPK1000011	A4	36	Y						
HPK1000012	A3	37	Y						
HPK1000013	A3	38							
HPK1000014	A4	39	Y						
HPK1000015	A3	40	Y						
HPK1000016	A4	41							
HPK1000017	A3	42							
HPK1000018	A3	43	Y						
HPK1000019	A3	44	Y						
HPK1000020	A3	45							
HPK1000021	A3	46							
HPK1000022	A3	47							
HPK1000023	A3	48							
HPK1000024	A4	49	Y	Y					

PLAN #	PRICE TIER	PAGE	MATERIALS LIST	QUOTE ONE®	DECK	DECK PRICE	LANDSCAPE	LANDSCAPE PRICE	REGIONS
HPK1000025	A3	50							
HPK1000026	A3	51							
HPK1000027	A3	52							
HPK1000028	A3	53	Y						
HPK1000029	A3	54	Y						
HPK1000030	A3	55	Y						
HPK1000031	A3	56	Y						
HPK1000033	A4	58	Y						
HPK1000034	A4	59							
HPK1000035	A4	60	Y				OLA010	P3	1234568
HPK1000036	A4	61							
HPK1000037	A4	62	Y						
HPK1000038	A4	63	Y						
HPK1000039	A4	64	Y						
HPK1000040	A4	65	Y						
HPK1000041	A2	66							
HPK1000042	A4	67							
HPK1000043	A4	68	Y						
HPK1000044	A3	69							
HPK1000045	A3	70							

PLAN #	PRICE TIER	PAGE	MATERIALS LIST	QUOTE ONE®	DECK	DECK PRICE	LANDSCAPE	LANDSCAPE PRICE	REGIONS
HPK1000046	A4	71							
HPK1000047	A4	72							
HPK1000048	A3	73							
HPK1000049	A4	74							
HPK1000050	C1	75							
HPK1000051	C2	76	Y						
HPK1000052	C2	77							
HPK1000053	A4	78							
HPK1000054	A4	79	Y						
HPK1000055	C2	80							
HPK1000056	A4	81							
HPK1000057	C2	82							
HPK1000058	A4	83							
HPK1000059	C1	84	Y	Y		OLA025	P3	123568	
HPK1000060	SQ1	85	Y						
HPK1000061	C2	86							
HPK1000062	C2	87	Y			OLA015	P4	123568	
HPK1000063	C3	88							
HPK1000064	C3	89							
HPK1000065	C4	90							
HPK1000066	C2	91	Y						
HPK1000067	C2	92	Y						
HPK1000068	C4	93							
HPK1000069	C3	94							
HPK1000070	SQ1	95							
HPK1000071	L1	96							
HPK1000072	C4	97							
HPK1000073	C4	98	Y						
HPK1000074	C4	99							
HPK1000075	L2	100							
HPK1000076	A4	101							
HPK1000077	L1	102	Y						
HPK1000078	A3	103	Y						
HPK1000079	A3	104							
HPK1000080	A3	105							
HPK1000081	A3	106	Y						
HPK1000082	C4	107							
HPK1000083	C4	108							
HPK1000084	C1	109	Y	Y					
HPK1000085	A3	110	Y						
HPK1000086	A3	111	Y						
HPK1000087	SQ1	112							
HPK1000088	C1	113							
HPK1000089	SQ1	114							
HPK1000090	A4	115							
HPK1000091	A4	116	Y						
HPK1000092	C2	117							
HPK1000093	A2	118							
HPK1000094	A1	119	Y						
HPK1000095	A2	120	Y						
HPK1000096	A3	121							
HPK1000097	C1	122							
HPK1000098	C1	123							
HPK1000099	A2	124	Y						
HPK1000100	A4	125							
HPK1000101	C1	126							
HPK1000102	C1	127							
HPK1000103	A4	128							
HPK1000104	A3	129	Y						
HPK1000105	A2	130	Y						
HPK1000106	A2	131							
HPK1000107	A2	132	Y						
HPK1000108	C1	133							
HPK1000109	C1	134							
HPK1000110	A4	135	Y						
HPK1000111	A2	136	Y						
HPK1000112	C1	137							
HPK1000113	C1	138	Y						
HPK1000114	A3	139							
HPK1000115	A2	140	Y						
HPK1000116	A3	141	Y						
HPK1000117	A1	142	Y						
HPK1000118	A2	143	Y						
HPK1000119	A3	144	Y						

PLAN #	PRICE TIER	PAGE	MATERIALS LIST	QUOTE ONE®	DECK	DECK PRICE	LANDSCAPE	LANDSCAPE PRICE	REGIONS
HPK1000120	A3	145	Y						
HPK1000121	A1	146	Y						
HPK1000122	C1	147	Y						
HPK1000123	C1	148	Y	Y					
HPK1000124	A2	149	Y						
HPK1000125	A2	150	Y						
HPK1000126	C1	151							
HPK1000127	C1	152							
HPK1000128	A3	153							
HPK1000129	C1	154	Y						
HPK1000130	A3	155							
HPK1000131	A2	156							
HPK1000132	C1	157							
HPK1000133	A2	158							
HPK1000134	A3	159	Y						
HPK1000135	A3	160	Y						
HPK1000136	A2	161	Y						
HPK1000137	C1	162							
HPK1000138	A3	163	Y						
HPK1000139	C1	164							
HPK1000140	A2	165	Y						
HPK1000141	A3	166							
HPK1000142	C1	167							
HPK1000143	C1	168							
HPK1000144	A4	169	Y						
HPK1000145	C2	170							
HPK1000146	A4	171	Y						
HPK1000147	A4	172	Y						
HPK1000148	C1	173	Y	Y		OLA037	P4	347	
HPK1000149	C2	174							
HPK1000150	C2	175							
HPK1000151	A4	176	Y						
HPK1000152	C1	177	Y						
HPK1000153	C2	178							
HPK1000154	A4	179	Y						
HPK1000155	C2	180	Y	Y					
HPK1000156	A4	181	Y						
HPK1000157	A4	182							
HPK1000158	C1	183	Y						
HPK1000159	A4	184							
HPK1000160	C2	185	Y	Y					
HPK1000161	C2	186							
HPK1000162	C2	187							
HPK1000163	C2	188							
HPK1000164	A4	189							
HPK1000165	A4	190							
HPK1000166	A4	191							
HPK1000167	A4	192	Y						
HPK1000168	C1	193							
HPK1000169	SQ1	194	Y						
HPK1000170	A4	195	Y						
HPK1000171	C2	196							
HPK1000172	A4	197							
HPK1000173	SQ3	198							
HPK1000174	C2	199							
HPK1000175	C1	200	Y	Y			OLA014	P4	12345678
HPK1000176	A4	201	Y						
HPK1000177	C2	202							
HPK1000178	A4	203							
HPK1000179	C1	204	Y						
HPK1000180	A4	205	Y						
HPK1000181	C2	206							
HPK1000182	A4	207							
HPK1000183	A4	208							
HPK1000184	A4	209							
HPK1000185	C3	210							
HPK1000186	C1	211	Y						
HPK1000187	C2	212	Y	Y	ODA012	P3	OLA024	P4	123568
HPK1000188	C2	213							
HPK1000189	C1	214							
HPK1000190	C3	215							
HPK1000191	C1	216							
HPK1000192	C3	217							
HPK1000193	C1	218							

PLAN #	PRICE TIER	PAGE	MATERIALS LIST	QUOTE ONE®	DECK	DECK PRICE	LANDSCAPE	LANDSCAPE PRICE	REGIONS
HPK1000194	A4	219	Y						
HPK1000195	C3	220	Y	Y					
HPK1000196	C2	221							
HPK1000197	C2	222							
HPK1000198	C3	223							
HPK1000199	C4	224							
HPK1000200	C4	225							
HPK1000201	C4	226							
HPK1000202	C1	227							
HPK1000203	C2	228							
HPK1000204	SQ1	229	Y	Y					
HPK1000205	C3	230	Y	Y		OLA038	P3	7	
HPK1000206	SQ1	231							
HPK1000207	C3	232	Y	Y		OLA038	P3	7	
HPK1000208	C3	233							
HPK1000209	C4	234	Y						
HPK1000210	C2	235	Y						
HPK1000211	C4	236							
HPK1000212	SQ3	237							
HPK1000213	C3	238							
HPK1000214	C4	239							
HPK1000215	SQ1	240							
HPK1000216	C3	241	Y						
HPK1000217	C4	242	Y						
HPK1000218	C3	243	Y						
HPK1000219	L1	244							
HPK1000220	SQ1	245							
HPK1000221	C3	246							
HPK1000222	L1	247							
HPK1000223	L1	248	Y						
HPK1000224	L1	249							
HPK1000225	SQ1	250	Y						
HPK1000226	SQ1	251	Y	Y					
HPK1000227	L1	252							
HPK1000228	SQ1	253	Y						
HPK1000229	SQ1	254							
HPK1000230	L1	255							
HPK1000231	L1	256	Y						
HPK1000232	SQ1	257	Y						
HPK1000233	C4	258	Y						
HPK1000234	SQ1	259							
HPK1000235	SQ1	260	Y						
HPK1000236	L2	261							
HPK1000237	SQ1	262	Y						
HPK1000238	L2	263							
HPK1000239	L2	264							
HPK1000240	L1	265	Y	Y					
HPK1000241	SQ1	266	Y						
HPK1000242	SQ1	267	Y						
HPK1000243	SQ1	268	Y						
HPK1000244	SQ1	269							
HPK1000245	L2	270							
HPK1000246	SQ1	271							
HPK1000247	L2	272							
HPK1000248	C2	273							
HPK1000249	C4	274							
HPK1000250	SQ1	275							
HPK1000259	C2	8	Y						
HPK1000260	A4	19	Y						
HPK1000261	C1	32	Y		ODA012	P3	OLA010	P3	1234568
HPK1000262	A3	57	Y						

Why settle for a home that's less functional, beautiful, and affordable than what your family wants? Take a leading role in the design of your next residence and let breathtaking spaces like these welcome you every day to the home you love. For more of plan HPK1000005, please turn to page 22.